AF478135

Autonomy, Ethnicity, and Poverty in Southwestern China:
The State Turned Upside Down

Chih-yu Shih

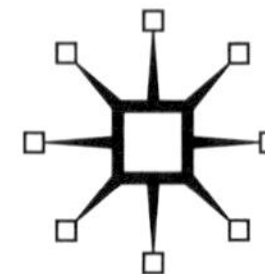

Autonomy, Ethnicity, and Poverty in Southwestern China
Copyright © Chih-yu Shih, 2007.

First published in 2007 by
PALGRAVE MACMILLAN™
175 Fifth Avenue, New York, N.Y. 10010 and
Houndmills, Basingstoke, Hampshire, England RG21 6XS.
Companies and representatives throughout the world.

PALGRAVE MACMILLAN is the global academic imprint of the Palgrave Macmillan division of St. Martin's Press, LLC and of Palgrave Macmillan Ltd. Macmillan® is a registered trademark in the United States, United Kingdom and other countries. Palgrave is a registered trademark in the European Union and other countries.

ISBN-13: 978-1-4039-8446-3
ISBN-10: 1-4039-8446-8

Library of Congress Cataloging-in-Publication Data

Shih, Chih-yu, 1958-
Autonomy, ethnicity, and poverty in Southwestern China : the state turned upside down / by Chih-yu Shih.
      p. cm.
    Includes bibliographical references and index.
    ISBN 1-4039-8446-8 (alk. paper)
     1. Minorities—China, Southwest. 2. Poverty—China,Southwest. 3. China, Southwest—Politics and government. I. Title.

DS730.S522 2008
951'.306—dc22   2007001437

Design by Scribe Inc.

First edition: December 2007

10 9 8 7 6 5 4 3 2 1

Printed in the United States of America.

Chapter 1 is an edited version of "The Teleology of State in China's Regional Ethnic Autonomy: A Review of the Chinese Writings in the International Workshop on Ethnic Autonomy," *Asian Ethnicity* 3, 2 (2002)

Chapter 3 is an expanded version of "Reforming China's Anti-Poverty Policy from Below ? Experiences from Western Hunan," *Asien* 99 (April 2006)

Chapter 8 is a revised version of "Lost Agency for Change: Diasporic Identities of Yizhou's Shui Community," *Social Identities* 11, 4 (2005)

Chapter 11 is an edited version of "Living with the State: Ambivalent Autonomy in Jinxiu's Yao Community," *The China Review* (November 2007)

Contents

Part 4 Riding the Citizenship

Introduction: Performing Unity

Ethnic communities in China demonstrate their ethnicity, as defined by those acting in the name of the state, in ways that state officials at various levels have not anticipated. The state, so to speak, acts to define ethnic groups, but then ethnicities can create their own interpretation of what their ethnic identity means, which ultimately affects the state's agenda. Nevertheless, the stories of this sort are not always beautiful, and noticeably different feelings are often registered toward the same stories. These various feelings may come from actors in different positions and perspectives. They may also come from the same actor facing different people, issues, or events. The seemingly monolithic state, represented by officials, cadres, and the system of ruling, manages this disarray of feelings and judgments by uniting them into a few specific discourses to keep otherwise potentially disintergrated local narratives from emerging. Although the officially approved discourses on Chinese ethnicity never incorporate all of them at the same time, frequent visits to the villages enabled the interviewer to summarize them into a grand hegemony of Chinese multiple ethnicities.

At this point, it is plausible to conceptually divide the ethnic communities of the Chinese state into three different dimensions. This conceptual division is not from any theoretical perspective. It is a product of the orientation brought about by the continued visits to villagers in ethnic Hunan, Guangxi, and Guizhou, beginning from the summer of 2001. In fact, local officials and cadres report their work on the ethnic townships with respect to three aspects: autonomy, ethnicity, and poverty. While autonomy is the general principle of ethnic affairs in the governmentality of China, poverty concerns specific policy issues dealt with through specially designated administrative channels. As for ethnicity, except for the pervasive celebration of multi-ethnic unity, it mainly refers to arranging exemptions or privileges to ethnic jurisdiction. Together, the three aspects discursively lock the local communities within the policy agenda of the state. Despite that these three dimensions rarely take place at the same time or are experienced by the same interviewee, they all point toward one big direction—the unity of the Chinese nation, which means autonomy points to political unity, ethnicity to cultural-national unity, and poverty to economic unity.

The evolution of larger discursive contexts explains the division of ethnic citizenship into three aspects. From the earlier obsession with national unity, which has led to the top-down granting of autonomy to ethnic communities by the central authorities, post-Cultural Revolution attention to modernization has added the dimension of poverty to ethnic citizenship. The latest faddism of globalization has further developed interest in ethnicity, as displayed in the form of tourism that submits images of local ethnicity to be consumed by global visitors, whether they are electronic or physical. Accordingly, the central authorities of the state intervene heavily in defining autonomy and poverty, while local communities have, through interaction with the outside world, made room for participation in providing meanings to their own ethnicities. However, intervention does not guarantee control as local communities begin to familiarize themselves with the official rhetoric and make use of it comfortably.

In the visited villages, local ethnic communities are seen to be at a disadvantage when forming a counter-discourse to the institution of autonomy. They are more capable of giving meaning to their own ethnicity rather than accepting the state's monotonous narrative of multi-polar unity. They are occasionally capable of forming an alternative self-understanding when falling into the designated status of poverty, distinguishing accordingly between bottom-up and top-down perspectives. Therefore, what one can learn about ethnic politics is quite different from what one would have expected. If not for this learning, one would have expected that autonomy would allow room for the local communities to breathe, while the discourse on poverty would have easily locked them into a passive, backward position. It should be stressed that these experiences are not necessarily universally true; this book reports them with the intention of showing the possibility of their mere existence.

The filed learning in this book is that the central authorities in China have reduced autonomy into an administrative mechanism used for mobilizing support for national unity. The central authorities do not need the local communities to enforce autonomy, which has occurred mainly in the form of recruiting ethnic cadres to serve as administrative heads. The local communities (which are supposedly autonomous in administrating central government policy) have little room for new languages or possibilities. What the state officials care about is the local communities' performance in executing policy goals. This preoccupation with achieving policy goals results in such paucity of language that the term autonomy is not useful in understanding ethnicity or any locally sensitive identities.

In addition, by contrast, the state's intervention in defining ethnicity is mostly dubious. Based on an a priori preoccupation with origin, the state recognizes that each specific ethnicity is in itself retrievable from a distinctive origin, but is not interested in knowing how this is so. This attitude encourages and allows local communities, when motivated, to rediscover their own past. Participation in the state in this sense enables an ethnic community to assert its uniqueness.

Moreover, there is the issue of poverty. The addition of this dimension to the discussion on ethnic citizenship should be a major breakthrough in scholarship. Note that both autonomy and ethnicity provide discourses conducive to the sense of subjectivity as well as difference in local communities. However, most ethnic communities fail to explore their full potential partly because the central authorities want to use these two discourses to achieve national unity in opposition to local distinction. However, another reason for the inability of the local communities to take advantage of autonomy and ethnicity is that they lose a position of articulation due to their poverty status. This status gives them a culturally backward image whenever dealing with the state. Since they are not supposed to know anything meaningful either in the state or in the market, it is difficult to confidently assert autonomy or ethnic distinction. Although poverty is seemingly unrelated to ethnic citizenship, it is critical to understanding the loss of agency for change in many of the ethnic communities.

Here is an example of how poverty and identity are mutually constituted. During the period of research for this book, there have been a number of similar incidents regarding the self-restraint on profit making exercised by members within the same ethnic group. These instances revolve around restaurants in ethnic communities opened by villagers to accommodate tourists. The restaurant owners often refuse to charge their friends or relatives for products and services consumed. Government officials as well as local cadres find these practices unwise, or even unnecessary, in the age of market reform. Nonetheless, one should suspect that this reluctance to charge fellow villagers for meals is due to the concept of making money that has already become an issue of identity among ethnic groups. This means that as the government, at all levels, consistently and continuously accuses local communities that are in poverty of being culturally backward, the local villagers respond by treating Han tourists as no more than sources of revenue. As a result, the act of making money among ethnic groups becomes an indicator of strangeness and perhaps even a form of revenge to defend themselves against the downgrading of their self-respect. By contrast, free treats imply a we-group and relaxed self-representation. Accordingly, poverty and identity are indirectly but forcefully connected.

This book stresses the opportunities for local communities to develop their own discourse on poverty, even to the extent that some may retort when the state tries to unilaterally impose certain identities upon them. The designated status of poverty (which deprives most villages of self-respect) may generate the quest for local subjectivity. This is especially true when the work to alleviate poverty increasingly relies upon the preservation of local ecology. Ecological thinking sensitizes the local communities to an ancestral consciousness, which implicitly puts the state in the awkward position of being an intruder.

The Interpretive Approach

The book adopts an interpretive approach. It is the first academic attempt to break down official Chinese discourses on ethnic citizenship in accordance with the existing practices of the state. Specifically, central authorities have developed three separate discourses to deal with ethnic citizenship: autonomy, ethnicity, and poverty. Each section in this book deals with a different consequence of these three discursive regimes. Each chapter stresses the different functions of each regime in formulating local communities' self-knowledge, and provides at least some clues about the contribution of the state to the self-representation of the local communities.

Like those who want to rescue Chinese minorities from the state's monopoly over identity discourse, an earlier work of mine—*Negotiating Ethnicity: Citizenship as a Response to the State*, (London: Routledge, 2002)—attempted to demonstrate the point that the state cannot control the fate of the minorities; neither can it suppress their participation in identity politics nor unilaterally absorb them into a teleological mission toward modernity. One would think that this way, the previous book had successfully shown the coincidental and contingent nature of identity. According to *Negotiating Ethnicity*, it is unlikely that the ethnic communities would completely subject themselves to the state's determination of their self-understanding. There is always room for creativity as well as for unintended subversion. *Negotiating Ethnicity* followed the literature on Chinese minorities and minority identities in celebrating the hybrid characteristics of minority identities. This approach shows respect for each ethnic community's hybridity. However, this is not enough.

This book makes a revision and realistically presents the possibilities that hybridity may lead to inaction and that, backwardly, evolution may reduce hybridity to a name that masks assimilation. However, assimilation can sometimes contribute to the construction of identity rather than to the destruction of it. This book will examine how the national state, or the Chinese identity, can constitute a part of the ethnic identity through the deliberate choice of a local community. The state contributes to the emergence of subjectivity in the local community both positively and negatively—positively because the local community uses the state to achieve a certain identification effect, and negatively because the local community cannot escape from the state in determining its self-representation.

More than Resistance

The conclusion of *Negotiating Ethnicity* was hasty. The inference results from its author's inattention to ethnic citizens' potential to face, comment on, or use the state to support their pursuit for self-representation. The major argument in *Negotiating Ethnicity* was that local ethnic minorities are often able to satisfy the needs of the state. In return, the central authorities allow these minorities to develop their own cultural identities in areas that the authorities care very little about. If the ethnic minorities use the state, according to *Negotiating Ethnicity*, they use it to avoid it. One would honestly think that this observation, based upon fieldwork experiences, undermined the rationality of the state.

In the meantime, the majority of related literature on Chinese ethnography supports observations made in the previous publication. However, most writers did not make general statements in the way the earlier book suggested. It looks that *Negotiating Ethnicity* recorded a kind of experience with the ethnic minorities who creatively cope with the demands of the authorities. All of them have their own ways of coping that are attuned to their own local conditions. In a sense, the book betrays its own discipline, which is political science, by recounting stories of how the state matters in manners alien to political scientists. Implicitly, in this earlier research, the problematiqué rested upon a discursively assumed subjectivity in each ethnic community that is outside the state. These subjectivities enable each community to cope with the state's intervention in their life so that each is able to avoid the state's quest for national unity in their own way, even though they typically appear submissive to the state at the moment they encounter someone carrying the name of the state. Accordingly, the book never conceived the state as an intrinsic element constituting ethnicity. This assumption of discursively determined subjectivity is somewhat flawed because it failed to account for the situation in which ethnic minorities do not simply escape from the state by participating in it. On the contrary, they actively involve themselves in providing different meanings to the state, while those usually intervening in the name of the state do not feel threatened. The state could actually constitute an important part of ethnic identities in some communities. It does not always have to be exclusively an intervening outsider. In other words, the relationship between the ethnic community and the state is more complicated than one could figure it out by reading the previous book.

The state is definitely not a monolithic entity. The authorities acting in the name of the state hardly remain consistent over time and issue, or with one another. The assumption that the state exists is, however, very powerful and relevant to local identity politics as ethnic communities struggle to incorporate the notion of the state as they see it into their worldviews. The assumption that guides the Chinese authors of the statist narratives in the form of policy papers, academic analyses, and media reports camouflages the assortment of encounterings, each radiating into meanings that are unfamiliar to those authors. This book, therefore, moves beyond the quest for wisdom in the localities that serve to avoid, or even deceive, the state, to reach the acknowledgement that the state has been an intrinsic element of ethnic identity in many places, albeit in ways not anticipated or understood by the authors of the state narratives. The book first reviews what the dominant narratives have to say about the local ethnic communities and then reports on the practices and reinterpretations by the local communities in order to appreciate how the seemingly monolithic state has either unexpectedly led to fresh strategies of self-representation, ruthlessly fixed their self-understandings, or incidentally contributed to the evolution of self-knowledge.

The Structure of the Book

The Statist Discourses on National Unity

In the first section of the book, Chapter 1 introduces the mainstream discourse on autonomy, ethnicity, and poverty. The book begins with a review of the Chinese literature organized by the Commission on Ethnic Affairs for presentation at a conference on regional autonomy for ethnic minorities. On the whole, teleology of state prevails in all writings by Chinese authors. All except one paper praise regional ethnic autonomy as the most effective mechanism in perfecting state governance.

Papers by Chinese authors generally begin with a legal framework that stipulates the state's minority policy regarding autonomy. This way, ethnic autonomy and state sovereignty are connected, and the installation of autonomy should necessarily be a unanimous decision.

State officials acquire the duty of implementing autonomy in ethnic areas under their jurisdiction. Those officials who attended the workshop repeated this sense of duty in virtually every session. Supporting autonomy is therefore more of an issue of attitude. The pedagogical function is important, as almost all Chinese writers believe, be they Han or ethnic authors. Thus, national unity and the common prosperity of all ethnic groups are the final destiny of autonomy. Exposing how they reduce autonomy to an instrument of the state to co-opt ethnic communities, Chapter 1 primarily treats the views expressed by these Chinese writers.

Chapter 2 touches upon the area of ethnicity where the state has a vested interest but is seldom specific. The intersection between ethnicity as a kinship and ethnicity as a culture is where Chapter 2 begins. Ethnicity as a kinship is maintained through policy privileges exclusively available to ethnic citizens, which are predominantly economic in nature, with a teleology leaning towards statist modernism. Ethnicity as a culture is designed to maintain the symbolic characteristics of each ethnic community, hence the absence of teleology.

In practice, these two dimensions of ethnicity meet in the promotion of tourism, which is economically motivated to achieve universal modernization. So liked by the state, and symbolically embedded in the claim to authenticity, tourism satisfies the local communities' need to be represented differently. For the state, the important thing is that tourism consolidates the claim of authenticity, while at the same time, it adds to local economic growth that hopefully unifies all the groups in the state more cohesively.

The site of the field research is the Guilin Municipal Museum of Folk Ethnicities. The program shown by the institution is entertaining; the modern facilities and air-conditioned environment add pleasure to the ambience. The audience learns to see the ethnic groups from the external state or the Han point of view. When the ethnic category achieves the status of authenticity, it no longer matters if ethnic groups are interested in reinterpreting the cultural representations of their ethnicity. The variety of cultural representation is unable to affect the teleology toward the ever-higher unity of the state.

Chapter 3 begins by acknowledging that there is no shared meaning of poverty among liberals, Marxists, institutionalists, Confucianists, and socialists. As a result, their approaches to poverty differ widely from one another.

Chapter 3 also reports on field interviews of poverty-eliminating teams conducted in Yongshun.

Poverty can be measured by income, life necessity, productive infrastructure, motivation for higher profit, or ecological condition. County officials, team members, village cadres, and villagers all participate in negotiating the definition of poverty. The theoretical implication for political anthropologists is that the state is no longer able to monopolize the poverty discourse. The Helping-the-Poor campaign gives the privilege of a special mix of statism and liberalism—a state-promoted, top-down mobilization to alleviate poverty through the enhancement of market competitiveness ability. The campaign is illuminative in the sense that the "practical" side of poverty at the basic level serves to mediate among various theoretical perspectives in a silent yet autonomous manner. Interviewees tell stories that uncover the limitations of the official Helping-the-Poor institution. Peasants, like practical theorists, act on the notion of poverty from somewhere outside the pundits' circle.

Toward the end of the chapter, the introduction of the notion of "ecological Helping-the-Poor," a kind of anti-poverty campaign that preserves rather than exploits the nature, can be a topic of special interest. This seems to have empowered some local county officials in developing a discourse on poverty that is distinctively different from, yet still compatible with statist liberalism. This dubious and yet nascent empowering effect should shed light on the pursuit of economic unity in the future.

Unity for the Sake of Local Identities

In the second section, the book discusses how the state's intervention in defining ethnicity may result in its use for the purpose of self-representation in the very styles unrelated to national unity. Ethnic communities living on sovereign borders often face the problem of double identities. Chapter 4 reports on the identity strategy of the Jing (Kinh) people at the Sino-Vietnamese border. Basically, the Jing people identify culturally with the Vietnamese, but are able to separate themselves from the image of being backward by using their identity as a Chinese minority. The Chinese citizenship therefore means something concrete to the Jing community, to which the other side of the Sino-Vietnamese borders is not entitled. On the other hand, exchanges across the border show the world that there are not two separate communities. The Chinese citizenship also allows the Jing people to claim difference of their ethnicity before the Chinese State. The chapter studies how the preservation of cultural identity is parallel with the construction of a separate state identity. The state is reduced to an identity strategy, suggesting that the people living at the border are not always passively torn between multiple sovereign controls.

The Chinese state need not worry that the Jing people may turn their backs after reconnecting with the Vietnamese. Furthermore, the Jing people can enhance their social status when the Vietnamese on the two sides of the borders mingle. The Jing people demonstrate that the border communities do not have to totally surrender to the monopolized domain of national identity. They can use the state in the same manner that the state uses them.

Chapter 5 resolves the priority of ethnicity as kinship over ethnicity as a culture in a local community. Even though there is usually no direct mention of kinship or blood in the state discourses, the kinship narrative is pervasive in the government's policy, such as recruiting minority cadres, giving extra credits to minority examinees, allowing higher birth quotas to minority villages, and investing in local ethnic schools.

It is true that the experts sent by the government before 1956 to study ethnic demarcation considered both culture and kinship. The fact that cultural assimilation cannot change a person's ethnic identity suggests that the reference to the cultural narrative before 1956 was anything more than a double check of common kinship. Here, the "fusion" narrative may be useful in demonstrating that the Buyi people have joined the Chinese nation. On the other hand, however, the designation of Buyi ethnicity by the government makes it imperative that the Buyi people, the subject of this chapter, have an exclusively Buyi origin and ancestry. The cultural custom narrative embedded in ancestor worship insinuates a distinctive Buyi ethnicity that is not to be assimilated. Two cultural narratives accordingly camouflage two kinship narratives; first, the Buyi people and other ethnic groups practice intermarriage to achieve unity; second, the Buyi people remain somewhat unique due to their origin in a separate historical route, which points to distinction.

The rich local Buyi cultural activities enable the Buyi people to claim distinction, despite that these activities are not exclusively Buyi but are simultaneously Miao. The claimed distinction is not distinction per se in cultural terms, but a circular claim of distinctive kinship indicated by the cultural activities, which the Buyi community can happily accept.

Chapter 6 draws further lessons from the introduction of an ecology discourse to the Helping-the-Poor campaign in China. The ecological awareness has provided new possibilities for Western Hunanese to execute indigenous conduits of change regarding the enforcement of certain policies.

The new discourse gives the local villagers a tool with which to interpret the meaning of ecological protection.

Two ecological views emerge as a result: one interpretation asserts that villagers are a potential threat to ecology because they do not understand the importance of ecological preservation; the other sees modernity as the major threat because achieving modernity necessitates exploitation of the nature. The chapter reports findings from a research trip to a Western Hunan mountain site. It focuses upon the opening up of poverty discourse, which allows the representation of previously unheard identities and accommodates possibilities never discussed before. Xiaoxi interviewees were able to cite reasons why they do not favor relocation, but if not for the lack of anticipated support, the government would probably have moved them anyway. Xiaoxi villagers nonetheless have learned to speak their minds. They do not necessarily want to disobey the government or the Helping-the-Poor campaign, but there is a discursive string belonging exclusively to Xiaoxi villagers. They have formed opinions regarding the Helping-the-Poor campaign and the relocation plan, and have evaluated their merits from a perspective not apparent to outsiders.

Relocation is conceived of as being inconsistent with ecological policy. Ancestor consciousness emerges and transforms the outsiders into an awkward participant. Some indirect resistance at the subconscious level may be forming in the process.

Unity-led Disempowerment, Dependency, and Resistance

The focus of the third section is how the state discourses deprive the local villagers of their agency to cause disempowerment, dependence, or resistance. This section cautions cultural studies of hybrid identities that typically celebrate ubiquitous agency for change. Chapter 7 examines the meaning of Chinese multi-ethnic autonomy in Longsheng County, Guangxi Zhuang Autonomous Region. In China, although the ethnic policy is aimed at promoting national unity, the construction of multi-ethnicity comes into conflict with the purpose of autonomy because this construction strips ethnicity of its ability to mobilize people. Local cadres also cannot act meaningfully under the abstract concept of multi-ethnicity, to which everyone belongs administratively, but not ethnically.

In other words, multi-ethnicity cannot effectively represent any specific ethnicity. It also does not serve as an incentive for cadres of specific ethnicity to develop avenues for social change. One likely result is the widespread sense of "no way out" of the institutional rigidity caused by the rigid style of policymaking, which one could discover among interviewees at all social and political levels. Morale in Longsheng seems so low that the motivation to define local problems and to look for solutions is very difficult to generate. The multi-ethnic identity of Longsheng undermines the formation of a strong voice from the grassroots. Representation requires a unified voice, but the creation of such a voice in Longsheng is blocked by the sheer number of nationalities involved. This is true regardless of expectations that individuals will act in the interest of a shared multi-ethnic nationality, which is perhaps best described as a "policy-constructed nationality."

Chapter 8 reveals the possibility of an incorporated ethnic community, losing its avenue for change or subjectivity to face the state. Contrary to what a postcolonial writer wants to see, however, in the diasporic Shui community of Yizhou, there is a lack of avenue for change or self-empowerment.

Chapter 8 reports how the Shui identity is reduced to a by-product of ancestor worship within each family. The lack of avenues for change and the willingness to undergo acculturation do not necessarily confirm the state-promoted modernization theory's linear historiography. What the Shui example proves is that these avenues cannot be taken for granted.

Although the hybrid component in the Shui ethnicity is not obvious today, the chances that some revived ethnic consciousness can reinvent cultural customs should not be ruled out, as long as the Shui communities continue to carry the name Shui. The invention of "The Shui People Grabbing the Flower Lamp" and the interpretation of keeping the old trunks in the ancestors' place are two such possible points of beginning. However, hybridity of this sort is reinvented from their identity and not embedded in it. Nevertheless, the quest for being different from the larger community is both a matter of internal need and an external construction. This is why the simple name of Shui cannot be considered a basis for revival.

Chapter 9 reports the thinking of the township and village Helping-the-Poor cadres. They act as if they are able to narrate their poverty through a different perspective. Usually, the central government is the dominant player in formulating the discourse on poverty and the subsequent resource allocation to resolve the problem of poverty in accordance with its definition of the problem. This chapter examines the likelihood that those who execute anti-poverty policies can learn from the inexpressible needs and feelings of the poor villagers who have developed a different concept of poverty. If local cadres can develop their own perspective on poverty out of their interaction with villagers, they can feel comfortable to form opinions about the central government's stand on poverty. This means that the anti-poverty cadres may be affected by the poor villagers to the extent that the inexpressible emotion of the poor villagers can become a source of knowledge. Acquiring such local knowledge allows the cadres to formulate reactive feelings, which the central authorities believe indicate backwardness.

In their own ways, some cadres may empathize with the villagers when performing their role as Helping-the-Poor campaigners. In this way, subjectivity emerges, either in the mind of the lower-level township and team cadres, or the higher-level county officials, thus neglecting the creation of a unified image. In brief, it is not just what poverty means objectively and how to eliminate poverty defined by per capita income that matter. It is also how poverty can become a component of identity that affects the knowledge about poverty as well as the understanding of those who know poverty in its literal sense.

Creative Compliance with the Unity Discourses

The last section of the book is about how the local communities find room for their conciliatory participation in the process of the state and how they make a living in those areas encouraged by the state. The interaction between the regional autonomy and reform is discussed in Chapter 10. The chapter shows that the possibility for self-empowerment remains alive in autonomous areas. It divides previous research into rationalism and historicism, but incorporating both of them by sharing the possibilities of opening reform to various local interpretations, pertaining particularly to how identity politics leads to different forms of practice under the same political economic circumstance.

Specifically, a close examination of Luocheng's practices demonstrates how change in the county's autonomous status has caused identity consciousness. Consequently, there arises stronger motivation in using the existing institution for self-actualization, despite both institutions of autonomy and market assimilating, not distinguishing, the Mulao community. What characterizes the Luocheng case is its non-assertive style of self-identity—conciliatory, assimilable, indistinct, yet self-conscious, confident, and aggressive. The autonomous status that has been applied to Luocheng County under the guidance of rationalism affects the reproduction of identity. Yet, it does not monopolize the local response. The Mulao way of interpreting assimilation into the Han culture, i.e., conciliatory assimilation as a proof of deep-seated Mulao identity, shows a unique way of self-empowerment. In short, the reform does not determine behavior through incentives. Rather, how reform functions is in itself something to be explained.

Chapter 11 reports on the lessons learned in Jinxiu. Those high officials, who act in the name of the state, allocate resources and make decisions, often reducing ethnic communities to their policy performance. Their primary concern is how local cadres successfully develop local economy and recruit local children for school. History shows that some of these attitudes and their change and continuity have pushed local communities in directions that were jettisoned later on. On the other hand, the Jinxiu communities show some agency for social change, so that the Yao people are not completely and helplessly loyal to the state.

Cadres that carry Yao identities will play an important role when they decide their position between the universalist state and distinctive ethnic representation. They cannot act consistently or together all the time. Therefore, the state they represent cannot monopolize the meaning of being Yao.

Chapter 12 moves to the county of Fenghuang in Western Hunan, where the rational peasant and the moral peasant are not separable. To be rational during reform is to be socially responsible. To be socially responsible in a collective cooperative promotes self-interest at the same time. Reform arrives in Western Hunan in the name of the new culture, which in the local rhetoric refers exclusively to market consciousness. Both the government that promotes reform and the basic-level cadres who run the Helping-the-Poor campaign regard the market as a learned value. Teaching the peasants to become market-oriented is the common and only policy goal among officials at different levels. The primary target of their reform is the "backward" local culture.

Chapter 12 reports on the field research conducted in Fenghuang, suggesting a much richer range of responses from the peasants, which concerned how one can vicariously approach poverty and the market. In other words, the peasants' responses to the introduction of the market culture transmit knowledge on markets and poverty that abide by neither academic laws of behavior nor administrative goals of policy. This chapter does not provide an alternative theory; rather, it aims to qualify all existing theories.

Statism Suspected, Yet Acknowledged

The system of regional autonomy is associated with the expectation of unity and certain universalist standards in China. This concerns what the ethnic people mean to the state and vice versa. However, these are subjects of research left out by both political scientists and anthropologists. The concern of the book is still in line with the literature, since it continues to hold a suspicious view toward the state, and is concerned with the signs of subjectivity in the local communities and the opportunities for their self-empowerment. Nevertheless, this book allows the state a possible role in contributing to the self-representation of local communities. This means that local communities can willingly and actively participate in the affairs of the state while escaping them at the same time.

The ability of the local ethnic community to narrate a counter position of its own vis-à-vis the state's is most impressive. This is specifically so when the local narrators begin to comment on the state, its intention, or its performance, presenting a kind of subjectivity that is unheard of in previous writings on Chinese minorities (including *Negotiating Ethnicity in China*). In the past, by revealing "the weapon of the weak," anthropologists have lauded the agency for change or for hiding from the state in local ethnic communities. Few seem to be interested in how ethnic communities have fared in the discourse regarding development and unity contrived by the state.

This research reads more positive meanings into the state in the sense that ethnic communities can use the state as a tool to understand or represent themselves. The book continues to criticize the institution of the state, which suffocates the agency for change in local communities in many ways. However, the story is no longer invariably focused on how the state controls the agency for change or fails to do so, but also how the local communities survive within the state whose policies directly or indirectly affect their ways of life, ethnicity, and progress.

PART 1

—

Political, Cultural, and Economic Unity

Anyone acting in the name of the Chinese state would find it difficult to avoid the pretension of national unity. That is why, for the state, the issue of national unity is most sensitive in the minority areas. However, to spread the message of unity is not an easy task, as the situations vary widely among minority communities. This section introduces how the Chinese authorities have depended on local officials to propagate unity. Chapter 1 reviews what experienced local officials presented in an academic conference regarding how each of their regions has benefited from "regional ethnic autonomy." Chapter 2 reviews how performing teams in tourist sites indirectly but powerfully display the imperative of unity amidst cultural diversity. Chapter 3 discusses how Helping-the-Poor teams bring disconnected mountain villages back to the touch of the market economy. Both Chapters 2 and 3 describe how local officials in specific minority areas interpret the top-down policy platforms aimed at national unity. However, each chapter discovers some local agency for acting away from unity and toward diversity, though.

CHAPTER 1

The Teleology of the State: Top-down Regional Ethnic Autonomy

Writing China's Autonomy System

In the twenty-first century, relationships between ethnic minorities and their state will be among the most popular subjects of study in political science in general,[1] and in Chinese politics in particular. Officially, China has fifty-five minority groups. In principle, these minorities enjoy administrative autonomy in governing local public policy. Indeed, autonomy has gradually replaced self-determination to become an internationally accepted concept in dealing with domestic ethnic affairs. As compared to the notion of self-determination, autonomy does not require a change of sovereign borders and is thus a sellable solution to the governments in question.

However, the meanings of autonomy are equally, if not more, diverse than those of self-determination. Some might see autonomy as a confirmation of the central government's sovereignty over minority territories. In contrast, many writers find autonomy an attractive arrangement due to their respect for human rights that should, according to this view, have higher moral significance than sovereignty. Others might use autonomy as a conflict resolution mechanism. Still, others promote the idea of autonomy because it best maintains the ethnic identity of the minority group. A final possibility is that autonomy represents an emerging ethic of alterity that recognizes the local agency that is able to create meanings outside the familiar realm of the state.

The diverse meanings of autonomy composed the background as well as the result of the International Workshop on Regional Autonomy of Ethnic Minorities held in Beijing from June 22–25, 2001.[2] The workshop was sponsored by the Commission on Ethnic Affairs under the State Council. Scholars from twenty countries presented thirty-two papers, with fourteen covering issues related to ethnic autonomy in Africa, Asia, Europe, Latin America, and North America, and the remaining eighteen discussing China. The papers by the overseas participants touched on a variety of issues and raised different perspectives, but when compared with Chinese papers, they shared some interesting similarities quite different from the assumptions in the Chinese papers. Specifically, overseas participants were interested in an autonomous system that could protect the human rights of the minorities while the Chinese speakers focused on achieving national unity. In the latter, the role of scholarly research was obviously very pragmatic and even carried the mission of promoting the idea of ethnic autonomy. The normative concerns on the host's side were consistent throughout. This was different from the papers by overseas participants that focused on the philosophical or practical rationale of adopting the system. As concluded verbally by Wang Tieya of the Commission, the overseas writers analyzed autonomy from the human rights point of view, while the local writers were preoccupied with national unity.

In general, a teleology of the state prevailed in all the papers by Chinese scholars. All except one paper praised autonomy as the most effective mechanism in perfecting governance of the state. The papers generally began with a legal framework that stipulated the state's minority policy regarding autonomy. In this way, ethnic autonomy and state sovereignty became related, and the installation of autonomy was set as a top-down decision. State officials acquired the duty of implementing autonomy for ethnic areas under their jurisdiction, and officials repeated this sense of duty in every session. Supporting autonomy, therefore, is first an attitude. The pedagogical function is important as almost all the Chinese writers revealed, be they majority Han or ethnic authors. They introduced national unity and the common prosperity of all ethnic groups to be the final destiny of autonomy. The later sections of this chapter focus on the views expressed by the Chinese presenters.

In contrast to their Chinese counterparts, overseas writers took a bottom-up approach. Their rationale for installing autonomy among minorities revolved around the issue of human rights. Most of them considered ethnic identity a subjective determination that is not subject to the state's intervention. No overseas writer supported self-determination, but the reason was not the protection of national unity or sovereignty, but because the risks of potential bloodshed are too high. Implicit in this analysis is a recognition that ethnicity is cross-border and that sovereign states are not an effective foundation to deal with ethnic issues. Accordingly, sovereign states are no more sovereign than autonomous regions except that the national defense of these regions remains the responsibility of the state. Internally, autonomous regions should be sovereign. Their self-governing power comes from the delegation of residents of the regions, and not from the state.

The Chinese papers appeared to be of particular relevance because Chinese authorities did not allow academic papers on foreign policy, Taiwan affairs, or ethnic minorities to stray from the official positions in any way. However, this does not mean that there is no gray area on the borders of these positions. On the other hand, they must rely on scholarly writings to provide the substance for the guiding principles set up by the Chinese Communist Party. One cannot help but regard the initiation of these conferences by the Chinese authorities as a deliberate move to send some messages. Despite the inevitability that each Chinese author promotes the official positions in his or her own way, resulting in a variety of interpretations that the official positions cannot clearly deny or affirm, the overall messages are actually clear. Regional autonomy, as the Chinese papers try to demonstrate by using different local examples, is the best way to achieve economic prosperity—the key to the consolidation of national unity.

The Perfection of the Chinese State

The notion of minority nationality in Chinese politics was initially associated with patriotism. In 1912, the term "five-nation Republic," which included the Han, Manchurian, Mongolian, Muslim, and Tibetan groups, replaced the slogan "expel the Manchus," which was employed during the pre-1911 anti-Manchu revolution. For political leaders during the period of the Republic, minority issues were understood as contributing to anti-imperialism. The whole purpose of recognizing minorities was that minorities should unite with the rest of the Republic in opposing foreign intrusion. Winning the loyalty of the minorities and improving their status through "positive discrimination" were the two sides of one coin. In the first paper of the workshop, a leading scholar proclaimed the common destiny and common mission of all nations in China:

> China's social nature and the international environment since the Opium War determined that the close union of all ethnic groups is a prerequisite for the people of ethnic minorities to be their own masters and for their national unity and ethnic development and progress. In modern times, China is a

semi-colonial and semi-feudal country frequently suffering from imperialist invasion. The contradiction between imperialism and the Chinese nation was the principal contradiction in China's society. Only by taking the path of union and solidarity can the people of all ethnic groups beat their common enemy and achieve victory in their struggle for national liberation.[3]

Upon this historically determined goal of national unity and national liberation, the purposes of installing ethnic autonomy are to eliminate "the factual inequality caused by history," and to avoid "the aggravation of inter-ethnic confrontation as well as its contradictions." The destiny of all ethnic groups is "national unification and national unity."[4] If ethnic policy does not consider the significance of national unity, the national defense of China could run into serious problems. One writer reminds the audience that areas such as Tibet and Xinjiang will have to do with national stability, national development, and national security.[5] Under such guiding principles, the party secretary of the model Muslim County of Dachang then told of the great achievements the system of autonomy had brought about.[6]

According to one author, ethnic autonomy additionally requires that ethnic cadres accept and adhere to Marxist nationalist analysis, raise the self-consciousness in implementing the Party's policy, and take advantage of their own local conditions and effort to create political conditions favorable to unity.[7] Another author believes that this is why China could not adopt the Soviet-styled federation and instead decided to abide by the Marxist canonical teaching and stick with the unified, inseparable principle in devising state structures.[8] Ethnic autonomy guarantees the success of the principle of unity because ethnic autonomous governments must obey the superior leadership of the state government. On the other hand, Director Wu Shimin maintains that the support of the superior state government is a necessary condition to execute successful ethnic autonomy.[9]

It becomes obvious that the ethnic cadres are given the responsibility of implementing state policy from the state itself. The differences between an autonomous and an ordinary area should at most be two-fold, which means that cadres should have ethnic status, and they should have discretion over how to implement the state policy. The senior leading scholar cited earlier continues:

> The reunification of the country is the prerequisite for and the basis of regional autonomy. Those autonomous ethnic localities are an integral part of the whole country. The autonomous organs represent the will of the state and take charge of their local affairs in compliance with the Constitution, state laws, and regulations. In addition to having the same powers as other

regional authorities of the same level, the autonomous ethnic governments also have other powers according to the law. They have the power to manage the local economic, cultural, and educational affairs according to their specific situation, and they also have the power to administer international affairs to their own ethnic groups.[10]

Like all other local governments, autonomous governments are "bridges and key points to link the state leadership and the masses."[11] An official scholar declares that this is recognition of the greatest possible power of self-governance within a unified nation state.[12] However, recognizing local general conditions and local ethnic conditions should not inhibit the implementation (including expedient methods of implementation) of the state law or policy. Ethnic autonomy is thus no more than a kind of autonomy all local governments enjoy. There would be no ethnic autonomy if there was no state sovereignty. An ethnic Korean scholar from Nationalities University made it clear that there is no such a thing as an "autonomous nation" if it is not at the same time a "symbiosis" or "inseparable part" of a local government of the state.[13] Moreover, ethnic identity and autonomy are meaningless if not located in the ontological state.

Economic Orientation in Ethnic Autonomy

The teleology of the state is equally clear in the emphasis on economic development. It is the state's utmost responsibility to develop ethnic areas in order to reach the goal of common prosperity. One paper argued that the modernization of ethnic areas is the base of modernization of the Chinese state. In its introduction to the amended Law of Regional Ethic Autonomy,[14] all revisions are related to economics, finance, and social development. According to Wu Shimin's interpretation, the new law stipulates that it is the state's duty to "lead and assist" in the economic development of ethnic areas.[15]

Deng Xiaoping was quoted as saying that ethnic autonomy is quite meaningless unless accompanied by economic development. The current "Grand Development of the West" strategy follows this logic, especially since there is a greater concentration of ethnic autonomous governments in western China than anywhere else in the country.

[T]he areas inhabited by the ethnic minorities have been subject to historical and environmental restrictions for a long time, which has led to slow economic development and the widening of regional disparities. It seems that the system of regional ethnic autonomy plays an unnoticeable role in the economic field, and the poverty and backwardness of most of the ethnic autonomous regions can testify to this. Therefore, to quicken up the pace of the economic development of the ethnic autonomous regions, narrowing regional disparities and achieving common wealth and prosperity are the main issues in the ethnic autonomous regions. The solution is not only the pressing demand of the ethnic minorities and the masses in the ethnic autonomous regions, but also the fundamental principle of the Chinese system of regional [ethic] autonomy.[16]

Although ethnicity is more a cultural than an economic phenomenon, and indeed, the newly revised Law of Regional Ethinic Autonomy mentions the promotion of ethnic cultures, there was, to the best of one's knowledge, no serious discussion on ethnic cultures at the workshop. The superior government comes to the ethnic area only to examine how well the autonomous governments have improved their economies. This means that tourism is given pride of place in the cultural sphere because the most important ethnic cultures are those with commercial potential.

This ignorance of ethnic culture contributes to the evaluation that the persistence of economic backwardness has to do with the human quality of ethnic people. That is, to cure the disease of poverty is not much different from curing "stupidity."[17] One participant puts the situation as follows:

> It must be seen that poverty in ethnic regions is not only due to being poor materially; it also includes lack of intelligence, information, culture, and technology. On the surface, these destitute villagers lack food, clothing, and money. Behind these, in fact, lies the destitution of culture, knowledge, technology, and intelligence. Therefore . . . input on education and culture should be increased. Works on increasing information import, knowledge spread, idea transformation, and technology guidance should be strengthened. Only through this can they achieve poverty alleviation and common prosperity in real terms.[18]

Bilingual education receives some attention in this regard because it helps children to adapt to school teaching and transfer to a mandarin system in later years. This long-term plan cannot compete with the idea of utilizing ethnic cultures for quick money in the tourist business. Yunnan Province, well known for its complicated and diversified ethnic mosaic, serves as the model of ethnic tourism, according to a Yunnan official:

> [T]he distinctive natural and ethnic cultural resources of Yunnan should be fully utilized to build Yunnan into a province of rich ethnic cultures with unique characteristics, a province with a strong green economy and a grand international channel that leads to Southeast Asia . . . By showing tourists the

buildings, their daily lives, ethnic costumes, folkways, music and dances of various ethnic groups, it offers tourist attractions in a way that the ethnic culture can be directly perceived as a unique tourist sight. This is a good example of development and utilization of the folk traditional cultures by a commercial enterprise in the socialist market economy.[19]

From the Chinese writings in the workshop, it appears that the top-down style of ethnic autonomy is a matter of policy, law, and criteria of success. These criteria are similarly top-down determined to the extent that local ethnic cadres have no say in what counts as successful autonomy. Gross National Product (GNP), income level, food production, paved road mileage, electricity, growth rate, financial surplus, and investment are among the most often cited indicators. These indicators pitch autonomous areas against non-ethnic governments in realms irrelevant to ethnicity. The meaning of ethnic autonomy is accordingly more about autonomy than about ethnicity. This ignorance of ethnicity implies that a minority is a minority because of blood, not because of culture or subjective choice. In brief, practices of ethnic autonomy in China define, as well as privilege, a kind of ethnicity that cannot be changed.

Ethnicity as Genetic

Ethnicity is categorized in accordance with factors such as language, customs, religion, and level of development. Once categorization is complete, however, one's ethnic identity is fixed. While children of mixed marriages get to choose their ethnicity, once chosen, they are not allowed to change their identities even when significant changes take place in terms of their language, custom, religion, or level of development. In other words, ethnicity is about something cultural in the beginning, but it is nothing more than genealogy now. Probably because of this, the Law of Regional Ethnic Autonomy uses the term "intra-nation" comfortably. For the Chinese government, citizens cannot belong legally to cross-ethnic groups nor can ethnic groups that cover cross-sovereign borders belong to two sovereign countries. Children of an ethnic group belong to that group not because they were categorized by the state into the group, but because of their inheritance of their forefathers' blood.

If members of ethnic groups feel culturally unrelated to their groups, their identity might become a source of self-alienation, if not anxiety, especially if ethnicity carries the mark of "backwardness." The fixation of identity by state law might enhance self-alienation. With the state's exclusive focus on economics, a self-alienated person will not be able to abide by the law of the market that presumably gives an individual his or her self-respect.[20] The resultant profiting behavior that violates certain market norms can easily be interpreted as a sign of backwardness, creating a vicious cycle. From the Chinese writings presented at the workshop, this does not seem to be an issue at all. Most discourses continue to flow under the assumption that ethnicity is a matter of inheritance.

Cultural convergence thus means very little to the drafter of the Law of Regional Ethnic Autonomy and to ethnic officials. As a result, ethnic education refers to the education of ethnic children into a mainstream society. Ethnic education has absolutely nothing to do with common-sense ethnicity. The assumption is that children do not lose their born ethnicity when cultural convergence takes place. Indeed, with the fixation and later separation of ethnic categories, national unity can be an ongoing process. The irony is that ethnic fusion is legally impossible, even if it is culturally desired by the state. For the time being, the state is satisfied that a privileged economic policy has ethnic targets so that ethnic groups are separated and united at the same time. All the other policies, such as exemption from the one-child-per-couple policy, extra points for school entrance examinees, allowances allocated to ethnic students, and so on are based upon genetics, which legally defines ethnicity today.[21]

The most important policy that reproduces ethnicity in blood is the recruitment policy of the ethnic autonomous governments. The law states that autonomous governments must be led by local ethnic leaders, which means that policy dictates the need to recruit, prepare, and promote ethnic cadres. One writer explains: "The training, selection, and use of cadres of ethnic minorities are keys to better work on ethnic affairs and settlement of ethnic problems. After setting the political lines, cadres become a deciding factor. Cadres of ethnic minorities have natural connections with the masses of their own ethnic minority, and they are links in connecting the masses of ethnic minorities to the Party. They are also bridges for implementing lines and principles from the Party to ethnic minorities. So such special roles played by cadres of ethnic minorities are irreplaceable by cadres of Han ethnicity."[22]

Overseas scholars joined most actively in the discussion on the policy of positive discrimination. European scholars generally oppose this policy and favor a policy that enhances the competitive capacity of the target group members so the state would not intervene at the point of recruiting. The philosophical difference, which did not surface in the conference but is pertinent, is that European scholars looked at the recruiting state from an individualist point of view. Consistent with this view is the aforementioned position that ethnic identity is a personal choice instead of being inherent, so it means little to compare one ethnic group with another on the base of fixated ethnic identities. For Chinese scholars who worry about the slow effect of education given to a certain group fixated by lineage, the most effective egalitarian policy has to be collectivistic so that a floor quota must be set to protect the minimum recruitment of members of each minority group.

Likewise, there is the reservation about "positive discrimination" on the Chinese side. Both overseas and Chinese scholars mention the irony that students benefiting from the privilege policy most often are from well-to-do ethnic families, many of whom are culturally and totally assimilated into the mainstream. It is unlikely for many of them to contribute to the welfare of their groups in the mountain regions. Few ethnic children from the inland or peripheral areas can compete well with their well-to-do counterparts in the urban areas. This partially explains why ethnic conflicts occur between lower- and higher-class members. For example, radical Uygurs in Southern Xinjiang target Uygur cadres working for the state much more often than Han cadres.

Globalization and State Teleology

Globalization potentially challenges the teleology of the state. What characterizes the power of globalization is participation in the World Trade Organization. It is expected that the privileges the autonomous regions are accustomed to enjoying today will be removed. These privileges include the recruiting policy that privileges or exempts ethnic members, as well as the allotment of subsidy for ethnic enterprises. A director of a Chinese Social Science Academy worries about the direct challenge that globalization poses to the teleology of the state: "We do not agree on the theory of 'limitations over sovereignty' that has ulterior motives, but political globalization is indeed developing along with economic globalization. It exerts direct impact not only on the exercise of traditional state functions, but also on our regional national economy . . . the implementation of relevant preferential policies on the ethnic autonomous regions will be tremendously restricted."[23]

Globalization similarly affects the cultural sphere. Clothing, entertainment, and art that display ethnic cultures will all witness continuous disappearance, decline, and demise. Ethnic languages will be ignored to different extents or will be jettisoned. If all this takes place at a time of economic weakness, nationalism will likely spread toward autonomous regions. The same author warns:

> Suppose the ethnic autonomous regions cannot make the same progress in development as other areas in the globalization process, or are even totally marginalized, it is hard to imagine that nationalism which has been rampant throughout the world will not expand and drop seeds in China's multi-ethnic areas. Separatist influences in Tibet and Xinjiang do not have a direct bearing on China's economic development and globalization, but it is obvious that the scale of the antagonistic forces and the length of their survival cannot but have a direct bearing on the level of economic development, particularly that of the ethnic autonomous regions.[24]

In fact, the economic prospects do not look good in the age of globalization. The financial capacity of many of these autonomous regions is often devastating. The situation has been exacerbated since 1994, the year the new taxation system was installed. According to another Chinese Social Science Academy fellow, autonomous regions witnessed rising deficit while the financial support from the government declined. When there is support, there is the demand for a local relative fund. Under this circumstance, he sees no chance to achieve autonomy:

> The Law of Regional Ethnic Autonomy as amended in 2001 provides that the purpose of financial transfer payment to ethnic autonomous regions is 'to increase capital investment in ethnic autonomous regions, to accelerate the economic development and social progress of ethnic autonomous regions, and to gradually narrow the gaps with advanced areas.' However, viewed from the operation result of financial transfer payment from 1994 to 1998, this purpose was basically unachieved. Compared with the deficits of ethnic autonomous regions that have exceeded RMB50 billion, the financial transfer payment, the total amount of which was RMB6 billion, was like a glass of water offered to dwindle a whole car of firing wood. In the financial quagmire characterized by 'eating finance' and large amount of wages and medical expenses left unpaid, ethnic autonomous regions are already basically incapable to mobilize local financial resources to develop local economy, not to mention narrowing gaps with the advanced areas.[25]

There is no optimism for the future, either. The current financial difficulties "have hindered the autonomous governments from even managing [daily chores well]." Furthermore, the decline of financial capacity has "in reality reduce[d] the autonomous governments' power to represent autonomous nations to govern their internal affairs." He believes that the current centralization system is no better than a federal system in which local financial capacity would be higher. The current system provides the autonomous regions a degree of support that is no more than "dribbling raindrops."[26]

Possibilities of Opening

Although most authors, especially those in official positions, only want to perfect the state by enhancing national unity and development, and they have no intention of allowing boundary-crossing identities, the characteristics of ethnic identities nonetheless influence their writings. The notion of autonomy cannot rule out the element of deconstruction, as well as reinterpretation, because participants in the system of autonomy have the potential for shifting identities instantly. Even the possibility of shifting, rather than actual shifting, might be sufficient to change the meaning of autonomy.

The room for an ethnic citizen to interpret the meaning of carrying the ethnic identity that the introduction of the notion of autonomy has created is yet to be recognized. The seeming fixation of ethnic identity in accordance with one's blood in fact provides a foundation for cross-border ethnic solidarity. Moreover, because the system of autonomy presupposes the relevance of local conditions in determining the meaning of state law and policy, the state loses monopoly over the interpretation of law and policy. The granting of autonomy in the process of implementing law and policy to adopt different ways presupposes the importance of local agency. Ethnic cadres acting on behalf of their agency thus gain legitimacy even if the agency is outside the range of state policy. This agency would assume a significant role in the future as regional ethnic cadres begin to raise their own criteria of success that are different from, if not contradictory to, the top-down criteria oriented exclusively toward economic development.

The aforementioned paper on the Muslim Dachang model is worth recalling in this regard. While the praise of the Dachang model concentrates on displaying loyalty to the state, it ironically reveals a tendency that has no function in the familiar teleology of the state, that is, on the exchange relationships the county has established with Islamic countries. The relationships developed were ironically the result of the state's diplomatic strategy to win recognition from Arab countries in Beijing's tug of war with Taipei. In exchange, the Arab countries gained access to Islamic disciples in China. The previously fixated national identity in Dachang began to flow across Chinese borders. Dachang's search for new meanings in these contacts is both economic and religious, and surely beyond the teleology of the state.

The workshop itself is an opening of orthodox views on ethnicity as it provides opportunities for dialogue between the autonomy embedded in the teleology of the state and that founded on human rights in Europe. In addition, scholars from Nigeria, Spain, and India, as well as Singapore, each presented a complicated case that directly suggested the indeterminate nature of ethnic identities. In addition, a British scholar's lenient attitude toward a potentially independence-seeking Scotland could be shocking to the audience if they understand the implications of her presentation to China. Many European practices of joining the Union or the World Trade Organization preserve the possibility of national participation and regional non-participation, such as in the cases of Norway and Denmark. The conflicting positions between the national and local authorities allowed in the initial design of autonomy could not be more subversive to the teleology of the state. The purpose of holding the workshop was to promote the system of ethnic autonomy in China. Almost all of the guests agreed to the system of autonomy, although their decisions are based entirely on unacceptable rationales.

The top-down meaning of ethnic autonomy might still prevail in China today. However, autonomy could be creating more local agencies, since it would compel regional ethnic cadres to think hard on what they might do in order to be different. Difference can sometimes be an exotic way of attracting tourist attention or soothing hollow self-respect. Nevertheless, new meanings of ethnic autonomy might still arise. Since the state only cares about the economy while giving the best lip service to cultural development, economically and politically cooperative cadres, left alone in each locality by their trustful superior government, actually open a wide and wild field for themselves to try cultural creativity. What was lacking in the workshop is a language of alterity that is sophisticated enough to respond cooperatively to the teleology of the state, and to report, without being threatening, on the state of the local agency outside the realm of the state.

CHAPTER 2

Performing Ethnicity: Politics of Representation in Multi-Ethnic Guilin

Constructing Authentic Ethnicity

Ethnicity is meaningful only if there are symbolic representations of it through people, things, places, and so on. Words and actions conducted through these representations reproduce ethnicity over time. It is considered common sense among anthropologists that the boundaries between ethnic groups cannot be fixed.[1] Defining ethnicity is essentially a political decision. However, the existence of liminal groups, which move in and out of the arbitrarily set boundaries, endangers any set definition of ethnicity in the long run. Without the institution of state, the changeability of ethnic representation poses no problem to political leaders. However, since the state remains the most powerful organizing frame in the world, the relation between the fixed boundary of the state and the ambiguous, fluid boundary of an ethnic community has to be managed.

The politics of ethnicity likewise applies to China. The act of officially defining fifty-six ethnic groups faces challenges in terms of their representation. The suspicion is that the majority of Han people, who are in a universal position to define ethnicity, are themselves subject to redefinition. This means that the practices of those carrying ethnic identities affect the meaning of being Han or Chinese. This could potentially rock the foundation of the Chinese state, which presumably contains all fifty-five minorities and Han people in a fixed boundary.

Those who must first cope with this potential are those in the position of defining ethnicity. The difficulty being faced by the state and the Han majority lies not in the minorities' denial of their ethnicity but in their cooperative responses to reproduce ethnicity, which unintentionally lead them to disputing the arbitrary boundaries that the state assumes to be natural. In fact, to obtain representation within the state, ethnic minorities readily accept their own identities, each being essentially and authentically distinctive from other groups. While the state enjoys both clarity and stability that this seemingly submissive attitude offers to the management of ethnic affairs, the state loses its monopoly over the politics of representation. The minorities supposedly have better knowledge of the boundaries of their groups. As a result, the state succeeds in imposing a clear identity on minority groups but ironically loses the power to determine how they distinguish from the others, especially with the majority Han. Consequently, any ethnic community might achieve narrative power and psychological subjectivity outside the official understanding of ethnicity. If this subjectivity threatens the state's universal position on leadership, confrontation is likely to happen. The heart of the Chinese politics of ethnicity depends on how to deal with the need to fix ethnic identities and the likelihood that identities are subject to constant redefinition.

In any event, the understanding of authenticity and ambiguity are contradictive. Both of those acting in the names of the state and the ethnic minorities operate under the assumption of authenticity. Therefore, they are not open to implications that ethnicities are the products of practice and interpretation. To avoid the embarrassment where the state and ethnic communities have different opinions on what specific ethnicity means, some tacit exchange of benefits between the state and the ethnic communities seems to occur in China. On one hand, the state, so to speak, depends on policy privileges exclusively allowed for ethnic citizens to co-opt the recipients to remain silent on this issue. Their silence is sufficient for the state to continue operating under the assumption of fifty-five minorities. On the other hand, the state deliberately avoids intervening in the cultural activities of local ethnic communities, which are useful in reproducing ethnic identities. For the state, authenticity thus achieved is efficient enough to mobilize the ethnic communities' loyalty toward the state. For the ethnic communities, they are free to substantiate their claim of authenticity in accordance with the local conditions. In brief, the state defines ethnicity through genealogy or blood, which is fixed and indisputable, while the ethnic communities might want to add some cultural dimension, which is fluid and ambiguous.

The chapter begins by discussing the connection between ethnicity as genetic and ethnicity as a culture. Ethnicity as genetic is maintained through policy privileges that are predominantly economic with a teleology toward statist modernism. Ethnicity as a culture aims at maintaining the symbolic characteristics of each ethnic community, and hence it is not a teleology. In practice, these two dimensions of ethnicity coincide in the promotion of tourism,[2] which is both economically motivated to achieve universal modernization, and symbolically embedded in the claim to authenticity, which satisfies the local need to be represented differently. For the state, the important thing is that tourism consolidates the claim to authenticity while at the same time contributes to the economic growth that unifies all groups in the state. More significantly, the state is invisible in tourism. This makes the claim to authenticity in tourist programs conform to the state's objective to the extent that the ethnic communities presenting their supposed uniqueness feel no pressure from the state. The following discussion focuses on the implications of ethnic tourism to the authenticity of ethnicity as assumed by the state. The site of research is the Guilin Municipal Museum of Folk Ethnicities.

The Stereotype of Primitive Ethnicity

Guilin is among the most popular tourist sites in China. It is well known for its river scene and uniquely shaped Karst terrains. Guilin belongs to the jurisdiction of Guangxi Zhuang Autonomous Region where a variety of ethnic communities, including Miao, Dong, Yao, and many other small groups are located. Travel agencies always arrange ethnic programs for tourists between visits to the scenery sites. In fact, in many local restaurants, waiters and waitresses are dressed in ethnic-styled clothes to entertain the diners. Ethnicity and the natural scenery are two sides of one coin in the local tourist program. The implied connection between ethnicity and nature is indeed everywhere in Guilin. The program designed by the Municipal Museum of Folk Ethnicities follows this mode of thinking.

Physical Strength

Nature can be vividly implicated in the image of physical strength of the local ethnic people.[3] This connection between the physical minority and nature is not unique in Guilin.[4] Guilin is just another example of this construction of image. In one of the indoor programs, a man carries a woman who grapples with him in order to stay on him while swirling in the air. In a series of very impressive moves, the man is able to swing the woman swiftly into the air. They have to hold on to each other very tightly to avoid falling, and their body contact is always swift and very loud. These types of body contact between men and women are very typical in indoor programs. They are characterized by quick movements, strong contact, strength, and the show of muscle.

In one of the outdoor programs called "Up on the Knife Mountain, Down to the Fire Sea," a bare-chested man climbs up a thirty-meter tall bamboo stick on which sharp knives are attached and on which he has to step on as stairs in order to reach to the top. Before climbing, he tries the knife with a flat object and neatly cuts it in half. A woman climbs after him, reaches the middle, and turns herself upside down with her legs on the knives supporting her body. A third person at the bottom begins to move the stick around to make the two people in the air go around in a circle with increasing speed. The two then change positions so that the woman is on top, and they move swiftly around in a circle once more. They return to the ground where three metal pieces burning red-hot are stuck into a long iron stick. They both step on the stick and on the metal pieces several times.

In a less dangerous program where the audience is invited to join the challenge, the dancers jump over moving sticks that follow certain paces of step with the accompanying music. When the dancer misses the pace, his or her foot is squeezed by the quickly moving sticks, and this inflicts minor pain on the dancer. This program is what a tourist would often encounter in southern China's minority areas. These shows of physical fine-tuning are not ethnically specific but are associated with the notion of ethnicity in general. Those invited to be tested are presumably Han tourists who are theoretically not as physically fine-tuned as the performers.

Another program where tourists might be asked to join is the tug-of-war. The contest involves two groups and lasts for up to three rounds. This purely physical activity is very popular among tourists. Strangers become attached to one another with the cheering teams clothed in ethnic dresses, shouting loudly on the side. The competition is not always close each time. The winning teammates often fall upon each other so that in the end, everyone is on top of each other. As physical distance disappears, cheerleaders lead the participants to dance in a circle. They move forward and backward so that the members of the crowd are squeezed into one another as the circle shrinks during the forward movement. The pace of the music is not easy to follow, and disorderly movements lead the participants to bump into each other until they burst into laughter. During the dance, the participants stomp their feet forcefully on the ground together at each interval to make a very shocking sound that creates a physical feeling.

Wildness

The style of clothing is equally noteworthy. Bare skin is the common theme in all the programs. In all indoor shows, women bare their shoulders, waist, and back, while men bare their chests. Bare skin suggests the spirit of liberation and the desire to return to Mother Nature. Moreover, all dancers are told to smile all the time. This reinforces the feeling of happiness of returning to nature. The only exception is a program in which four male dancers dressed in feminine attire play geese. They sport very serious looks while deliberately fumbling all the time in order to achieve an amusing effect. This last incidence suggests that the way the dancer poses is all part of a play. The laughing poses in the other programs must have also been specifically done to create the effect of happiness and liberation.

Since there is a stereotyped image of the ethnic minority being alcohol lovers, the scene of drinking alcohol is constantly brought up onstage. One of the short stories describes how the bride's friend forces the groom to drink until he collapses. No one could wake him up until the bride comes. He recovers and carries her home. Alcohol and love are discursively locked together. Alcohol represents courage, with which the groom dares to take his bride home. The scene of alcohol implicitly makes marriage an institution of liberation, rather than of constraint.

This reflects one of the typical writing techniques in Chinese folk novels, that is, alcohol and meat represent liberation, according to Hsia Chih-ching. The famous novel Heroes on the Water Margin is a good example of this.[5] There is also the story of the beggars' party in swordsmen's novels. Swordsmen are heroes of martial art who are away from the official control and always able to restore justice when it is broken, while the beggars' party organizes lower classes to achieve the same goal. However, both the heroes on the water margin (a metaphor of being away from the official control) and the beggars' party subscribe to Confucianism at the same time. To reconcile the spirit of liberation and the norm of loyalty is the novelist's challenge. Likewise, to reconcile the image of the primitive and the claim of cultural distinction for a specific ethnic community also requires special attention.[6] This is where ethnic music and clothing play a role. In the tourist programs, each ethnic identity should specialize in a specific musical instrument, and make use of particular colors or combinations of colors. As a result, bare skin, which symbolizes liberation, is presented with shining colors and loud music, indicating distinctive cultural styles.

It is not a coincidence that ethnic programs are always about love. The neighboring Xiangxi (Western Hunan) Tujia and Miao Prefecture is the home of the famous Miao writer, Shen Congwen. The tourist programs in

Western Hunan also talk about love stories between young men and women, the practice of marriage customs, and the birth of the new generation. This performance is related to the reproduction of genealogy and blood relationships.[7] These programs are accordingly based upon the perception that Han tourists come to watch the origin and the reproduction of ethnic people. The metaphor of genealogy, once enlisted and repeatedly shown in these programs, essentializes the notion of ethnicity.

Contrast with Han Sophistication

As a result of the aforementioned essentializing programs, liberation, happiness, and authenticity provide the audience a sense of certainty. This assures them that the state is in unity with the minorities and that the ethnic minorities are well taken care of. The living reality in these minority areas, where poverty characterizes their economic conditions, is not expressible. Frustration and sadness in the abortive love story become exclusively Han related. In fact, the Guilin Municipal Museum of Folk Ethnicities uses one of the most classic tragedies—Liang Shanbo and Zhu Yingtai—to characterize Han ethnicity. The story is about how a woman who disguises as a man to attend a cram school to prepare for a dynastic examination falls in love with another student. Unfortunately, intervention by a politically powerful family causes both of them to die for love. The story is about the feudal examination system, suppression by the court official, and the special love between two Han students. The contrast with the other programs implies that there is no feudal suppression—either institutionally or socially—in the minority areas, and that the Han style of love is too sophisticated for primitive ethnic lovers to experience.

The Liang-Zhu story is sharply in contrast with ethnic love stories. In the first of these programs, a large group of young men and women embrace while dancing and singing together. In the second program, the stirring of the groom by the bride's friends effectively leads the audience away from politics. In comparison, the political struggle between different classes and the manipulation of human emotion in the Liang-Zhu show take away the possibility of liberation from the Han people. After all, it is from the Han that the state recruits most national leaders and officials. It is not appropriate that the leader of the majority of the state behaves in a liberated manner or is self-involved in his own family reproduction. This further implies that Han, as an ethnicity, is not about genealogy or blood, but about cultural sophistication. It is the Guilin Municipal Museum's innovation to let the Liang-Zhu show appear in its ethnic programs. No such practice could be seen in other tourist programs.

Chicken Wrestling

Another innovation in the Guilin Municipal Museum is chicken wrestling. In this game, a total of four chickens compete against each other. Held every Spring Festival, this game brings much excitement to the audience. However, one could tell from the Han tourists' excitement that chicken wrestling is hardly an ethnic game. However, the host claims that ethnic minorities living near the Li River (whose scenery Guilin is famous for) are known for this type of game. He further assures the Han audience that once they see this game, they could claim having understood the ethnic minorities in Guilin.

There is a danger in his remark, though. He tells the audience that a triumphant chicken fight depends on experience and strategy. The language seems politically driven. In his definition of ethnicity, he starts with strength and the primitive instinct, but he later slips into political sophistication. In other words, there is the danger of obscuring the boundary between the political and the non-political.

Generally speaking, tourism should not involve politics. It is this seemingly political irrelevance that makes the naturalization of ethnic people powerful. It is not politically appropriate for the state to openly connect ethnicity with being primitive. Nevertheless, the state can take advantage of tourist programs, which spread the image of primitive ethnicity. They cannot be challenged. It is not about defining a specific ethnicity, but about the general characteristics of being an ethnic minority. Even if ethnic communities dispute the state on what it means to be ethnic in its community, it is at best a technical dispute since it only inquires how to be ethnic in person and not how to be essentially ethnic in concept. The dispute cannot be about being essentially ethnic because being ethnic is being natural. The common theme running through these tourist programs is that ethnicity features the primitive nature, and the non-Han reduces the complexity of being ethnic into a technical and local issue.

The Unity Issue

Being primitive and demonstrating liberation are not always positive messages for the state. The state must demonstrate its ability to incorporate the primitive people into the modern institutional setting. The Guilin Municipal Museum tackles this mission of the state. The scene of the stage as well as the picture in the background give a clue on how primitive ethnic people are united with the sophisticated Han. Another common technique is the simultaneous presence of symbols representing various ethnic identities, such as the concomitant and invariable presence of the dancers dressed in the People's Liberation Army's uniform. In a number of occasions, the Great Wall or other well-known scenic sites in China were also in the background. In reality, one does not expect such an image of unity because people carrying different ethnic identities do not come together unless mobilized by the state to join an activity.

The person who confidently puts all the minorities in one picture could not be doing this from an ethnic minority perspective. In other words, this person must have assumed a universal position in order to imagine such an unnatural gathering. The combination of political symbols, historical images, and territorial confinement separated those minorities living on the border from their neighbors who formed the same ethnic community across the borders, which this book discusses in Chapter 4. Examples include Jing in the Sino-Vietnamese borders or the Koreans on the Sino-Korean borders. These groups do not celebrate ethnic belonging because border crossing is detrimental to the achievement of unity within the state. Other countries have witnessed similar attempts in their effort to achieve domestic unity. For example, the American Gymboree or Barney programs always bring together children of different colors or even of different accents. The background is often a playground. In an American setting, a meeting among children from various ethnic backgrounds is possible. Yet, the Chinese construction of unity is not as ideal as this.

In reality, the fifty-six Chinese ethnic groups do not get to meet on the playground. They only meet in the People's Hall. However, the show cannot use the hall as its background because bringing in the site of the People's Hall would defeat the purpose of avoiding politics. To use national symbols, such as the Great Wall or the national flag, is unavoidable. The fact is that the fifty-six groups do not meet either at the Great Wall or under the national flag. Therefore, the political construction of the Great Wall meeting or similar sorts is not as easily hidden. Rather than saying that the fifty-six groups unite together, it is more realistic to say that the fifty-six groups are actually made united by artificial representation.

The message of unity is pervasive in all those programs. One program shows groups of people walking with their feet tied together. To be able to walk, people in the same group have to move in harmony. One small difference would cause everyone to fall. The performers practice a lot in order to perfect their performance. Whenever the audience is invited to participate, all of them would surely fall, but they still enjoy the experience. The idea of foot tying came from the training technique of ethnic Zhuang troops to make the soldiers walk in harmony. Now, strangers who join the program become the potential fellow soldiers, implying the need for unity of all fellow citizens.

The climax of the program comes at the end with a grand scene of harmony and unity. Dancers representing fifty-six ethnic groups do a short performance. Each time, there are about ten groups present. They move fast and fluidly, with shining clothes representing their ethnic group. The movements are so fast that it is unlikely for the audience to tell which dancer represents which group. This should be all right since this last program is not purported to distinguish one group from another. The dancers' movements are in exact harmony. The message of unity here is ironically associated with the loss of characteristics. Different ethnic clothing is used as representations. The specific ethnicity each group represents is not relevant; the symbols used are meaningful only because they are in harmony with all the others.

There is a popular song in China that repeatedly praises the unity of the fifty-six groups. The song is repeated over and over from the beginning to the end of the program. The two phrases that come out clearly and repeatedly are "fifty-six nationalities are like fifty-six flowers" and "fifty-six brothers and sisters are one family." The metaphor in the use of "brothers and sisters" brings together those groups that are by themselves presumably related by blood. Accordingly, those who are no longer blood related still belong to the family by being citizens of the national state. The metaphor in the use of "flowers" reminds viewers of the 1988 U.S. Democratic presidential candidate, Jessie Jackson, who ran with the rainbow coalition slogan. His rainbow represented different colors of the skin. A similar metaphor was used in Guilin in which the colors pink, green, red, blue, and yellow are used to decorate the stage and to support the rise of a particular dancer in the middle, who appears as the "flower in the center" because literally, the meaning of China is "flower in the center." In this particular event, the state clearly represents the idea of unity.

Taiwan as a Target of Unity

One unique design at the Guilin Municipal Museum was the inclusion of a program about Taiwan's aboriginal group. This was a noteworthy addition because with the exception of the last program of fifty-six ethnic groups, there were no other ethnic groups represented except those in the neighborhood of Guilin, namely, Han, Zhuang, Miao, Yao, and Dong. This might have to do with Guilin being among the most popular destinations for Taiwanese tourists. In other words, there could be an economic motive in the addition of the Taiwanese ethnic group in the program, as Taiwanese tourists bring plenty of revenue to Guilin. Ladies dressed in ethnic clothing offering to be photographed with tourists charged Taiwanese tourists RMB10 instead of the regular RMB5 charged for Chinese tourists. Moreover, bananas sold to Taiwanese tourists are priced at RMB6 per kilogram, twice the price for a typical Chinese buyer. However, these private performers and peddlers are not very good references for interpreting the rationale of the Municipal Museum to include Taiwan in its program, which is concerned about public interests, mainly national unity.

The simple fact that Taiwan refuses to be part of China provides a strong motivation for Guilin patriots. The program designer must have considered political distance as a more important factor than geographical or cultural difference in selecting Taiwan as a guest group in the program. The Korean as well as the Mongolian identities, for example, which are both geographically and culturally remote to the four ethnic groups represented in Guilin, were not selected. In short, the unity of the country as a national goal prevails over the unity of ethnic groups.

With the dancers playing the Taiwanese aboriginals dressed in a very different style, there is a string common to other programs. Specifically, bare skin is still a feature and so is loud music. The male dancers each use a stick to knock on the floor to make a very powerful sound. They could not be much different if showing physical strength is what ethnicity is all about. They also stomp strongly on the floor to make a loud sound, producing an overall "heavy" performance. When the female dancers appear, the melody turns soft to induce an atmosphere of love. In the program, the director obviously stresses Taiwaneseness much more than aboriginality. The director's lack of knowledge on Taiwanese aboriginal characteristics is revealed in the programs' political nature. Lack of knowledge of this sort is worth further discussion.

The narrator of the program introduces the setting to be Ali Mountain. This is a famous mountain in Taiwan mentioned in Chinese students' textbooks. Chinese businessmen coming to Taiwan invariably want to include Ali Mountain on their itinerary. For many Chinese who do not know Taiwan well, Ali Mountain and Taiwan are synonymous. The most important aboriginal group that lives in the Ali Mountain area is Zou. On the other hand, the most famous Taiwanese aboriginal group to the Chinese is perhaps the Amei. Given this, the director announces that the performers represent the Amei people. In contrast, anyone who has knowledge of Taiwanese aboriginal groups would know that to represent the Ali Mountain through the Amei is politically and culturally inappropriate. However, what is politically needed in the Guilin program is something to represent Taiwan. Since the Chinese people have all heard about Ali Mountain and many have heard about the Amei people, putting them together to represent Taiwan seems intuitive. This suggests that the program is not aimed at the Taiwanese audience. Even if it was intended for Taiwanese tourists, psychologically, it could only be for those Chinese who are anxious about Taiwan being separate from China. In any case, this ethnic program is not about ethnicity but about unity.

Non-Political Narrative as Politics

The connection between tourism and politics is at best indirect. Note that political messages that are conveyed in a hidden, indirect way are usually the hardest to dispute because the message is treated as a premise of the way one understands the world.[8] In the case of Chinese tourism, politics is the premise of the non-political performing. It is the state's intervention in defining ethnicity that makes subsequent performance represent ethnicity meaningfully to the audience as well as to the performers. In the minds of both the audience and the performers, their collusion in the tourist programs reinforces the claim to authenticity of ethnicity. In addition, the contents of the program, which associate ethnicity to primitive development, further essentialize ethnicity into a useful category to divide and mobilize people. When the occasion requires the state to enlist these ethnic categories, other citizens would not question the validity of the category. At best, they can reflect or dispute the way this category is being treated.

Guilin Municipal Museum's program is more entertaining than those offered at other ethnic tourist sites due to its modern facilities and air-conditioned location. Moreover, the bilingual setting contributes to the participation of foreign tourists. What remains unchanged, though, are the hidden political messages and the mentality of both the designer and the director of the program. Through the programs, the audience learns how to see the ethnic groups from the external state or the Han point of view. When ethnic category achieves the status of authenticity, it does not matter any longer if ethnic groups are interested in reinterpreting the cultural representations of their ethnicity. The variety of cultural representation is unable to affect the teleology toward the ever-higher unity of the state.

CHAPTER 3

Silencing the Poor:
The Statist–Liberal Incapacity in Western Hunan

Bringing Poverty back to Political Science

Poverty is not a subject matter familiar to most political scientists, although their research agenda refers to poverty in one way or another. There is no shared definition of poverty among liberals, Marxists, institutionalists, Confucianists, and socialists. Their approaches toward teaching the state how to define and intervene with poverty differ drastically from one another. This chapter reports on field interviews of Helping-the-Poor teams conducted at the Xiangxi Tujia-Miao Autonomous Prefecture. From the interviews, it appears that poverty has a different meaning when different people living in different places refer to it at different times. Poverty can be defined by income, life necessity, infrastructure, motivation for higher profit, distributional justice, or ecological condition. In China, officials at various levels, Helping-the-Poor team members, village cadres, and villagers all participate in defining poverty. The theoretical implication for political anthropologists is that the state is no longer able to monopolize the poverty discourse.

Political scientists as well as anthropologists cannot avoid the issue of poverty although they rarely deal with it in the familiar agenda of power, value, public management, indoctrination, and so on. However, poverty is implicitly connected to political research. Poverty is an important topic for research agendas focusing on revolution, justice, and modernization, to the extent that the level and distribution of poverty already conditions political participation. When poverty is not endogenous to the analysis, it is nonetheless an implicit condition. For example, research on conflict resolution has to cope with scarcity of resources, which incites a confrontational approach. The study of state-society relations analyzes the struggle between national defense and social welfare budgets. Democratization is a conceptual frame related to the interest articulation that differentiates the haves from the have-nots. Globalization enters the research agenda along with the rise of class-consciousness and human trafficking. Therefore, it is quite reasonable to see political science as indirectly a study of poverty.

Unfortunately, political scientists rarely treat poverty as a serious issue. They borrow the notion of poverty without communicating other similar uses that convey completely different meanings. Both the poverty of political science in this regard and the ability of the state to abuse the notion of poverty are different aspects of the same phenomenon. Being always top-down, the state machine uses the poverty policy to indoctrinate a chosen ideology, whether it be modernism or Maoism. Once it grants poverty a working definition, the responsible bureaucracy will be able to demonstrate politically correct improvement by manipulating statistics accordingly. Likewise, political scientists take the dubious definition of poverty in their research, without further thought. As a result, when politicians approach poverty or political scientists explain political behavior through the notion of poverty, it is quite common for both sides to discover that no shared meaning of poverty exists between them. As the next sections show, the simple confusion about the meaning of poverty affects the self-images of ethnic villagers in the mountains and their ability to formulate their own discourse on poverty.

The Chinese government has been determined to tackle the issue of poverty, especially in the minority areas, since the early 1980s. However, there has been no systematic attempt to clarify the definition of poverty. In theory, most documents and public rhetoric regard poverty as a matter determined by low income or wealth. The issue of poverty has always been portrayed in a negative fashion. The widespread Helping-the-Poor campaigns seem to leave behind the positive meaning of poverty during and before the Cultural Revolution. That was the period when poverty meant purity, which empowered peasants. In contrast, the promotion of harmonious society by the authorities since 2005 shifts some attention to distributional justice in order to prevent peasants from dissatisfaction due to relative deprivation. Under globalization, a different view of modernization suspects that underdevelopment can be a state closer to the beauty of nature, which is being destroyed by industrial exploitation in developed areas. There is also a futurist view. Local governments in Western Hunan actively participate in the idea of the ecological Helping-the-Poor campaign, to the point that poverty turns out to be a blessing.

This chapter sets forth possible meanings of poverty that political theories have provided. The Helping-the-Poor campaign privileges a special mix of statism and liberalism—a state-promoted, top-down mobilization to alleviate poverty by enhancing market competitiveness. The campaign is illuminative in the sense that poverty is at the basic level. It serves to mediate among various theoretical perspectives in a silent yet autonomous manner. Interviewees tell stories that uncover the limitation of the official Helping-the-Poor institution. Peasants, like practical theorists, act on the notion of poverty from somewhere outside the pundits' circle.

Toward the end of the chapter, a topic of special interest is the introduction of the notion of ecological Helping-the-Poor. This seems to have empowered some local county officials to develop a discourse on poverty that is distinctively different from, yet still compatible with, statist liberalism. This dubious and yet nascent empowering effect should shed light on the political science theory of poverty that is to come in the future.

A Statist-Liberal Mix toward Poverty

Poverty in Political Theory

The study of politics deals with the institutional capacity of the state to manage the society, pertaining particularly to the extraction and distribution of resources. The state takes an active role in determining what is to be extracted and from whom it will be extracted. Perhaps, due to the influence of the modernization theory, political science—particularly the knowledge on poverty—is typically about income and wealth. The modernization theory, which tackles the function of the state, does not intervene in defining poverty directly. However, since growth is intrinsic to modernization, the state is responsible for lifting the constraint on growth. This is why the Chinese government's poverty policy has picked up momentum since it was decided upon in the late 1970s that modernization must be given priority attention. The theory that Chinese authorities have applied to the understanding of the Chinese state apparently affects how it conceptualizes and treats poverty.

In fact, the rhetoric of "what is poverty" and "what causes poverty" is often indistinguishable—causes are confused with definition in both theory and practice. For example, take the issue of "poverty as income." Poverty policy should be aimed first at increasing and then at stabilizing income. Tackling the reasons that cause low income ironically diversifies the definition of poverty. Depending on the theory employed by the state, the causes of poverty might include factors such as the lack of infrastructure, education, information, or investments, or a dependent mentality, injustice, incorrect values, and so on. Little by little, poverty as low income easily slips into the discussion of poverty of information, poverty of opportunity, or poverty of culture, and so on. The meaning of poverty expands to reflect the worldviews of the state and its ability to make income per se a less relevant piece of information in making a poverty policy. On the other hand, those state agencies in the street can further gather information about how the poor explain their life conditions and participate in the redefinition of poverty. This process might lead to the revision of the worldview held by the state. The street level workers who are between the state and the low-income level might encounter embarrassing situations where the theoretical standards that evaluate their performance and the expectation of their clients are not reconciled.

Liberalism is among the most popular theories that attempt to define poverty. From the classic liberal perspective, low income is a result of low market value. This refers to the low ability to purchase as well as to earn in the market. Therefore, the aim of an antipoverty policy should be to improve the ability to earn. The state would not question the market institution at all as it is conceived of as a solution to poverty. The more competitive one is in the market, the more one is willing to invest in the state, hoping to consolidate the market. Low income and low competitive abilities are two sides of the same coin. Those factors unrelated to the exchange value in the market, such as spiritual, ideological, as well as psychological needs, do not belong to the discursive scope of poverty. The responsibility of the state is to protect market exchange so as to stimulate the producers to supply. Direct intervention in poverty is incorrect.

Institutionalism that revises liberalism by shifting emphasis from market exchange to property reproduces the fundamental role of the market. Institutionalists believe that the lack of incentive is the cause of low income. Thus, the state should enforce the appropriation of property in accordance with specific and clear property rights—preferably with individualized rights. Under institutionalism, profit incentives are essential in motivating participation in market competition. Minimal income must be guaranteed in order to provide working incentives for low-income families. Institutionalism directs policy toward privatization of public property. Villagers or workers of a collective property unit should be transformed into stockholders. Low income and low incentives are mutual. Hence, to alleviate poverty is to reformulate property institution.

By contrast, a Marxist would consider the state as the cause of poverty because the state survives the control of the ruling class only if it reproduces the property institution that benefits the accumulation of the ruling class. The state and the ruling class are allies in suppressing the working class, which suffers low income and alienation. The state propagates and legalizes the market institution to blame low income on the low competitive ability of individuals, individualizes property rights to distract the workers from class consciousness, and transfers welfare payment to placate the proletarian class. Even though the working class fairly enjoys a stable income, workers still live under poverty. Poverty is defined in terms of ownership of the means of production. In order to minimize poverty, policy makers should encourage direct investments, allowing local villagers to put up businesses using their own capital. Notably, the Chinese socialist reform has relied on both Marxism and institutionalism. However, institutionalism is currently gaining ground, while Marxism is losing its foot. The evolution toward private property rights parallels the development of other post-socialist countries.

State-promoted Liberal Discourse

The contemporary Chinese Communist Party is a Marxist party attracted to the liberal theory. Despite the disintegration of the Soviet bloc, the Marxist discourse continues to guide post-socialist development in the Chinese academic circle. Indeed, neo-Marxists in the West place post-socialist development under the framework of north-south division. The country has a high birth rate in the south, which aggravates the problem of poverty and widens the north-south gap. Immigrant workers move in large numbers from the south into the northern cities, forming the new poor. A similar trend has taken place between Chinese inland provinces (the South) and the coastal cities (the North). Both poverty and crime characterize the poverty issue.

On the whole, however, the Marxist worldview has lost its popularity among the Chinese authorities. The Chinese state has quickly adopted the liberal discourse as reform continues. The new-left intellectuals who continue to embrace socialist perspectives are no longer the prized advisors of the authorities as they once were in the aftermath of the Tiananmen massacre. Yet, there is no open denouncement of socialism. In fact, the theory of the primary stage of socialism, which ex-premier Zhao Ziyang talked about and which has been picked up again since Jiang Zemin, preserves a socialist string. However, the major direction is that China should make up the lacuna of the capitalist stage before entering socialism.

With the lack of liberal tradition in Chinese culture, the institution of a market promoted by the state encounters lukewarm responses from the countryside. Scholars and officials involved in the Helping-the-Poor campaign often feel frustrated with the "stupidity" of the population under poverty. Consequently, they find the notion of human capital attractive:

> Enormous evidence suggests that the low cultural quality of the population is both a result of past poverty and a cause of future poverty. The previous ignorance over education or investment in human resources, which costs the Helping-the-Poor campaign double the work load with only minimal achievement, is a serious lesson. Managing poverty requires managing stupidity first; managing stupidity requires an investment in education. The Helping-the-Poor practice in some areas has demonstrated that educational development to enhance the scientific cultural quality of the population under poverty is a powerful and fundamental way to stop the vicious cycle of poverty and stupidity and resolve the problem of poverty.[1]

In ethnic Western Hunan, "traditional" thoughts and "pessimistic, lethargic mentality" are manifestations of stupidity. The idea is that the poor must participate willingly, knowledgeably, and voluntarily in the Helping-the-Poor campaign. Top-down investment in poor areas does not suffice. However, cultural reformation lacks a clear focus, since it involves too many aspects. For example, cultural reformation has pointed to so many various missions where reformation remains conceptual. These missions include cultivating a sense of responsibility amongst local cadres, raising the level of awareness of an exacerbating dual economy, and encouraging local government to make more investment. The key issue is to improve the profit capability of the local population. Western Hunan thus witnesses a poverty discourse embedded in both the modernization theory and a kind of statism whereby the state is entitled to "appropriating, coordinating, controlling, and supervising the use of economic resources." In the meantime, the state should also teach the poor people to do the same for themselves:

> To structure a bottom-up anti-poverty environment by recruiting the poor population to participate is an important element of the Helping-the-Poor campaign. International experience shows that having the poor population participate in a development project in order to collectively adapt to a market economy is the guarantee in winning the anti-poverty war. The experience in China also suggests that without active, universal participation of the

poor population in the Helping-the-Poor campaign, it will fail. At present, the participation of the poor population in the Helping-the-Poor campaign is a result of top-down mobilization by the government. There is no active, self-conscious, or initiative moves from within the poor population. Some measures must be taken to enable them to participate actively.[2]

In brief, the state is worried because poverty impedes growth and modernization in two aspects. First, modernization might lack sufficient momentum without the full participation of the population in question. Second, the poor might fall further into the lower echelons of a dual economy. This hinders development and does damage to the legitimacy of the Communist Party. To carry out reform and achieve harmony, the state wants to see the poor areas develop. This is difficult because the poor are not comfortable with market competition. Eventually, cultural reformation becomes an inevitable end of the Helping-the-Poor campaign.

Practical Perspectives on Poverty

The theoretical implications gathered in the streets are different from the aforementioned hypothetical abstractions. Three kinds of practical theories are worth noting. The first concerns the culture of poverty. Cultural reformation is to an extent consistent with Confucianism, which sees the importance of mind over matter. Self-cultivation aimed at reaching a high status is more of a culture rather than an economic purpose. Poverty of the mind is a serious drawback. In this sense, poverty refers to the lack of motivation. To rectify the mind, one relies on the emulation of models which education should have provided. Under this cultural context, local village cadres should play the role of success models in the market. Their success can eradicate suspicions toward profiting behavior that previous socialist indoctrination has denounced. Leadership provided by local party secretaries is more persuasive to the poor villages than the profit incentives provided by the state. Cadres cash in on the policy privileges, and the neighbors follow. This would be a forceful demonstration to conservative villagers who prefer to adhere to the existing way of life.

To avoid embarrassment of appearing calculative in a socially harmonious network, the Helping-the-Poor team can take advantage of Confucianism by re-conceptualizing success in the market as a form of contribution to the growth of one's hometown. This eventually reconciles individual and collective interests. Moral incentives of this sort are equally, if not more important than the material incentives. Treating the problem of poverty requires one to step outside the market, and to tolerate collective property in the backward areas so as to maintain a minimal level of courage in the local leadership to join the market.

The theory of the primary stage of socialism, which is the second practical theory, treats poverty as a historical stage to be transcended. The theory encourages those who have the capability to get rich to get rich first, and not to worry about those lagging behind. The Sixteenth Party Congress further raises the theory of the "Three Represents" to welcome the bourgeoisie into the Communist Party. As a result, poverty is legitimately considered a maladaptation to the progressive force of the market.

If poverty of culture is so severe to the point that the prospect of joining the market is slim, the emphasis of the Helping-the-Poor teams will be refocused upon providing basic needs instead of cultural reformation. The most typical projects in this regard include clean water, electricity, and village roads. While central authorities see the goal of the Helping-the-Poor campaign as eliminating poverty, teams in the field are satisfied with supplying basic needs. For those in the field, low income is not the most relevant criterion of poverty.

Finally, the understanding of poverty is practically revised in areas where the preservation of ecology substitutes for development. The lack of development in previous years makes it possible for Western Hunan communities to return to ecological resources to cope with poverty, defined as low income. Attempts to enhance the level of income might result in ecological deterioration. The ecological thinking of local communities breaks up the familiar contrast of development with poverty. By the same token, becoming rich could possibly lead to ecological poverty.

Poverty, as defined by low income, could also serve as an indicator of ecological preservation. Under the ecological mindset, the economy of scale is a concept destructive to natural preservation. The role of liberalism and institutionalism in justifying market forces is reduced to the cause of long-term poverty in ecological terms.

There is no doubt that the modernization theory remains dominant in the state's policy toward poverty. However, Helping-the-Poor teams are able to access local worldviews. These perspectives are rarely available to the public forum. Working as Helping-the-Poor team members might open their eyes to local attitudes toward poverty, ones that are not heard of elsewhere. It is likely that the belief that local communities must go through cultural reformation is not as firm or natural in the local teams as in the central government.

The Top-down Helping-the-Poor Campaign in Western Hunan

The Overall Policy Rhetoric

Economic development has been China's top priority since the 1980s. Imbalanced growth leading to distorted distribution of wealth has concerned top state officials. Poverty in the agricultural areas is believed to hinder national growth as well as social harmony in the government's efforts to modernize.

Following the Sixteenth Party Congress in 2003, the newly inaugurated General Secretary Hu Jintao stated at the first Political Bureau session that dealing with poverty should be given top priority. The Helping-the-Poor campaign, which began in the mid-1980s, has faced serious bottlenecks for some time. In addition, reflecting the widening economic gap, there has been a steady increase in the number of inland immigrant workers entering coastal areas since 1992. In response, the central authorities formulated a more comprehensive version of the Helping-the-Poor campaign to tackle the bottlenecks, followed by the long-term national project entitled "Grand Development of the West." The goal of the Sixteenth Party Congress is to eventually upgrade living conditions and alleviate the plight of the poor.

The government is used to employing a definitive level of income to define poverty. However, in Western Hunan, the Helping-the-Poor teams concentrate on basic needs, rather than on profit-making projects. The first priority is to improve living conditions. Economically related work includes setting up infrastructure. In most cases, it means paving village roads and reducing administrative fees. Western Hunan stresses the importance of infrastructure in resolving the problems related to water and electricity supply, roads, and telephone and radio facilities. Hopefully, this will facilitate the transport of goods and the flow of information. The government branches out at provincial, prefecture, and county levels to organize and staff the Helping-the-Poor teams and train village cadres into becoming Helping-the-Poor agents.

The Helping-the-Poor staffs selected by each government branch are sent to the village. Each member stays for a year, and the shift rotates among them every year. Each team is responsible for a particular site for three years. The team moves to a different site after the three-year term expires. Since individual villages are unique in all respects, each government branch has its own specialty, and each branch's Helping-the-Poor capacity differs greatly from the others. It is almost certain that each Helping-the-Poor project is in itself a specific story. In this regional effort, few have not in one way or another participated in the Helping-the-Poor campaign. This is not unlike the style of the "Great Leap Forward." Government officials are able to establish contacts with the bottom level of society during their one-year service with the team. This learning experience echoes Mao Zedong's idea of learning from peasants. While teaching villagers how to make profit is the mission of the team members, learning from villagers is likewise significant. The team members evaluate their careers after living in poverty for a year.

The official document records all success stories of the Helping-the-Poor campaigns. The reported success is doubtful, however, as a good number of these success cases slip back into poverty soon enough. However, the learning that takes place among Helping-the-Poor cadres is worth noting. These team members are both agents of the government and the village. The mix of perspectives takes place among them. They are both sympathetic and familiar with difficulties at the local level. It is likely that they are the backers of reformulating the poverty discourse. Only those reflections considered "creative" are reported. Others that reproduce the mainstream view of cultural reformulation will not be repeated, except for the sake of providing contrast.

Limited Administrative Leverages

Poverty is not going to vanish simply by reallocating resources to poor areas. Likewise, central authorities cannot possibly formulate specific Helping-the-Poor projects for specific villages. Despite stress on the common senses that one should teach how to fish instead of giving fish, it is up to the Helping-the-Poor team to decide if joining the market is a viable option for its client. For central authorities, the belief is that as long as villagers are properly motivated, they will eventually learn how to survive in the market. Once they taste the fruits of their efforts, they will stay in the market.

The key to eliminating poverty is accordingly a cultural reformation, which is a top-down rather than a bottom-up approach. From the point of administration, there are two incentives for township and village cadres to strive for market performance. The first is the setting up of indicators, which superiors will use when evaluating the performance of cadres in charge of the area. Frontline cadres will find a way to accomplish the designated level of growth in order to pass the administrative check. These indicators are invariably per capita income, the number of acres cultivated, and public revenue. Specific indicators might include social welfare, school enrollment, specific crops, crime rate, and the like. The second is moral incentive—to persuade the local cadres away from the fabrication of statistics or to nurture their sense of responsibility toward the poor.

The top-down approach might have some positive effects on income. However, most township governments only arrange trips for top officials to tour the more successful projects. The county officials also face similar administrative pressure from the prefecture (or the province); thus, they have to find out the reality about the work of their subordinates. However, officials have promotion concerns, and therefore, it is a disincentive to disclose the unresolved poverty in their jurisdiction as this could affect the evaluation of their work. Therefore, administrative incentives exist for officials to exaggerate the achievement of the Helping-the-Poor campaign.

Specifically, almost all counties would fall below the national standard poverty line in Western Hunan. As a result, the county government is not forced to have the ability to eliminate poverty. There is little pressure for exaggeration in Western Hunan except that townships usually still have to meet the designated level of revenue imposed by the superior counties. In other areas where a single county below the poverty line threatens the whole region to be administratively out of poverty, the pressure to exaggerate is quite strong. Exaggeration at the county level is the subject of many complaints at lower levels because the lower levels would not be eligible for the financial appropriation available in the following years that is specifically reallocated to poor areas.

Two examples from a personal case reservoir are worth mentioning. In 1999, a poor village in Beining City, Liaoning was under strong pressure to report a comparatively higher level of income. The cadres would be penalized through deductions in their personal income if they were to report less than the suggested level. To prevent this, they had to fabricate statistics for their boss to show to top officials. Beining is not poor. In fact, it was just upgraded from a county to a city in the previous year. The year was the same year when everyone looked at Premier Zhu Rongji who promised an annual growth rate of 8 percent.

In southwest Hunan, poor Chenbu County forewent the extra-financial support by beating the poverty line in 2000. Local cadres severely criticized the "achievement" which they claimed was only fabricated for administrative reasons. Not only was the income level exaggerated, the rate of enrollment was clearly false. The squeezing effect took place immediately as ethnic schools did not get the expected funding for ethnic clothing. The ethnic schools even considered raising funds from the parents at a certain point. The education commission was opposed to it because the parents might not be able to afford the extra expense. Interestingly, the poverty that killed the ethnic clothing project and the achievement of transcending poverty co-existed at the same time.

Reaching out to the Poor

Western Hunan Autonomous Prefecture is a designated poor area according to the project called the Grand Development of the West. The Hunan provincial government also lays emphasis on the poverty issue in Western Hunan. All counties in Western Hunan are assigned to a Hunan city, which will then be responsible for alleviating the plight of the poor residents in the counties.

Poor schools and individual households may be assigned to the provincial enterprises or officials. The case is Yongshun County, which falls under the 'responsibility' of Xiangtan City. Yongshun is situated near the city of Chongqing. The Mengdong River, whose rafting is well known in the country, is under its jurisdiction. The award-winning film "Furong Township" was shot in Yongshun. In recent years, a unique pool of genetic species (jiyin yinhang or, literally, "gene bank") had been discovered in Xiaoxi Township. This township became a national level natural reserve in 2001. In 1986, the central government designated Western Hunan a national-level poor area. The political sensitivity lies in the fact that Western Hunan once housed the red armies before 1949, and that it has been home to the ethnic Tujia and Miao nationalities.

Hunan's Communist Party Commission issued a document in 1994 that formally declared the Helping-the-Poor campaign in Western Hunan. In April, the city of Xiangtan passed its Helping-the-Poor plan for Yongshun. Villages in Yongshun were eligible to receive Helping-the-Poor teams from the provincial, prefecture, and county levels, depending on the level of poverty of each village. Among the poorest villages, the village leadership (composed of the party secretary, director, and school principal) was taken over by a staff sent to the village by the county government.

On the whole, the Helping-the-Poor teams, the three-year intensive campaign, and the county and township governments all shared a collective responsibility for the long-term Helping-the-Poor campaign. In Yongshun, each village was assigned to a township leader. This individual lived in the village and carried his or her county work to the village office. These in-village cadres were from the superior government, unlike the Helping-the-Poor team (which had no administrative relationship with the village). In addition, at the county level, Xiangtan and Yongshun had an exchange program whereby the former sent Helping-the-Poor officials to the latter area and the latter sent its members to the former to learn governance. These movements of cadres and officials contributed to the growth of all the participants:

> [T]he immediate benefit is to strengthen the leadership. There are more and more people working in the village to resolve all the problems caused by poverty. Cadres assigned to villages understand villages much better. They are able to improve their work according to their experience in the village once they returned to the office. Some younger cadres are developed in the process and stay in the village. They show competent leadership. Others take the opportunity to learn from the senior colleagues also assigned to the village and learn how to deal with real world problems. Leadership at the basic level is crucial to the Helping-the-Poor campaign. The right leadership can always discover a right road for the village. Wrong leadership misreads the information and sinks the village into problems. The Helping-the-Poor campaign actually develops little by little. In 1992, it was decided to let only part of the population to get rich first and then help the rest. However the coastal areas grew too fast. Some administrative intervention was necessary in order to facilitate the exchange of experience and talent.[3]

In Yongshun, a total of thirty-eight county officials have been dispatched to fifteen villages. These villages are less poor than those assigned to the provincial and prefecture Helping-the-Poor teams. The mission of these county officials is to make sure that all the help coming from the superior or the enterprise have local agents. Furthermore, all funding and projects must have a direct contact in the village. When executing a Helping-the-Poor project, the officials must also make sure that they have contacts with each participating household. They are also responsible for choosing the village leaders and supporting them. County-level officials are required to set up a model Helping-the-Poor village, and the bureau-level officials are each responsible for facilitating the Helping-the-Poor projects in the most-poor households. As for annual checks, those who are considered "irresponsible" or have "no achievement" will receive the penalty of downgrading or may even be laid off.

The field trips to Yongshun included visits to six villages once and two villages twice, and meetings with many officials from different levels—the county, prefecture, and provincial offices in Yongshun, Jishou, and Changsha. In almost all the interviews carried out with officials below the township level, village party secretaries provided active assistance. In some cases, county secretaries were present. The county's Office of Taiwan Affairs assigned escorts each time to arrange for transportation, meetings, and visits. Interviews with villagers were conducted where it was possible. On a few occasions, villagers came to chat in the hotel room. Since the visitor's family originally came from Yongshun's ethnic Miao community, the government officials knew him well and the local villagers always welcomed him with great enthusiasm.

The Institutional Incapacity to Read the Society's Silent Response

Culturally Conditioned Poverty

The Helping-the-Poor campaign cannot cope with those areas where there is absolutely no resource or no motivation. Despite investments made in some areas, the prospect for growth remains slim. In some of the remote sites, the installation of electrical cable is even impossible. In others, no water is available; rain is the only source of water. Building roads in these areas makes no economic sense. In the past, logging was the only source of income for these places. Yet, lumbering is no longer legal today, which leaves mountain villages with no means of production. In other areas, hunting used to be the source of living, but this has been outlawed, too. The alternative is to relocate these villages. Relocation requires tremendous efforts of persuasion, especially in communicating with the village elders. Even after relocation, the villagers tend to return home after a while. Relocation can only be the last resort because land for the immigrants is also hard to find. The residents of the would-be host villages would have to concede land to the immigrants. With land, relocation can still fail anyway because mountain dwellers familiar with hunting are not necessarily good farmers. Learning agriculture is a long-term project since most immigrants cannot read, remember certain techniques, or learn new skills.

Equally insurmountable is the psychological condition of peasants who see the Helping-the-Poor teams as miracle workers. Poor villagers expect quick results, but Helping-the-Poor teams rarely bring in cash except for handicapped persons. Even county government officials are psychologically unwilling to share the financial burden. In Yongshun, the Helping-the-Poor teams could not complete their construction projects since the local government who shared half of the funding often made last-minute rearrangements to the budget, reallocating the funds to other urgent cases.

The county government is not happy that outside Helping-the-Poor teams still demand relative funding from the county budget, even though they know perfectly well that Yongshun is a national-level poor county. Another serious problem is the dependent mentality of the villagers, who imagine and expect that the Helping-the-Poor teams are there to resolve whatever problems they have.

Local villagers welcome the provincial level teams, since their financial back-up is far superior to the prefecture or county teams. Unfortunately, the provincial Helping-the-Poor teams themselves reproduce the unrealistic expectation that they are miracle workers. They do this by exaggerating the achievements of their campaigns, using terms like "turning the heaven and the earth upside down" to describe them.

The Western Hunanese style of taking over village leadership complicates the situation. This approach usually leads the villagers increasingly into dependence although the Helping-the-Poor leadership always tries to prepare a prospective group of leaders. Villagers typically lack confidence when their own people step up at the end of the three-year campaign. Indeed, old factional confrontation usually returns to village politics when the team leaves. On one hand, the villagers rely heavily on the teams. On the other hand, the teams enjoy an omnipotent image. Consequently, matters that villagers should be able to handle themselves become the teams' responsibility. Neighboring villages also become envious. They come to seek help as well, but rarely incur the sympathy of outside teams, who plan to depart in three years and rarely shift attention to neighboring villages. At most, the water tower, a favorite project of any Helping-the-Poor team, can also supply water to the neighboring villages. The county Helping-the-Poor teams are more adept at agricultural reform, the result of which can be easily shared by the neighboring counties. Besides, neighboring villages belonging to the same county are actually the responsibility of the county government.

Typically, this kind of Helping-the-Poor campaign cannot bring any significant change to the mentality of the local villagers. In Yongshun, what the villagers need most is housing. Once they earn enough money to build a house, they would think that all their problems would be solved. This conservative attitude toward growth or material profit makes the teams disappointed and pessimistic. Villagers engaged in business brought by the team report fear upon seeing the Helping-the-Poor teams leave at the end of the third year. The provincial government forms an impression that the poor Western Hunanese villagers are trapped in the psychology of "waiting, asking, and depending." Some of them actually call on the government branches, which send in the team after the termination of the campaign for further help. Some team members believe this is fundamentally a cultural problem. They see the poor villagers do nothing during the day except play mahjong. The seeds given to the villagers are sold to buy alcohol. The rabbits given for them to raise and sell become part of their meals. Many continue going to the river to fish. There was even a case in which the team built houses for the villagers, leaving them to make the doors themselves. Five years later, when the team returned, no doors were installed. The worst case was when a team that once visited an area incurred the suspicion and ire of other residents, citing that the team played favorites. The incident led to serious fist fighting.

A provincial Helping-the-Poor team leader believes that the so-called cultural backwardness is a matter of historical coincidence. In his view, mountain dwellers are heirs to those barbarians defeated in the past. This analysis is obviously difficult to substantiate, but nonetheless reflects the impression of the team about poor ethnic villagers.

Another explanation points to the problem of conservatism. The cadres of the poor villages had no education, but had assumed leadership roles for decades. In one extreme case, the ages of three village council members added up to over 220 years old. There is no chance for them to find opportunities beyond the mountains. Neither is there any motivation to work in factories put up in the village. In one case in Yongshun, the brick factory invited by the government to invest in the village hired workers from the city because no one in the village was interested. A team member likewise has criticized mountain villagers for being freeloaders.

No reaction to these criticisms of cultural backwardness was gathered for this book. However, it is not difficult to see the prejudice some team members hold against the poor villagers. The villagers' view of their environment and of poverty is not sympathetically heard. Once induced into the poverty discourse, the villagers are left with no alternative but to rely on the Helping-the-Poor teams. This is a kind of constructed dependence because the villagers are not able to form their own discourse. In an ironical sense, silence or dependence is perhaps the best one can do in a poor village in order to be recognized as a legitimate participant in the Helping-the-Poor campaign, which the villagers have no way to get out of anyway, just for the sake of a quick and easy gain.

Unsustainable Campaigning, Inaccessible Poverty

Many villages incorrectly operated the facilities introduced by the Helping-the-Poor teams after the teams left. The worst thing that could ever happen to the Helping-the-Poor teams is that the campaign seemed to have succeeded, but it actually did not. The teams discover this upon their return. A provincial level Helping-the-Poor official confessed that at least 10 percent of the successful villages returned to poverty the following year. In one of the successful villages, a senior villager described the situation after the Helping-the-Poor campaign: "Food is still food; mountains are still mountains; our lives remain the same." In one case, the Helping-the-Poor teams purchased special machines to dig sand. When they checked on the village the following year, they found out that inhabitants of one village still could not operate the machinery. Another village lent the machine to outsiders. In another case, the machine was stolen. Another village sold it. A similar development took place in another area where the Helping-the-Poor team installed the machine to manufacture bathroom tiles. The villagers used it to build a schoolhouse, which later collapsed. Stories of mismanagement are abundant.

Maintenance is another serious problem. The villagers are either incapable of managing the funds or they simply do not have the funds. In the Xiaoxi Township of Yongshun, the road constructed with the help of Helping-the-Poor funds was destroyed in two months. It left the village completely beyond the borders of civilization, as in the past; a four-hour rafting trip was the only way to reach the village.

Neighboring Sichuan Province has faced the same problem. The road built to connect Meigu County, which is of national-level poverty to Xichang was completely ruined three years after it was completed. What used to be three-hour trips on this road later took nine hours. In Western Hunan, flooding is a frequent phenomenon. The maintenance of paved roads demands constant care, which is beyond the means of a technically and financially fragile county. In 1998, for example, in thirty-one counties in southern and western Hunan paved roads worth RMB2.6 billion were destroyed. Since all of these mountain villages in Western Hunan are vulnerable to flooding, any quick increase in income in a particular year can be reversed the following year.

Yongshun has asked the Helping-the-Poor officials to work down to the household level. In poor households, the problem centers on the sick, the old, the handicapped or the obtuse, and the victims of natural disasters. The problem is that they have no connection to the outside world. One villager who came from a place that suffered frequent natural disasters had told the interviewer that when he took his cow calf to the mountains with him, he knew it had no chance of leaving the mountains for the rest of its life, insinuating his own situation.

Most Helping-the-Poor teams would rather avoid poor villages of this kind. They choose settlements close to the provincial highway to facilitate their work, and to show they have accomplished much in less time. To connect to the civilized urban areas, the teams only need to build village roads.

Those deep mountain poor villages are left to care for the county Helping-the-Poor teams whose members have no means to handle the situation.

By the end of year 2000, 5,374 villages had a per capita income of less than RMB800 in the prefecture. By the end of 2002, a total of 2,500 villages had no roads leading to civilized sites. Of the villagers themselves, 300 had no electricity, 3,500 had no phone line, 1,500 had no radio, two million residents had no access to safe drinking water, and 2,000 villages owned less than three acres of arable land per capita. A provincial official sarcastically puts the situation of Western Hunan as a "serious backward situation said to be a beauty of heaven simply because there is clean air and wonderful views." In reality, this description is completely out of touch.

The provincial official summarizes four serious problems.[4] One problem is egalitarianism. For example, when a special fund is set up to help specific households, the village is usually in disagreement about who should be eligible for it. In the end, every household receives a meager amount of RMB200. The second problem is the lack of financing. The few who receive household loans never intend to pay back the amount owed because they do not know what a loan means. The third problem has to do with the weakness of a crop economy. In Western Hunan, it is all "buyer's markets." The crops are always overproduced. The coordination among peasants is so weak that the purchasing company can easily pass on the cost of the market fluctuation to the households. The fourth problem is that village businesses are generally not qualified for loans. This is especially true after China joined the World Trade Organization, which prohibits low-interest subsidy to domestic producers. Besides, few households can come up with collateral to convince the bank. The risk in the mountains is too high for the bank. Consequently, the more loans the villagers need, the less likely they will get it.

In most villages, the Helping-the-Poor teams are able to resolve certain problems pertaining to water and electricity supply and roads. Yet, they cannot cope with the financing problem. The situation worsens as national enterprises, which used to give privileges to village factories for the sake of policy, lose significant market shares under a regime of reform.

To make things worse, the poor villages' administrations are fragile and not capable of any active search for funding. Social relations are sometimes useful alternatives, as one village director tells of how he relies on his cousin's connection to the county-operated pavement truck company to pave roads supplied by the Helping-the-Poor teams. In contrast, another village, located in the middle of the mountains, could not do anything to recover from the misfortune arising from a woods-rebuilding project. The project was given to the poor mountaintop villages as well as low mountain villages whose view was important to the image of the government.

The villagers complained that the truth was that they did not know anyone in the government, and they were too poor to bribe the officials. They reported that two brokers called on the village, promising government funding for village projects in exchange for a commission as high as 10 percent of the funds received. Another broker demanded kickback from the anticipated gains to the village—either all the money given for the number of the trees planted, at the rate of RMB15 each, or all the reimbursements for the loss of arable land conceded to tree planting. Responding to the inquiry of why they had not sought help from the people's congress, political consultative conference, or other Offices of United Front, they simply replied that they have never thought of these agencies as relevant. It is widely believed that the only way out is to become an immigrant worker in coastal areas. They have a low school enrollment rate and a high birth rate, and portray themselves as "barbarians to whom nobody cares."

For the government, however, the more villages that are above the poverty line, the better. At the macrolevel, the central authorities do not care which poor villages are upgraded first. Social relations therefore come in handy. After all, these villages are all poor even though those who receive the most help are not the poorest. In fact, the "less" poor villages are expected to have a lower rate of slipping back into abject poverty. If these villages return to their original standards, it makes no sense to first help those who will more likely return to their impoverished state. The bottle neck of the Helping-the-Poor campaign is precisely that the poor villages left on the agenda are extremely hard to support.

Teams Between the State and the Society

The Helping-the-Poor cadres sit between the state and the society. Their concerns are not the same as those of the central authorities or those of the lowest echelons of society. Officials involved in choosing the site for the Helping-the-Poor campaign tend to put their own hometown near the top of the list. Other villages or counties criticize that favored sites are the first ones to receive Helping-the-Poor assistance, or they enjoy broader, thicker paved roads. Prefecture and country officials do not have to demand preferential treatment for their hometowns because lower-level officials would have already taken steps in their behalf. There is allegedly a policy rationale for the officials to begin from their own hometowns. This is because they know the conditions of their hometowns well. To begin a new campaign with inherent difficulty, it is reasonable that they need a familiar environment in which to test the policies. Lower-level cadres explain that their sympathetic sequence of campaign actually saves time, since no detailed investigation is needed in places where the officials know the environment well. However, projects such as reforestation require no site investigation. The hometown bias is obviously present in some places.

Each Helping-the-Poor team has to depend on how much support its affiliated organization can supply. Villages supported by organizations that receive steady revenue from service charge or levy are definitely better off. The specialty of such organizations makes a difference, too. For example, the Bureau of Foods as a Helping-the-Poor unit is able to provide seeds or transfer agricultural technology. Banks as Helping-the-Poor units can arrange low-interest loans. Power companies can install or renovate electric cables. Offices of Foreign Affairs or Overseas Chinese Affairs can introduce foreign charity funds. These organizations with advantages and their villages might achieve something concrete. Yet, this does not necessarily mean that the income level of villages will increase.

This is the Western Hunanese style of Helping-the-Poor—focusing on ameliorating living conditions instead of generating income. This particular style is not coincidental. Since the villages are culturally and financially unfit for market competition, it makes little sense to bring them into the market. In addition, anything related to money would inevitably lead to the problem of distribution because any monetary input could produce enmity among poor villagers. For example, investments in education lead to intense competition among villages on the issue of where to build the school. Even building a water tower might cause a dispute. In Western Hunan, where various nationalities live in the same neighborhood, dispute over limited resources among different ethnic communities can become politically sensitive. In one case, parents in one ethnic community refuse to let their children attend a school built in the neighborhood of a different ethnicity. In another case, the upper stream villagers refuse to pay the water fee since they benefit the least.

All these experiences suggest that the Helping-the-Poor campaign is more than a technical transfer of resources. It is also management of social relations. The state tries to calm troubled waters, so to speak, by intervening in village life with a top-down goal of eliminating poverty, defined as "low income." However, when there are problems, the teams and the county officials are held responsible. A provincial official blames the Helping-the-Poor team members for their "lack of patience or a serious attitude with a problematic working style."[5]

Because, Yongshun is in itself a county of poverty, roughly 180 cadres are sent to the village to work on the Helping-the-Poor campaign each year. In the end, over 80 percent of the county employees have served on the Helping-the-Poor teams. A good number of them appear to be reluctant. Since they need to serve for one year, these reluctant crew members avoid serious engagement. There are villagers who complain about this attitude. The county government can only do so much about the attitudinal problem, lest any sanctions further destroy the morale of the Helping-the-Poor teams.

There is no doubt that most team members feel sympathetic to their clients after witnessing the hardship. However, they cannot effectively respond to the villagers' wistful expectations of them. For the team members, they are in the villages to perform a "moral virtue," and not to work miracles. One provincial team member has made this observation:

> From the perspective of the Helping-the-Poor team members, they face enormous challenges in terms of work habits, living conditions, and even the use of language once they arrive in the village. Many do not know how to adapt. Sometimes, even the meal interval causes a problem. For example, villagers may eat only two meals a day. The Helping-the-Poor colleagues really have a hard time adjusting. Some suffer from diarrhea for quite some time. Others have to live in the peasant house for months with only pickles and rice as sustenance. No air-conditioner or electric fan is available during the summer. In terms of work habits, these team members are used to bureaucratic procedure and paper work. Giving verbal orders as usual, many are incompetent communicators in the real world. There is no doubt that many have an attitude problem.[6]

Team members complain that their work does not earn them enough recognition. The complaint is especially pertinent to what constitutes proper relations among team members and villagers. It is a strict rule in Western Hunan that the Helping-the-Poor teams should impose no additional expense whatsoever on the village. The team members' affiliated organizations must pay for everything they use in the village. For those who have provided really good service, villagers naturally want to show their appreciation. Yet, this is not allowed. In one case, a well-respected team member accepted a dinner invitation on the day he left. He was severely punished and publicly shamed by his superior for accepting the invitation. He was even forced to pay for the dinner. It seems that the superior's "drama" of helping the poor undermines the fundamental tenets of a harmonious society.

Institutional Incapacity

The final stage of the Helping-the-Poor campaign is to eliminate poverty in villages and to consolidate those having risen from poverty. This is an extremely difficult mission. The manpower that has been invested into the Helping-the-Poor campaign is so great that it involves over half of the middle-level officials in the county. Praises of achievement are typical, while complaints are indirect and personal. The central authorities raise the Helping-the-Poor rhetoric toward the final stages of the campaign, creating pressure for the provincial (as well as lower-level) officials to expedite the campaign. Nevertheless, the prospect of total success is still doubtful.

The adjustment in Western Hunan to concentrate on uplifting living conditions instead of raising income has a good rationale. Yet, this approach goes against the trend of using income as an indicator. For the central authorities, the use of a "universal" indicator is a convenient sign of national unity and equality. This presumption reflects the socialist nature as well as the benevolent rule of the Communist Party. In reality, no such national institution is available to enforce a nationwide Helping-the-Poor strategy. On the other hand, in light of the vast differences existing among poor areas in the country, there should probably be none at all.

The top-down income-oriented Helping-the-Poor campaign intervenes in local village life and generates unexpected consequences. Few of these consequences end up as feedback to the central authorities or lead to a different conceptualization, although different practices have already generated responses of various kinds, including creative ones, to which this chapter turns.

An Ecological Alternative to Mediating Between the State and the Society

Once a Typical County

Yongshun's Helping-the-Poor discourse follows the mainstream, which abides by income level. There are various quotes identifying the poverty line, from the initial RMB400 to RMB800, and then to RMB1,200 in 2002. The official quote from the provincial Helping-the-Poor office is RMB625. What is between RMB625 and RMB865 is considered the "difficult" zone. However, since villages reeling in poverty might slip below the line, specific poverty lines, which could be met in one year but broken in the following year, are not as useful as to whether or not the effect of the campaign can be long lasting.

There are also cases where the income level is intentionally underestimated, in order to qualify for the Helping-the-Poor fund. However, the official Yongshun Helping-the-Poor campaign continues to attend to income. Since the ability to generate income is low, the county has decided to ease the financial burden of villagers as much as possible. In 2002, the county enforced the reorganization of all local fees into a one-time government tax. Accordingly, all the levies imposed on villages by the townships were cancelled. In return, the county government took over all the payrolls for townships. Furthermore, charges for water and utilities were reduced. All school fees were condensed into one flat fee. The collection of tax for killing animal stock was also stopped. When the expenses were finally controlled, the income level was reported to be higher even if there was no actual increase in the income. Worse, township officials began to fine violators of trivial regulations in order to maintain the level of revenue.

On the other hand, the county government believes that it is important to establish local enterprises to support village finance. The Helping-the-Poor team is expected to provide market information as to what to invest in, while the bank (or the team-affiliated organization) should provide the funding. In most cases, the Yongshun villages do not operate businesses by themselves. Rather, they call for experienced contractors to use village land in exchange for rent. Nonetheless, the rent received is not sufficient to enable any village to engage in a serious livelihood or to raise the income level. It might cover some expenditures of the village, such as those allocated for schools, water reservoirs, or roads. The major source of income is the cultivation of fruit trees, especially kiwi and orange. To transform a rice field into a fruit tree plantation will take five years. For peasants, the required time appears unaffordable and risky. The government will have to send agricultural professionals to assist village cadres in planting fruits. Once there is evidence of success, they could then persuade the rest of the community to follow.

The county government also encourages villagers to participate in the flower industry. However, if fruit farming proves adequate for their everyday needs, they are more likely to engage in such an activity than venture into unfamiliar territory. In short, the villagers do not consider a steady increase in income a necessity.

However, the aforementioned Helping-the-Poor focuses on living conditions, rather than making business profit, which is widely accepted among the Yongshun Helping-the-Poor teams. The installation of infrastructure aimed at generating income and improving living conditions are different strategies. To generate income, infrastructure, which facilitates information flow and transportation, is important. To improve living conditions, the first priority is to install both running water facilities and reservoirs to irrigate rice fields, to cushion the impact of flood or drought.

Yongshun villagers generally lack interest in business investment. If the county government wants to raise the income of the population, the solution has to be top-down cultural reformation to install a leadership embedded in market consciousness. From past experience, successful cadres who can promote market earning come from four different sources: People's Liberation Army retirees, college students seeking opportunities outside the city, returnees who have learned business management from the coastal employment experience, and specially selected postgraduate trainees. Their leadership style is market-oriented, trustworthy to peasants, and technically equipped. One county official believes that recruiting cadres from these four categories can resolve the problems of alienation and abuse of leadership. In short, income level is not a local priority.

Provincial party secretary Wang Maolin has recognized this attitude toward the market. From the experience gained during the first four years of his term (which began in 1992), he concluded that agricultural development, in addition to business, should be the priority of the Helping-the-Poor campaign. His Helping-the-Poor strategy was to enable peasants to live in their natural environments. He is perhaps among the first of the Helping-the-Poor practitioners who conceptually linked the living ecology to the Helping-the-Poor campaign. His remark coincidentally warmed up the movement of ecological Helping-the-Poor that came in a few years later:

> For the sake of establishing a perpetual and stable base of agricultural development, mountains, flood, and drought are the key issues to ecological protection and amelioration. Protecting the ecological environment is protecting the life line of agriculture. Ecological erosion is not much different from "killing the chicken to get the egg"—speedy [development] means [ecological] failure; progression causes regression. . . . Turning dirty sand ditches into clean brooks, presently allocating 15,000 acres to forest trees [in the past few years] has effectively controlled territorial erosion. Eight of the 13 wells around where the X township government is found and which has dried up have witnessed steady streams. In comparison, other places where the trees are cut down to produce timber were to be exactly the same places seriously

affected by floods. Serious penalties await anyone who does not follow the law of nature.[7]

The Ecological Turn in the Yongshun County

Immediately after the Western Hunan Prefecture designated itself as an ecological prefecture, Yongshun also designated itself an ecological county. For the government, the substitution of the ecological Helping-the-Poor campaign for the previous style is still mindful of income level. The government believes that ecological consciousness is an attractive image to the well-to-do city residents, who may be willing to spend money on an ecologically sensitive environment. For example, organic fruits and vegetables are one of these profit-making projects. Nonetheless, the addition of the ecological focus is fresh enough to go beyond the conventional understanding of Helping-the-Poor. Western Hunan and Yongshun are among the poorest residential areas in the country, but they have embraced new thinking quickly. It is very likely that eventually, the value attached to ecological protection might overpass those of Helping-the-Poor.

The central authorities play a role in the promotion of ecological Helping-the-Poor. It was in the early and mid-1990s when the whole country suffered from serious flooding. Both Western Hunan and Yongshun recorded high death tolls and damages. The central authorities responded through a national ban on logging in order to preserve fragile soil from further deterioration. In Hunan, Dongtin Lake (the largest in China) was selected as a target. Peasants around the lake were ordered to "return" the rice fields, which they acquired through paving and expanding the lake bank during the Great Leap Forward, back to the lake.

There have also been nationwide projects of retreating from the woods by replanting trees. Western Hunan—now seriously ruined by paved roads, barren fields, and bare mountaintops—has historically been well known for its green surroundings and serene beauty. The problems of soil erosion and frequent flooding also hurt tourism. Reforestation has become one of the most serious ecological projects in Yongshun.

Another nationwide project that Western Hunan actively executes in an effort to preserve its trees is one aimed at generating marsh gas to substitute for firewood. Some five thousand households installed gas devices in 2002. More households followed afterwards. In order to accrue excrement, each house must breed swine or oxen; animal excrement serves two functions—it produces gas and fertilizes fruit-bearing plants. The nutrition from excrement is better than chemical sources because organic vegetables and fruits also serve as tourist attractions. Marsh gas likewise serves dual functions—one as a source for household energy and another for keeping fruits fresh in the storage room during off-season sales. Marsh gas is currently the core of the ecological Helping-the-Poor campaign in Yongshun. The theme aligns perfectly with the emphasis on the county's current economic investment in orange tree planting. It is hoped that marsh gas, fruits, energy, woods, storage, household animals, and tourism together compose an ecological circle.

The technology needed to build a gashouse is critical to the success of ecological Helping-the-Poor. In fact, the early stage of the project was a failure because staff members were unable to install the pressure-reducing device. Several months later, technological breakthroughs enabled the county government to begin experiments in all villages, each with a selected number of participating households.

The installation was the responsibility of the county government, which also provided the cement subsidy needed to build the gashouse. Subsequent stages involved the building of ecological villages where urban dwellers can pick organic vegetables and fruits, thereby encouraging them to have a vacation in ecologically-friendly lodging houses. The policy is to avoid building hotels. Instead, family lodging amidst an ethnic environment featuring the Tujia style of up-ground house is encouraged. Furthermore, Mengdong River rafting in the neighborhood adds to the tourist attraction.

In addition to the gas-fruits-tourism circle, another nascent ecological Helping-the-Poor project is the national reserve in Xiaoxi Township, which was approved in order to protect the unique ecological woods in the locality. The European Union's environment experts call on the reserve every year. A fund of RMB40 million has been set up by the EU to protect the woods, which its experts have nicknamed "The Museum of Genes." The county has been planning a relocation schedule to move all the villagers out of the reserve, turning them into employees of a tourist company and setting up warm spring sites. The Xiaoxi example connotes a message contrary to the Helping-the-Poor campaign as defined by the income level—the money invested is not for exploiting natural resources to support businesses but to keep natural resources from being exploited. In previous eras, poverty has been attributed to the incapacity to utilize natural resources. Today, such incapacity is considered an advantage.

In Need of a Comprehensive Discourse on Poverty

Not Always a Market Competition

For a modernized state like China, the nascent institution of the market nurtured by a liberal political economy leads to an income-oriented indicator of poverty. Yet, applying this indicator to real villages does not necessarily result in a liberal economy. The official Helping-the-Poor campaign is aimed at creating autonomous interest pursuers who are able to generate and control resources to enhance their competitive participation in the market. The Helping-the-Poor team members, as well as their clients, do not always share the same attitudes. Despite Helping-the-Poor team members' occasional references to backward culture, few entertain the notion of cultural reformation beyond the rhetoric level. The profit incentive is not a popular subject in the Yongshun Helping-the-Poor campaign. Most Helping-the-Poor teams in Western Hunan, in general, concentrate on improving living conditions.

The reality is that the Helping-the-Poor teams never seriously engage in cultural reformation. Western Hunan scholars are also alerted to the notion of cultural reformation. Their lukewarm attitudes toward modernization or market competition have different roots. For the Helping-the-Poor teams, there is no preparation for cultural reformation. The goal of ameliorating living conditions is too burdensome to allow room for distraction. Besides, the widespread phenomenon of "falling back to poverty after rising from it" warns against any cultural overture or optimism. Villagers are not interested in repeating the state-level Helping-the-Poor discourse, except in adapting to the arrival of the Helping-the-Poor teams. This adaptation is hardly permanent. Nevertheless, some dependency emerges to put pressure on the Helping-the-Poor teams, making cultural reformation increasingly difficult. At the macrolevel, the state stresses the importance of enhancing income on one hand, and bans the use of natural resources for the purpose of protecting the environment, on the other. This seeming contradiction confuses the villagers. Many have to leave for good to work in coastal cities, causing further imbalance. Thus, if there is any cultural reformation, it is about immigration instead of modernization.

For many ethnic scholars in Western Hunan, modernization can attract a lot of problems. Reflective scholars believe that participation in the market does not guarantee commitment to the market culture. Even successful adaptation to market competition can be revoked whenever conscience resurfaces to keep progress checked. Moreover, the Western Hunan nationalities would survive the erosion of the natural environment only if the residents join efforts to preserve it. In a sense, dependence on Helping-the-Poor team is not bad since the villagers are psychologically not equipped for productive exploitation. They promote a different kind of "return." Instead of returning to poverty, they promote a "return to nature." A Jishou University professor is confident that this kind of return is a built-in feature of the traditional Tujia culture:

> Every nationality develops its culture out of some specific ecological environment. Whenever the nationality runs against the environment, its productive efficiency drops. To maintain the efficiency level depends on the exploitation of others' interests, making a case of cultural hegemony. One can detect some cultural tendency in every nationality's use of ecological resources. Other resources are typically not fully exploited. This is why a specific nationality's over-development is always done at the sacrifice of other nationalities' ecological resources. The consumption of one nationality is biased and single-dimensional. Multiple directions that exist among different nationalities are a kind of cultural check and balance. When external forces intervene to change the conventional culture, ecological balance is destroyed at the same time. This is a short-run phenomenon, though. In the long run, the culture is able to adapt at a deeper level to resume balance through self-restructuring. Let's take Dongting Lake as an example. The Han population paved the lake for new rice fields, ruining the upstream ecology. However, it is not clear if to return the field to the lake would ease the damage. The Han must think twice before sticking with its own productive mode if the Han wants to engage in restructuring while maintaining the basic cultural tradition. Most nationalities do not just learn new culture like a blind man. At the time of accepting the new culture, there is often the subconscious force of adaptation to reformulate the imported culture.[8]

Together with the rise of ecological consciousness in recent years is the difficulty to eliminate poverty as income levels have prepared Yongshun into the ecological Helping-the-Poor campaign. In other words, the ease that Western Hunanese have taken in accepting ecological Helping-the-Poor is not a planned result. The idea of ecological Helping-the-Poor substantiates Jishou professor's confidence in self-adjustment. The discursive incapacity of poor villagers to respond to the state's Helping-the-Poor campaign does not foreclose their behavioral response. It is senseless to resist it. In fact, local villagers often willingly cooperate with (and long for) Helping-the-Poor funds. The villagers' dependent mentality has strengthened the image of cultural backwardness, which shifts the Helping-the-Poor attention away from enhancing income toward ameliorating living conditions. Underdevelopment continues, but it makes the whole area a perfect place for ecological Helping-the-Poor.

Ecological Helping-the-Poor is qualitatively different from economic Helping-the-Poor: the former considers human agents subordinate to the greater environment, while the latter believes that natural resources are for human agents to exploit. According to ecological Helping-the-Poor, the villagers should not abide by their own need in determining how much they would exploit from the environment. Instead, they should judge the environment first and adapt their strategy to the requirements of environmental preservation.

Under this rationale, it should not be the priority of the state to intervene in behalf of the poor villagers to enhance income level. Furthermore, even though not all villagers might appreciate the emancipative potential of a liberal economy, they are, under ecological Helping-the-Poor, nonetheless able to assert that they are part of the natural ecology if forced to relocate or banned from logging. In short, ecological Helping-the-Poor provides the village with a discursive position to regard the state as an outsider.

Creative Politics of Poverty

For anyone who takes modernization as the goal of the state, it is accepted that a socialist country should adopt liberal indicators to define poverty. For a subsistence economy where monetary income is at best secondary to basic needs in terms of surviving hardship, modernization cannot provide poor peasants with the incentive to join the competitive market. The state's technical concern over income level standardizes the criterion of poverty in terms of the level of development.

Accordingly, peasants living under a subsistent economy are "transformed" into poor citizens. This means that those who are behind the modernization schedule are either dismissed or brought up. Redefining their identity might render them a place in the modern state system, but it is not sufficient to further turn them into competitive participants in the market. Without the process of redefining, poor peasants would remain no more than poor peasants outside the modern state. Yet, once redefined by the state, poor peasants are reduced to a constraint of the continued development of the state. They are a constraint because the state is embedded in the modernist discourse, and because the state is supposedly accountable for the welfare of all its citizens. Without doing anything, poor peasants become the burden of the state overnight.

Between the poor peasants and the state, their relationship is not derivative of competitive market exchange. The state intervenes unilaterally and top-down. This distrustful relationship leaves poor peasants in a permanent status of poverty. Interestingly, under this scenario, their income earned in the coastal cities is not always correctly reported or counted. Unsold and unreported crops are not always calculated, either. Sometimes, other similar income sources cannot be reported, for they are not technically included in the state's crop category. For the poor peasants, the Helping-the-Poor campaign is a source of income, not an inroad to modernization. Their seemingly dependent mentality cannot be cited as cultural backwardness because the poor peasants' purpose to squeeze as much as possible from the state without being absorbed into the unknown process of modernization is not against modernization, but a result of it.

Interestingly, the Helping-the-Poor teams' desire to establish village business runs against the market mechanism, which recognizes individualized property rights, though not village property rights whereby the shares of peasants of the village are equitably distributed. From the perspective of modernization, collective property belongs to the past. Under Yongshun's productive condition, however, collective property is but natural. Many villages own rights to the road, the water reservoir, the ditch, and other public infrastructure. Peasants feel secure only when they can invest as members of a collective group. Under this arrangement, they equally share the burden as well as the profit. To expect individual peasants to come out to join the market competition can bring about only sporadic success and at best, enrich cadres. For those who prefer to stay where they are in terms of income, neither the Helping-the-Poor teams nor the state are willing to recognize its attitude as a legitimate preference.

In any case, the eventual choice of most Helping-the-Poor teams to stress the amelioration of living conditions echoes more of a Maoist, rather than a liberal concern. On the other hand, in the process, there are additionally Confucian elements of industry, hard work and deferring to gentlemen's leadership, which contrasts with the liberal stress on preference—to emphasize self-sufficiency of the village, to despise a dependent mentality, and to emulate cadres who must first demonstrate how to be a modern participant in the market.

Similar to the focus on living conditions, the county government also believes that to lower the levy of the peasants is a Helping-the-Poor measure. The original intention of preparing the peasants for market competition fades in the face of honoring the claim made by the theory of the primary stage of socialism that China is a country of a large population with a shallow productive foundation.

Finally, the ecological Helping-the-Poor campaign further questions the validity of modernist historiography. The nascent project connects the contradictive concepts of economic backwardness and advancement in postmodern values. This final note combines transnational funding from the

European Union, local ecological consciousness, and the national Helping-the-Poor campaign.

Political scientists are concerned with the distribution of resources under the state system. Under this context, the issue of poverty is intrinsic to the management of state affairs. The state must define poverty in order to run national affairs. However, in real life, actors including the state, the local government officials at various levels, the Helping-the-Poor team members, and poor villages work together in revising the meaning of poverty on a constant basis. Concepts incompatible with one another are connected through this mixed, huge, and exhaustive Helping-the-Poor campaign. If the state cannot monopolize the meaning of poverty, the comprehensive and rigorous mobilization of peasants into the market should not monopolize political science research agenda.

PART 2

———

The State Turned Upside Down

While regional autonomy aims at national unity, for the Jing people discussed in Chapter 4, it is an extension of identity useful to distinguish the Jing from the Vietnamese, presumably from a superior position to avoid inferiority for being culturally Vietnamese and to willingly continue practicing Vietnamese customs. While the cultural discourse on the multi-polar unity of the Chinese nation mediates among ethnities, the Buyi people discussed in Chapter 5 exemplfy how the same discourse can imply an ethnicity that is oriented toward genetic authenticity instead of unity. While the recent innovative Helping-the-Poor campaign that relics on ecology aims at economic intergration, the Tujia people, as discussed in Chapter 6, develop an ancestor consciousness to make the external helpers become awkward intruders. There is no intention to resist the state or its discourse on national unity, but there is always room for the strategy of adaptation that turns the state upside down to become a discursive foundation for the local communities to assert their distinction.

CHAPTER 4

The State as a Borderline Identity—Distancing the Jing Ethnicity from Vietnam

Recognizing the Strategic Room for the Border Community

Contemporary political science and international relations studies take for granted the modern sovereign state as its analytical unit. To recognize a state is to fix it within its geographical borders. This statist assumption faces serious challenges from emerging cultural studies literature that problematizes the borders.[1] Reducing the borders to a discursive construction supported by the power practice of those acting in the name of the state, the new literature inspects those micro-practices that use the state to serve functions as well as fulfill meanings outside the familiar scope of international relations. Unlike those political scientists who reproduce state institutions by treating the state as given, students of cultural studies deconstruct the state by approaching the issue from the perspectives of those who are supposedly loyal to the state. In the latter research strategy, the scholar no longer looks at the citizen in a top-down position presumably embedded in statism. Instead, cultural studies provide the bottom-up possibility so that the citizen can look at the state in different perspectives.

According to the new literature, the state's survival depends on the idea of an enemy. It is the enemy threat that allows the protection offered by the sovereign borders to make sense—the "border" promises the exclusion of foreign enemies. Ironically, those who are either geographically or culturally in the closer neighborhood pose the stronger threat to the clarity of the borders. Enmity and intimacy are closely intertwined. While there is mounting literature focusing on both communities residing on sovereign borders and immigrants crossing borders, what their actions mean to the state is always less attended to as compared to what the state means to them. From the critical as well as humanitarian points of view, the literature accuses the state of maltreating people on the borders. But it is not necessarily optimistic about the potential of those caught in the seemingly embarrassing situation to extend, revise, and undermine the position of the sovereign state. On the other hand, contemporary studies on ethnic minorities living at the borders attend more to the difference of the group under study that the state cannot represent, rather than how this group takes advantage of the state in support of its own purpose, such as maintaining difference.[2] Consequently, critics of the institution of the sovereign state might unexpectedly confirm, rather than rock, the predominant power of the state, simply by disclosing how vulnerable the border communities are to state intervention.[3]

The creativity of border communities in strategically responding to the state's intervention in their political lives can exist in both actuality and possibility. To understand how it is possible that the state can be useful to a border community, one is required to move away from the state's standpoint and toward the border community's. This approach is in itself a challenge to the statist perspective because it increases the room to read potential resistance into practices of the border community. The communities might lack such awareness. The cultural studies literature has already begun to look at the state from the perspective of the ethnic community in general.[4] However, few consciously learn from the border community in order to reflect upon alternative meanings of the state. In the interaction between the state and the border community, to what extent the border citizen's seeming loyalty could convey the messages of obedience, appeasement, utilization, collusion, avoidance, resistance, or a mix of these demands deeper interpretation. Under this interpretation, all sides are participants, whether they are state officials, community members, or scholars. There is no innocent, neutral observer.

The act of studying border communities indirectly acknowledges that the sovereign order is an existing fact of life. It is at the same time a study of change in the sense that it opens up the meaning of the border to reinterpretation to the effect that local people are able to escape from fixed identification with specific borders.

Cultural studies thus turn the familiar research design upside down. Instead of disclosing how the state constructs the border through the representation of a border community, cultural studies simulate how the border community presents the state in their daily practice, suggesting that there is room for local residents to make decisions with regard to freedom from the state's imposition of identity. For this purpose, this chapter presents the Jing Community in the Chinese Dongxing City on the Sino-Vietnamese border. Given the strong nationalist tendency of the Chinese and the Vietnamese state, the room for the local reinterpretation of the meaning of the state is rather limited. However, there does not seem to be any trouble as to how the Jing people look at themselves. This is very different from the Korean community on the Sino-Korean border. Their different strategies show the creativity of the border community in responding to the state representation of their identities.

The Border Communities Between Two National Identities

Border communities are the major source of conflict in contemporary world politics. This is because border communities reside in areas that do not strictly abide by sovereign divisions of geography.[5] One cannot deny that the institution of sovereign border can significantly affect the image of the border community, to the extent that identities of the pre-sovereign time become obscure, divided, or reconstructed.[6]

In some of these cases, the potential for confrontation is particularly high, especially when the border community is consciously torn between different identities. One noticeable border community in China that harbors such threat is the Uygur community in Southern Xinjiang. Though not seen as a high-risk group that leans towards confrontation, the Korean community between China and North Korea nonetheless demands conscious reconciliation. The Jing community, as well as the Yao community along the Sino-Vietnamese border, both show almost no potential for confrontation. Their different strategies illustrate how the state is not only the premise of action, but also an instrument or even an object or target of action. The strategy of the Jing community is among the least mentioned in the literature.

The primary subject of this chapter is the majority Jing community, which resides in the three islands off the shores of the township of Pingjiang under the jurisdiction of Dongxing City, Guangxi Zhuang Autonomous Region The three islands, namely, Wutou, Shanxin, and Wanwei historically, culturally, and linguistically belong to the same community residing within the Vietnamese borders today. Both the Jing people and the Korean people have a clear and conscious ethnic identity. However, there is no such need to cope with the problem of double identity in the Jing community as is in the case of the Korean community. Even the effect of the Sino-Vietnamese war in the late 1970s was limited. War did not seem to cause too much embarrassment for the Jing people. The Korean War was different in comparison. With the two Koreas in confrontation, the Korean Chinese population was not able to maintain emotionally neutral. It appears to the Han people that this event should be no more than an objective matter of Chinese national interest. The Jing people are ready to apply different identities on different occasions and toward different people. The mechanism for maintaining the Chinese identity and those for maintaining the Jing identity are so arranged that they do not conflict with each other. The similar ease appears in the neighboring Yao community, which is also found in Pingjiang. Yet, the Korean Chinese has no such luxury.

A few notes on the Korean people in northeastern China are useful for the sake of comparison, pertaining particularly to how much strategic room is available to the border community in representing its ethnicity. The Korean community receives more attention, due to both political and social reasons in addition to its size. First, the border-crossing movement grows dramatically in the age of internal reform and external globalization. More recent controversy over the history of Koguryo has further attracted media attention. The political atmosphere during official diplomatic gatherings is embarrassing, if not intense, because of the historical issue.

Indeed, since 1949, the Chinese state has treated the Korean identity with care. Sensitive about the development of any situation on the Korean Peninsula, the Korean community in China is strongly conscious of its difference with the mainstream Han populace. In addition, motherland consciousness registered in the Korean community is unusually strong, compared with that of most minority groups in China. This makes the Korean community a special subject in the Chinese government's minority policy. After Beijing and Seoul established diplomatic ties in 1992, aid and investments from South Korea have seen a steady increase. An interesting social hierarchy is formed among the three Korean communities, as more Northern Korean women marry Korean Chinese men in China, while more Korean Chinese women marry South Korean men in South Korea. Many of these Chinese women are highly educated. In comparison, an increasing number of North Koreans of less education have emigrated to join the Korean Chinese community. The Korean identity has increasingly become a touchy issue. This is also because, in recent years, rumor claims that after the reunification of the two Koreas in a foreseeable future, the Korean Chinese community would be a potential addition to the reunited Korean state.

The Chinese state adapts to the Korean situation much faster, more willingly, and more sensitively than the other cases. In brief, the Chinese state is actively involved in the reconstruction and reproduction of the Korean identity within the community on the Sino-Korean border. While the maintenance of the Korean identity requires differentiation from the ethnic Han mainstream, state participation in the identity formation decreases the potentially explosive nature of this process. The state sponsors Korean language education, as well as publications of Korean textbooks and newspapers. Most Korean high school graduates take the college entrance examination in Korean.[7] The state and the Korean identity are therefore mutually complimentary. Despite occasional conflict between the Koreans and neighboring ethnic communities, the Korean elite stratum feels a high degree of dignity. In fact, the relative number of Korean college professors surpasses the relative size of the Korean population.

Ironically, the identification with the Chinese state coexists with probably more intensive identification with the Korean nation. One schoolteacher has experienced this double identity in a distressed mood because, according to him, these are the only two nations that still suffer from a split. The interviewee expressed his sympathy and understanding toward the Chinese, who are thought of as suffering. Note that this is a gesture that only a Korean can take.

Most Chinese would feel the split of the Korean nation, if they cared at all, from their experience of the split with Taiwan, not vice versa. When a concerned Chinese citizen reads about the situation in the Korean Peninsula, he or she could not be emotionally attentive to the dispute between the two Koreas. A yet-to-be-published research study suggests that support for North Korea among the Korean Chinese has begun to tilt toward the South.[8] A Chinese citizen, who is familiar with the ideological or interest-driven perspective can rarely feel excited at the Korean situation. In other words, for the Korean Chinese, their Chinese identity is focused on legal and political citizenship. In contrast, the Korean identity has been historical, social, cultural, and even economic in more recent years. The ability of the Korean Chinese to move between perspectives allows them to identify with two different nations, even though these two national identities are often presented in opposition to the other's interests.

This creative distinction between the political economy and the cultural and historical spheres is neither automatic nor natural, and requires effort to formulate. Political economic citizenship is the product of the top-down mobilization of the Chinese state while the cultural, historical identity is the answer to politics in the two Korean states. The Korean community is in an unusual condition because the Chinese state intervenes in defining both cultural and political identities. This is unlike other ethnic groups whose religious and cultural identities are often left unquestioned by the state, as long as they effectively demonstrate political loyalty. No such leeway is available in the Korean community. Both states watch their responses.

Jing as a State-granted Identity

In the Jing community, there is no effort to cope with the Chinese and Vietnamese identity problems. In fact, they oppose each other in the sovereignty discourse. Some patriotic effort exists in the Han and Zhuang neighborhoods. Surprisingly, this effort does not arouse any unease in the Jing community. For example, in the streets of Dongxing, private homes voluntarily put up Chinese national flags. Local officials report that in the streets of the county of Mangjie (across the Beilun River that separates China from Vietnam), Vietnamese national flags are seen fluttering in the wind. The three Jing islands belonging to Dongxing do not witness the same patriotic performance. Local residents report that they do not have to deal with national identity issues because they are all doubtlessly Chinese. This does not mean that they have completely settled the identity issues, although their ability to remain psychologically outside of border war is nonetheless worth noting.

In 1979, the local populace witnessed a border war right in their midst. In the aftermath, Chinese Vietnamese spilled over the Chinese borders. These Chinese Vietnamese included both the Chinese living in Vietnam and the Vietnamese who once lived in China. In fact, there was the historical Sino-French war in 1885 that also involved the local residents. Yet, in this earlier war, the Jing people served on the French side.

Evidence suggests that the Jing community remains tightly within the discursive confinement of the sovereign state. Note how local cadres explain the origin of the name "Jing." They unanimously report that the name bestowed by the government indicates the Jing community member's heart is toward Beijing. The late Premier Zhou Enlai allegedly bestowed the word "Jing" (literally capital) on today's Jing ethnicity. This is hardly believable, but it reflects the pride that local cadres have in their connection with national leaders. The Jing people were already called Jing long before 1956, the year the name sank into their consciousness. Jing is pronounced in accordance with the local dialect. It is the term "Kinh" from the Bai dialect, with which the Jing people identify themselves. The Jing cadres leave aside an origin that carries more distinctiveness for the sake of an imagined connection with Beijing. This decision is not without motivation. However, there is no evidence to determine when this contemporary story of naming became popular. The early 1980s is perhaps a good guess.

In the past, the Jing population in the three islands (then numbering about twelve thousand) depended on fishing for a living. The central government invested heavily to gradually fill the sea gulf between the islands and the continent. This new "pavement" creates both land for cultivation and road for transportation. As a result, the three islands have been artificially changed into a peninsula. This kind of economic reform has improved the living standards of the Jing community. Moreover, a number of interviewees mentioned that Han women are now willing to marry Jing men. This is dramatically different from the past, when interviewees had to identity their Jing membership in order to win sympathy from the sellers and to receive a more favorable price or quantity.

In recent years, the development has even been more impressive. Tourism has been the key to the growth of the local economy. The Jing people now return to the sea, and sea products are in such great demand that even Han immigrants visit the islands to look for jobs. The tourist industry continues to grow. One famous site is the Golden Beach in Wanwei, a name that suggests a higher quality than Silver Beach in the far more famous Beihai city, Guangxi, which is roughly three hours away. In addition, Dongxing has become the transit point to Mangjie where the Vietnamese government has invested in casino and horse racing. All these developments since the 1970s condition the politics of identity.

The central government's investment generates noticeable growth, which should have contributed to the identification toward the Chinese state. This might explain why there has been an enthusiasm to embrace the Chinese identity in the 1980s. The competition between Dongxing and Mangjie also contributes to the sensitivity toward identity over the recent years. A Jing official working in Dongxing's Department of United Front expressed his anxiety several times during an interview that Mangjie could eventually outperform Dongxing. More serious is that distinctions between the Jing and the Vietnamese communities have been blurred, as tourist activities dominate local business.

More and more Vietnamese come to the Jing islands and Dongxing to work, and more Jing people work in Vietnam. The majority of these transnational workers commute from home, crossing national boundaries twice a day. A Jing official of the Dongxing Bureau of Education is working to promote the Vietnamese language program in the hope that the Jing people will be able to do business more efficiently with the Vietnamese. However, the mingling of the border communities generates pressure on the Jing people to decide who they are fundamentally. If the political economy has propelled them to a higher economic, social status, it is natural that the Jing people will stick with the Chinese identity.

The irony is that continued growth depends on further interaction with the Vietnamese community. The local government is actively involved in pushing the Jing people into the Vietnamese market. The neighboring Pingxiang City has signed an exchange program for the Pingxiang Occupational School with a Vietnamese school. They will select students for a year for language exchange. Dongxing officials are anxious upon seeing this development because language is supposedly the strength of the Jing people. Dongxing's efforts to negotiate a similar exchange program for Jing students has yet to bear results, but there is a new adult language class helping Jing people familiarize themselves with written Vietnamese so that they could negotiate and sign transnational business contracts. The problem is that the Jing people do not enjoy being identified with the Vietnamese, who are historically as well as economically considered inferior to Chinese, especially by other Chinese groups.

From the Han or Zhuang outsiders' point of view, there is no clear distinction between Jing and Vietnamese. Indeed, all the tourist products sold in local stores or food in restaurants feature Vietnamese exoticness. Chinese tourists see Jing girls working in Vietnam as Vietnamese girls. The Chinese identity seems to be an identity that connotes a higher social status. One such female worker says that she feels insulted every time Chinese male tourists speak to her in poor Vietnamese as a gesture of friendship. She says, "My own people still treat me as Vietnamese even when I speak to them in Chinese." She continues, "Han is the primary group in China while Jing is the primary group in Vietnam." She is a Jing, but also a Chinese who sees other Chinese as her "own people." In short, she has no difficulty identifying herself as a Jing culturally, but insists that she is basically Chinese while in front of another Chinese. To them, being both Jing and Chinese is natural. Otherwise, the Jing people would be regarded as lacking integrity.

However, unlike the Vietnamese Kinh identity that needs no conscious effort to maintain, the Chinese Jing identity is learned and requires much effort to maintain. The Jing people are happy to undertake such a task, for both political and economic reasons. However, the mobilization through the Chinese identity, even during the war, does not lead to the weakening of the Jing identity. This might suggest that the Jing identity is actually very strong and deep, thus making the alleged Chinese identity superficial. The next section will demonstrate the strength and depth of the Jing identity and, then, argue that the Chinese identity in the Jing community is functional with regard to the enhancement of social status. While the Jing identity is an intrinsic identity that separates the Jing people from other Chinese, the Chinese identity is functional with respect to separating the Jing people from other Vietnamese.

Jing as a Cultural and Border-blind Identity

Virtually everyone interviewed in the three islands have relatives in Vietnam. The Dongxing officials estimate that seventy thousand Vietnamese refugees currently settling in the foreign land are relatives of Dongxing residents. During the war in 1979, some Jings were recruited to be interpreters for the Chinese intelligence. No one can recall any social tension with either the Vietnamese or the Han Chinese during the war. In fact, not even a single shell landed on Piangiing territory. The Jing interviewees were confident that the Vietnamese would not terrorize the Jing community. (Only outsiders have become paranoid, they claim.) How can such confidence be maintained? Why does the Chinese identity not intervene in or weaken the cultural identification with Vietnam?

According to the interviewees, there are three areas where the Jing people engage in identity reproduction: engagement in religious Ha'ting worship, revival of the single-string zither, and installation of an egret reserve. Ancestor consciousness, cultural consciousness, and indigenous consciousness are beyond the concerns of the state. The Chinese Jing and the Vietnamese are connected through their ancestors and cultural consciousness. At the same time, indigenous consciousness provides a vague territorial basis for the local identity to thrive upon. All three dimensions together compose a discursive foundation outside of the Chinese state, and create a basis for the Jing people to claim an authentic difference.

This sense of difference allows the Jing people to feel secure while deferring to the state of the Han and Zhuang majority. In return, the Chinese identity that is added to the Jing identity becomes useful to the extent that it serves to distinguish the Jing people from the Vietnamese people. In this second-order interpretation, the Jing community incorporates the Chinese state into becoming a part of its identity strategy. This strategy gives the Chinese state a meaning that is hardly comprehensible to those acting in the name of the state. The latter have no idea that the Jing identity, which the state installs for the convenience of ruling, now engulfs the state. The state's policy toward the Jing community is at the same time a policy toward the state itself because its policy affects how the state is received and reproduced by the local people in the next round. The state loses its universal, neutral, and external position.

Ha'ting worship is widespread among the Jing people. Each of the three islands has its own Ha'ting temple. Ha'ting worship combines legends, religion, and ancestor worship. Initially, the Ha'ting festival was typically celebrated in the beginning of lunar June. Later, in order to avoid conflict with the harvest season, Wutou changed it to August 1, and Shanxin to August 9. Wanwei decided to keep it close to the original date and set it on June 9. During the opening, a Ha'ting ritual first invites the God of Peace at Sea who, according to legend, conquered the Ghost of Centipede. The creature's power is believed to have caused the three islands to form the shape of a centipede swimming ashore. In fact, the first island is named Wutou to literally mean the head of a centipede.

Another major purpose of Ha'ting worship is to summon rainfall. Once the God is in the temple, the ritual is centered on the worship to ancestors. One of the elderly villagers leads this ceremony. The selection is based on a lottery. Every household prays to its ancestors and reads sacred texts. In the meantime, a group of Ha'ting sisters sing the wish for the God's and ancestors' blessing. A family reunion is the final stage. Most family members working in other cities return to join their family. In recent years, Vietnamese priests have been invited to lead the prayer in the role of the God of Peace.

The Jing community is highly attentive to existing tradition and long lasting phenomenon, even the age of trees. In Wanwei, the village council makes tablets for trees over a hundred years. All households keep their ancestors' plates. The Ha'ting temple is filled with Chinese calligraphy, praising common ancestors. Most of these paintings trace the origin of the Jing people to an imagined, remote past, and each in its beautiful, imaginative style. Some of these paintings promote national consciousness and unity. There are also many paintings expressing gratitude for good fortune enjoyed by the current generations. The interior of the Ha'ting temple is full of Chinese calligraphy.

One interviewee reveals that many of the writings are works of Han residents. The Vietnamese on the other side of the border share both rituals and ancestral worship. Interestingly, the message of national unity that appears conspicuous among all the rituals discursively connects the Jing people to the broader Chinese nation. In addition, Ha'ting worship is carried through a patriarchal lineage to such an extent that girls are not allowed in the temple. Anthropologist Zhang Zhaohe observes that Vietnamese prostitutes are not allowed near the temple, while those married into local families can stand outside and watch. Zhang suggests that this practice reproduces the myth that the Jing community is composed of "pure blood".[9]

The other identity practice that has attracted attention is the revived tradition of the single-string zither, which is unique to this ethnic community. The instrument has a history that can be traced to the Tang dynasty. It is well known for its love songs and blue melodies and is still popular in Vietnam today. Traditional songs played by the single-string instrument are common to both cultures. These melodies play an important role in Ha'ting worship. Since the music records legends, customs, and old poems, learning to play the single-string is also quite an educational experience. Because younger generations are rarely attracted to this instrument, the succession problem appears imminent. In fact, today's Ha'ting sisters are all over fifty years of age, and few young girls can sing and dance for the ceremony. Both school and village party division are looking for ways to attract young people. A total of three single-string players from three different generations accepted interviews. According to their personal experiences, learning the single-string has been a conscious decision on their part. Indeed, it is not realistic for everyone to try making a living by playing the single-string. A learner must know that he or she is doing this specifically for perpetuating the tradition.

The senior player, aged forty-eight, nevertheless acknowledges that while one can make a living by playing the single-string, it can never be a long-term career. The youngest player of the three, aged twenty-three, teaches students who are mostly Jing kids. They come because their parents want them to be acquainted with the Jing tradition. These are predominantly girls, although the twenty-three-year-old once heard that in the past, the single string was taught exclusively to boys. Some of the learners come from the orchestra. These orchestra members are also from the Jing community. Their motive is occupational because adding this skill to their résumés increases their competitive edge in the job market.

The crisis is not as serious today because many feel the revival of interest in the single-string. The senior player has adopted a handicapped girl. He intends to train her into becoming a first-rate single-string player. Another twenty-nine-year-old junior player, who has won the award of the Flower of Jing with her single-string playing, once organized a group of forty to perform after only two weeks of training. The purpose was to promote the art of the single-string. She comes from a family inclined towards literature and the arts. Her father is an expert in Jing history and literature, and her mother is a cultural worker who introduced the single-string to her daughter. The "Flower of Jing" is nationally famous and is a favorite piece in their performances. However, she longs for more depth in what they are playing, and wants to learn how to write Jing melodies in the future.

The senior player runs a successful business. He once installed a huge trumpet on top of the building where he lives and works. He would play the single-string after dinner every evening. With a trumpet, his melody could be heard everywhere on the three islands. Fishermen could hear him clearly from the sea. A typhoon destroyed the trumpet on the building, but he is planning to reinstall it.

During the visit, he performed a number of melodies. The first melody was called "Vietnam and China," which ends with the phrase "Ho Chi Minh, Mao Zedong" being sung repeatedly. All the cadres sang loudly together until the end. (This performance reminds one of the deep relationship between the two late leaders.) He also sang "The Red Orient" to praise Chairman Mao who, in his lifetime, did not recognize the single-string, but is nonetheless given reverence by many melodies played with it. This reverses the relationship between the national leader and the ethnic citizens to the extent that Mao had no control over how and why the single-string player could find him useful in protecting the distinctive, and possibly inferior, Jing identity from sticking out.

The third dimension has to do with the indigenous consciousness present in the emerging environmental consciousness. Seasonal egrets come to the three islands every March, laying their eggs in August and flying away in September. An old man has established a "mountain reserve of ten thousand egrets" to protect them from poachers. There is no actual mountain, so the reserve is vulnerable to anyone determined to intrude, but watching all these egrets sit together in the trees is quite an experience, though one needs a local guide to go through the confusing trails in the bushes. A barrier set up by the "old man of ten thousand egrets" reminds the visitor where to stop.

Environmental consciousness did not exist in the past. A Han cadre, who married a Jing woman, recalls that when he was young, he could easily catch an egret. Today, however, the old man would save any single egret from typhoons. His conviction is to save every single egret because he and many villagers believe that the egret symbolizes fortune. A county official who escorts visitors confirms that every time he sees an egret, he finds good fortune.

The combination of environmental consciousness and local (as well as ethnic) consciousness has become a common development throughout the world. The rise of environmental consciousness has led to a reflexive understanding of past developments, including the investment in paving the sea gulf. Around the three islands, there are the so-called living fossils—the mangrove forests. Some local people regret that the rate of survival for mangrove forests had been reduced during the early stages of the pavement project. Paving the sea gulf was seen as a good policy then since the Jing people lacked arable land, but it becomes questionable today under the banner of environmentalism. The paving project had been a pet project of the state and still occupies a significant place in the official introduction of the township.

The presentation of the Jing identity is closely related to the state, to the extent that Ha'ting worship repeats the slogan of national unity. However, the reproduction of the Jing identity in the local community is not a state project, nor is it motivated by any reason related to the state, and it does not take place within the state. The force of reproduction varies, witnessing at least the three areas composed of Ha'ting worship, single-string zither, and egret protection. The spoken Jing language continues in the family despite the disappearance of the written language; the written language is still practiced across the border, however. The language distinguishes the Jing community from the surrounding Han and Zhuang populations, which speak Bai. Surprisingly, there is no national identity puzzle in the Jing community. With all the conditions met, the Jing community refuses to be identified with the Vietnamese state. They would rather consider themselves Chinese in the political sense, while remaining Vietnamese in areas that the state does not care much about, so that the state has no interest in intervening with identity-making in the non-political areas.

The State Identity Reduced to a Strategic Choice

The history that the Jing community does not speak about today does not fit the current identity strategy well. The relationship between the Jing and the Han people was not as harmonious as it has been in recent decades. During the Sino-French war, the relationship was actually quite tense. The literature suggests that the Jing people were on the French side during this historical conflict. In the aftermath, the relationship was so difficult that the Jing people had to dress up in Han style and speak in the Han accent to avoid discrimination. There was also the effort to promote the image of the Jing hero who fought the French troops alongside the legendary Liu Yongfu, a famous warrior in southern China.[10] A similar attempt can be recalled today in memory of the legendary Du Guoqiang, a Jing general who served the People's Liberation Army. He joined the Vietnam War to fight the U.S. troops while his children participated in the Sino-Vietnamese War in 1979.[11]

Another source of the problematic inter-ethnic relationship involves the competition over limited arable land. The competition has even led to sporadic fighting between villages. Once, there were attempts to establish borders, but demarcation was difficult to maintain. Furthermore, Han villagers wanted to cut down the forest to expand farmland, but the Jing community relied on the woods to prevent strong winds from blowing from the sea. The trade between the ethnic groups was not convivial either, as the Han merchants took advantage of the Jing fishermen. Many poor Jing people were left landless and had to work for Han landlords, creating a stereotyped caste image between the Jing and the Han people. While schools were open in the village temples, children of one ethnic group refused to enter the temple of another ethnic group.[12] These unpleasant memories quickly disappeared after the central government paved the sea gulf and built the road.

The state investment in the Jing community dramatically increased the Jing standard of living, to the point that the Jing people were much better off than the Vietnamese on the other side of the border. On the positive side, this provided material incentive for the Jing community to favor their Chinese citizenship. On the negative side, there was no comparable incentive for the Jing community to develop any sense of loyalty to the Vietnamese state. Their cultural identification with the Vietnamese tradition can actually be more secure in that their Chinese citizenship protects their cultural identity from being reduced to inferior social status—facing the Vietnamese neighbor, the Jing people enjoy a superior status; facing the Chinese, the Jing people are different and liked. This identity strategy works well during times of peace, but if war breaks out between the two states, they will have to hold on to their Chinese identity, since it is the more acceptable one, politically. This is so because political identity is obviously not as deep as cultural identity, which no one questions, and also because the Chinese state cares most about it. For the Jing people who could not decide for themselves, if they would like to get involved in war, they could only blame the Vietnamese government.

The war with Vietnam in 1979 significantly reduced both social exchanges and border trade. Sporadic exchanges of a smaller scale continued. Moreover, two informants reported that family visits were completely ground to a halt. The Jing people acted patriotically toward the Chinese state during the war, but kept their common ethnic identity shared by Vietnamese people. For the Jing people, the Vietnamese state is not attractive. Historically, in the eyes of the Chinese, Vietnam is a protectorate. At best, it is seen as a peripheral nation. The Qin Dynasty first conquered Vietnam. The statute built by the subsequent General Ma Yuan of the Han Dynasty, who stepped on the Vietnamese subject, was still talked about by the local people today.

Despite all this, history remains partial to the Jing people, and being politically and legally Chinese is certainly a reasonable choice. Their identification with the Chinese state makes them a bit insecure, though. For example, they fear that Dongxing might lose to Mangjie in terms of economic growth. War could still be embarrassing because it could disclose the discriminated Vietnamese blood inside the Jing identity, which could resurrect unhappy memories that should have already been left into oblivion. Some interviewees understandably blame the Vietnamese government for being unwise in fighting China. Moreover, they find the harmonious relationship between Mao Zedong and Ho Chi Minh memorable.

No tourist in Dongxing could miss the ubiquitous image of the late Ho Chi Minh. He is virtually everywhere—on stamps, souvenirs, huge photos in hotel lobbies, and in the single-string melody. Ho Chi Minh was the symbol of the golden age between Vietnam and China. It is true that remembering Ho Chi Minh today is a political decision by the central government, a gesture indicating the renewal of amiable bilateral relationship. However, the Jing people have their own perspective of the return of Ho Chi Minh in their life. Enthusiasm for Ho Chi Minh goes much deeper politically because its return releases the pressure for the Jing community to cope with the confrontation between two identities. The peaceful resolution between the two states exempts the Jing people from demonstrating their loyalty to the Chinese state or their embarrassment when dealing with the Vietnamese on the other side of the border.

Peace enables them to continue carrying both the discursively superior Chinese identity to face the Vietnamese neighbors, while using the exotic Vietnamese identity to attract Chinese tourists. The exodus of Chinese refugees in the late 1970s and the early 1980s further alienated the Jing people from the Vietnamese government. One Jing cadre describes the Vietnamese government thus: "They say bad things about you even if you treat them to a good meal, but they would say good things about you if you beat them up."

The Vietnamese government watches the border crossing more closely than the Chinese side. Even the fall of a rock on the Chinese side alerts the Vietnamese patrol, lest the rock squeezes the current of Beilun River toward the Vietnamese side. The same tension is hidden in the Jing people's mindset—they recognize that they are Vietnamese, yet they also discriminate against the Vietnamese. They say war does not affect them but act as if war had affected them. They criticize Vietnam's backwardness but worry that Vietnam might catch up one day. This seeming ambivalence makes the function of the Chinese identity much more obvious. For, it is the Chinese identity that allows the Jing people to conceptually treat their Vietnamese neighbor as "the other."

The identity strategy of this sort is not completely innovative if historical analysis is accurate about the Jing villagers speaking Bai and dressing up like Han in the aftermath of the Sino-French war. Today, the Jing people are much better off because they no longer need to act as Han to avoid discrimination. They could simply assert the Jing identity, which they say even Zhou Enlai liked.

In other words, Jing is neither purely Vietnamese nor purely Han. Compared with the identity strategy of other ethnic groups that lack confidence, the Jing community is different. During a previous visit to Jinxiu, Guangxi, a Yao cadre said that all the Yao people in the area had been acculturated into Han so that no Yao could ever claim the Yao identity anymore. In another research study, a Tujia school principal in Yongshun, Western Hunan, shied away from his mother tongue by saying that whoever spoke Tujia today could be derided by the bystanders; thus, no one spoke Tujia anymore (which is obviously not true). An ethnic Shui cadre in Yizhou, Guangxi said that she had decided that her child would register as Han for there is no advantage in being a Shui. This is not unlike the Jing people who had hid themselves beneath the Han appearance. However, a Yao priest endeavored to recover the Yao ritual. Similarly, a Tujia professor promotes the Tujia spoken language in order to record the Tujia legends. In addition, a Shui senior feels that Shui is like a name that needs no justification. In comparison, a Jing does not have to face any internal doubt that he or she is inferior, so to speak, to the Vietnamese because of his or her Chinese citizenship. The intervention by the state in the construction of the Jing identity is useful to the community in the sense that it gives the people a place to assert their difference and similarity to both sides at the same time. They no longer need to return to Han when they feel the lack of confidence.

The National Identity for an Economic Backward Minority

The neighboring Fangcheng Harbor City includes the Natong Township and the Banba Township, in which two different Yao divisions live. The home of Daban Yao presented both Gaolin village and Daken village to the visitor. Both villages are well below the official poverty line. There are Helping-the-Poor teams in both villages. Villagers typically have relatives in Vietnam. Some of them went to Vietnam in the early twentieth century. Others sought refuge in other places during the Cultural Revolution. The main motivation to emigrate was to seek arable land. Today, the economic conditions of the Chinese Daban Yao are a little better than the other side. The Yao community on the other side of the border belongs to the same Daban division but does not come from the same families. One village cadre calls them brothers.

Mutual exchanges across borders are common. These exchanges take the form of trade and family visits. Money from both sides circulates well among these border communities. In Daken, traditional market gatherings occur every three days. Each time, Vietnamese traders climb over the mountaintops to sell goods. They would rather save on the customs fee by spending two more days traveling in the mountains. Daken villagers sometimes visit the market gatherings in Vietnam, too. The Helping-the-Poor team, which was sent by the administrative superior to the village to improve the living conditions, paved a cement road leading to the Vietnamese along the border. The village road stops a meter away from the paved way at the borders. Once connected, the village road will belong to the jurisdiction of Foreign Service. More importantly, there would be a customs office set up on both sides, which defeats the purpose of saving money and time. Nonetheless, the symbolic function of the border is maintained because villagers must discharge the goods at the end of the village road and reload the carrier on the Vietnamese way, or the other way around.

Cultural exchanges are frequent, too. There is a Yao radio station in Vietnam. Its broadcasts aired in Vietnamese are well received by the Daken villagers. Whenever a mountain song contest is held, the Vietnamese Yao would come over to participate. Most of the songs they play are love songs. Daken villagers are used to singing in Bai while another Yao division, Huatou Yao, often sing in their own dialect. Border patrols on both sides rarely question these border-crossing activities. According to a Han Helping-the-Poor team cadre, "local people are very nice people who call themselves Vietnamese."

From the social point of view, the self-image of being Vietnamese makes sense since their living environment overlaps more with that of the people living on the other side of the border than with the rest of China. Recently, cross-border marriages have become increasingly popular. In the recent past, six new families had been formed on the Chinese side and two on the Vietnamese side. The Chinese families do not report the marriage to the government. All the rituals end up in the village. The villagers say that they will report the marriage only when the demographic investigation team visits the village at the end of the decade, as it normally arrives. They acknowledge with comfort that these new families are legally "black" families. The most frequent inter-village exchanges at a large scale are these marriages. It is obvious that villagers on different sides get to know each other easily.

Compared with the administrative chores given by the superior administration, these social activities seem to be the more important ones because the village seniors, who are the most influential in the village, care little about the administrative chores. The village councilmen who have to cope with the state administration are left to the care of those much younger villagers. In any case, senior villagers are not capable of handling these administrative chores, which involve many technical issues. In fact, Gaolin's Village Party is headed by a young man with a high school diploma. High educational attainment is definitely rare in the neighborhood. The division of labor between the party and the senior villagers is clear—the secretary is responsible for explaining and promoting government policy, while senior villagers make decisions on social affairs. In short, the state and the senior villagers divide their work according to their interests, and it appears that one has little interest in what is important to the other.

Civic consciousness in the Yao community is weak in comparison to that of the Jing community. For the former, the attitude toward the state is passive. Villagers recall little propaganda efforts during the Sino-Vietnamese war. Trade activities across the border continue. Perhaps due to the economic advantage of the Chinese Yao over the Vietnamese Yao being unimportant, their identification toward the state is more instrumental. The function of the state to the Yao community is, therefore, even more clearly related to the enhanced identity strategy of status. As a villager comments on the Sino-Vietnamese war: "War was a matter between troops, not between us. But Vietnam could be so over-reacting that a shell once fell in the village. How Dare? Even the Vietnamese Yao were angry. They complained at how the Vietnamese government wanted to fight with China. They said that their ancestors came from China, and China was their big brother."

Village cadres make fun of the Vietnamese patrols because of the latter's worry that the Chinese villagers would move the border toward the Vietnamese side. In the mind of the villagers, however, there is no reason for a "big brother" to behave so narrow-mindedly.

The Daban Yao's economic advantage is insignificant compared to that of the Jing people. The senior villagers care more about cultural and social activities than the administration. War has relatively little effect upon their lives. They even call themselves Vietnamese in front of the Han Helping-the-Poor cadres sent by the state. On the whole, the state is far removed from the villagers. However, when there is a need to make a distinction with the Vietnamese side, the state becomes discursively useful. The Chinese state is regarded as a big brother of the Vietnamese state. It is the big brother mentality that enables the Daban Yao villagers to simulate a sense of superiority, which they do not need at all in their daily lives. In this regard, the Yao villagers are comparable to the Jing villagers.

The Chinese State that Belongs to the Border Groups

The economic difference between the Jing community and the Vietnamese community is largely brought about by the Chinese state. The Chinese citizenship means something concrete to the Jing community, to which the other side is not entitled. On the other hand, exchanges across the borders show the world that there are no "two" separate communities. This also allows the Jing to claim difference in front of the Chinese state.

The outbreak of war embarrassed the Jing as well as the Daban Yao communities, just like how the historical Sino-Vietnamese War had embarrassed the Vietnamese Chinese. To maintain a politically higher (in terms of big brother) and socially advantaged (in terms of social and economic status) position toward the Vietnamese and to avoid an inferior position in the Chinese neighborhood, the Chinese identity becomes instrumentally useful. Eventually, the Chinese identity generates for the border communities a discursive foundation that they can look at the Vietnamese from the Chinese point of view. Ironically, the ability to point at the Vietnamese community makes the Jing people more secure in pursuing their cultural legacy, which is intrinsically Vietnamese.

The Korean Chinese have begun to reevaluate their identity since the end of the Cold War. As reform improves the economic conditions in the Korean Chinese community, North Koreans seek more opportunities. The diplomatic ties with the economically stronger South rocks Chinese Koreans' sense of superiority. At the same time, the reunification of the Korean Peninsula becomes an increasingly interesting subject. The Korean Chinese develop from these experiences a position that looks at the Chinese state from outside China. This development is especially real when the hotly debated issue concerning the historical origin of the Korean people dominates the front pages, an issue partly brought about by the celebration of the Koguryo heritage found in China.

The ability of the Korean Chinese to take advantage of their double identities is severely reduced, as both identities increasingly take the other as the point of differentiation in defining the self. In comparison, the Jing community is able to open up the monopoly of national identity by the state. The Jing people remain culturally Vietnamese and use the Chinese state to enjoy a better position than the Vietnamese. This is not what the state expects when bestowing the Jing identity on the Vietnamese Chinese in Dongxing.

The state cares very little about how the border communities use the national identity, and is unable to anticipate how the politics of identity will be played when the two neighboring states confront each other. There is no ready theoretical perspective in international relations to see the state through the eyes of the border communities. Both the state and the study of political science are concerned with dominance and resistance. Identity strategies that do not factor in the element of resistance are not expressible in political science.

Sometimes, the seeming silence and loyalty calms anxious state officials because they do not understand that working towards national unity by the border communities can be functional for these communities that continue to pursue their cultural connection with the motherland. This is the case in the Jing community because the Chinese state would not worry that the Jing people might turn their backs after reconnecting with the Vietnamese, and because the Jing people can enhance their social status when the Vietnamese on two sides of the borders mingle. The Jing people demonstrate that the border communities do not have to totally surrender to the monopolized domain of national identity. They can use the state in the same way that the state can use them.

CHAPTER 5

Imagined Genealogy: Behind the Cultural Formation of Huishui's Buyi Nationality

The Genealogy Narrative of the Chinese Nation

There has been a common understanding in literature about the nature of the Chinese nation, that is, the nation is a "cultural formation" as opposed to being a genealogy.[1] Therefore, any ethnic group can become Chinese as long it subscribes to the Chinese mainstream culture, especially Confucianism. The cultural argument has had a long history beginning during Confucius' time. Confucius was widely quoted as one who used the code of dressing to distinguish the Chinese from the barbarians. In fact, in the Chinese political narrative, "under-heaven" is a more popular metaphor than the territorial "state" when talking about the proper domain of the emperor. Under-heaven refers to a morally superior emperor reigning over those like-minded subjects, while the state is at most an extension of the emperor's genealogy. The early reference to "hua-xia"—whereby "hua" denotes being Chinese and "xia," the first recorded dynasty, as the representation of the Chinese civilization—further stresses the importance of culture, as opposed to genealogy, in the Chinese identity.

The Chinese nation, *zhonghua minzu*, is a contemporary self-representation.[2] This was an externally imported concept at the turn of the nineteenth going into the twentieth century. Thanks to the Han-led revolution that overthrew the Manchurian Qing Dynasty, genealogy nationality became a politically useful concept. However, for the sake of nation building, the notion of a cultural nation quickly returned in order to achieve unity among different ethnic groups, especially the Manchurian.[3] The Chinese Communist Party similarly enlisted the cultural narrative, hoping to demonstrate that the fifty-five government-designated ethnic minorities all subscribe to the Chinese culture. Furthermore, together with the Han majority, they jointly built a modern Chinese nation. In its nationality policy, the central government of China is preoccupied with the economic growth of the minority areas, believing that modernization is the common aim of all the ethnic groups. Modernization is the modern substitute for Confucianism in the cultural narrative. The constant component of the cultural narrative is the policy of assimilating ethnic minorities who were previously considered as barbarians falling outside the domain of under-heaven.

On the other hand, the genealogy narrative nonetheless continues. Note that Confucianism is about ancestor worship, and the notion of ancestors clearly belongs to the genealogy narrative. To argue that subscription to Confucianism is cultural instead of being genealogy oriented seems ironic. Take for example the most often quoted saying of "children of Emperors Yan and Huang," which is a popular idiom that school children learn to use in their writings to win extra credits. While "Emperors Yan and Huang" indicate particular cultural styles, the term "children" is unambiguously a genealogy narrative. In fact, the lingering of this particular expression is informative of the genealogy narrative in contemporary political discourse.[4] For example, Chinese authorities often accuse the separatists in Taiwan of forgetting their Chinese ancestors. The attention to the genealogy narrative seems especially intense to the Taiwanese. If cultural narrative is the major component of the Chinese nation, alienation from Chinese culture should give legitimacy to the separatist claim.[5] However, this is obviously not the case. The feeling that the Taiwanese separatists have betrayed the Chinese motherland suggests that the genealogy narrative can be more fundamental than the cultural narrative in representing the Chinese nation.

This chapter argues against the common belief that the Chinese nation is a cultural formation. On the contrary, the chapter proposes that the cultural narrative is often used to denote common ancestors that are no longer identifiable, hence causing a particular kind of genealogy argument. In other words, genealogy is the key to the imagined nation in the case of the Chinese. The function of the cultural narrative is to prove that there is a genealogy relationship among members of a particular ethnic group and among different ethnic groups in China. To complete China's nation-building process, one needs a genealogy narrative for each ethnic group and a genealogy narrative for the Chinese nation. When the genealogy narrative is not available, the cultural narrative is used in its place. Since it is a substitute to assist in denoting common ancestors, cultural alienation is not a legitimate reason to assert separatism. Rather, separation based on cultural alienation becomes a moral crime. By contrast, the non-separatist cultural narratives that point to a distinctive genealogy can have legitimacy. Unity is no longer the dominant purpose in the latter case.

The Narrative on Huishui Buyi Ethnicity

The research site for this non-separatist, distinctive genealogy is in Huishui County under the Qiannan Buyi and Miao Autonomous Prefecture, located in Guizhou Province. The name of the county does not designate an "autonomous" status because it already belongs to an autonomous prefecture. For the ethnic Buyi population, the county is nonetheless autonomous in their favor. Based on the 2000 census, the Buyi population makes up 36 percent of the total population and 61 percent of the minority population.[6] The county leadership is composed of both Buyi and Miao members. There was a plan to visit Changan Township in the deep mountain, which a number of township cadres claimed to represent "the original juice and the original taste" of Buyi ethnicity. However, bad weather stopped the plan of visiting the deep mountain site. The two research sites that were visited instead were the Yarong Township (twenty miles from the county government), a Miao community which has both the township middle school and the primary school, and the Dalong Township, a Buyi community which acquainted its visitor with the township government, Buyi families, and a township temple. The road leading to both townships is bumpy and rough, and travel takes over an hour from the county government.

The reason for selecting Buyi is that there has been an effort in Huishui's Buyi community to trace Buyi's exclusive common ancestor. At the same time, another effort exists to link the Buyi ancestors to other ethnic groups and to the migration of all groups in history. Anthropologists have studied the origin of the Buyi people. Their history goes as far back as the Old Stone Age. The one hundred thousand-year-old Shuicheng relics are believed to host the Buyi ancestor; hence, there are claims that the Buyi people are the true indigenous population.

There are many stories about the Buyi origins. Except for the Shuicheng one, all others point to some migration theory. They include the proposition that the Buyi people were the children of people living in coastal Shandong Province, whose ancestor followed the famous Song general Di Qin. Another theory proposes that the Buyi people migrated from either Jiangxi or Hunan and Guandong when an early Ming Emperor sent their ancestors in Guangxi. The Society for the Study of Buyi (SSB) denounces both propositions to be sheer fabrications.[7] Ethnic Buyi scholars do not deny that there had been migrants joining their ancestors, but they were few and became assimilated into the indigenous society. Their number is allegedly small. The reason that there have been such fabrications, according to the Buyi scholars, is because it was the Han scholars who first wrote the history. Han people migrated to the local society in later historical periods. The historians could only gather information from late Han immigrants whose personal experiences had misled the scholars. There was no Chinese record to allow the Han historians to do research on the indigenous society. The policy to assimilate the indigenous people in the early Qing Dynasty also had an effect, which compelled the Buyi people to hide their ethnic identity. Some married Han immigrants while others reported that they were Jiangxi immigrants. All these contributed to the misunderstanding that the Buyi people were migrants.

In contrast, Buyi scholars studied the historical remnants in order to trace the route of their ancestors' movement from the Shuicheng to the Huishui locales. They concluded that the Buyi people should be the so-called Puyue people noted in history texts. According to their studies, Pu and Liao were two local communities that joined the local Xiangke to form the mysterious, famous local kingdom of Yelang. Later, the Luoyue migrants from the north joined them. The scholars also gave details about how the Buyi people arrived in Huishui as a division and where all others have been. The rationale of their study is to give Huishui's Buyi people an unquestionable origin that does not belong to anyone else, especially the Han. Granting that in the long haul of history, different ethnic groups joined Pu to form the contemporary Buyi, still, their origin must be established because without which, the claim to Buyi would be baseless. Fortunately, this quest for an origin is compatible with Chinese multi-culturalism, which came about as a response to the emergence of globalization. Accordingly, there is no need to fear fusion between ethnic groups. However, the origin before fusion should be clear-cut to make the advocacy for fusion meaningful. The SSB scholars write:

> There is no pure ethnicity in the world. For the Buyi, Han, and other ethnic groups, to fuse is more than natural. Those stories of Buyi origin [from other places] reflected part of historical reality, but they failed to go beyond very late period and could not reach the origin. . . . For a very long period, the Buyi people have lived in the Buyi region, which is in the Guizhou high plains. Their style of living—that is, clustering together in habitation but overlapping with others—remains the same today. In the long haul of history, different nationalities have interacted and fused. In the formation of the Chinese nation, I have you in me and you have me in you. This is the basic trend of history.[8]

Fusion Instead of Separation

One cannot deny that the discourse on the Chinese or Huaxia has always been focused on nomenclature, ritual, and propriety, rather than on genealogy or origin. Benedict Anderson studied how contemporary settlers' states have constructed their national identities to differentiate themselves from the European motherland.[9] Embedded in European history, his analysis assumes that all nation states separated from an empire (e.g., Roman Empire) to form their own. The institution of sovereignty resulting from the Westphalia Treaty provided a territorial base on which nationalism later resides upon. Separating from a universal order (presumably the City of Gods) provides Anderson a clue as if creole nationalism is always about separation. He came to Taiwan to coach the separatists on how to construct a national narrative belonging exclusively to Taiwan. However, his advice could convince neither the Chinese nor the Taiwanese because Chinese history did not follow the same pattern he suggested.

Fusion, instead of separation, has been the major theme for writing Chinese history. Fusion first took place through cultural assimilation under Confucianism.[10] The under-heaven discourse encouraged barbarian nomads to assert their ascendancy by taking over the regime in China and playing the role of the emperor. The culturally sophisticated Chinese typically accepted the nomads' reign under heaven, once the conqueror willingly subscribed to Confucianism.[11] In comparison, modern Chinese narrators do not usually appreciate the institution of sovereignty that has emphasized exclusion and separation.[12] Confucius once worried that the nomads would make him dress in the barbarian way, but nonetheless felt confident that the barbarians would welcome his visit. The militarily weak, yet sophisticated cultural style of China has been open to migrants throughout history, making room for fusion among different nationalities.[13] In the Chinese discourse, the end of history should be a grand harmony among all people under heaven.[14] There is no anxiety toward fusion of blood, nor a need for any separatist claim.

The Chinese discourse welcomes fusion as a fact. Even the separatists in Taiwan have applied the logic of fusion in their argument that Taiwanese aboriginal people have joined the new Taiwanese nation to make Taiwan a new nation. Melissa Brown worries that this argument might defeat the purpose of independence since the fusion of genealogy is typically a Chinese argument.[15] Indeed, fusion explains the spread of the Chinese culture. In Chinese history, instances of separation occurred commonly during the time of the nomads—the North Wei period, Yuan Dynasty, and Qing Dynasty. The Han were discriminated during these periods. However, as legend says, the Han people eventually mingled both culturally and physically (by blood) with all the ruling nomads.[16] The contemporary Han are definitely more hybrid than the Han in the past. In other words, they feel superior not because they have been a pure kin, but because they have a superior culture.[17] The Chinese people's lack of sensitivity toward sovereign separation, shown by their obsession with the duty overseas Chinese should play in the development of China, probably leads both Lucian Pye and Ross Terrill to accuse the Chinese of being racists.[18] Ironically, Chinese racism welcomes hybridity, rather than purity.

This is why in the Chinese narrative, the commentators always try to show how different nationalities have fused their bloods. Fusion discursively assumes assimilation into Confucianism. On the other hand, assimilation into Confucianism is presumably incurred through intermarriage. Those who joined the Chinese nation through the fusion of genealogies would have their children carry the Chinese ancestors' blood, too. Fusion thus privileges genealogy expansion instead of territorial expansion. To assert separation is to betray common ancestors, violate Confucianism, and deny Chinese superiority. In this regard, the fusion of the aboriginal and the Han people in Taiwan should be seen as a form of expansion instead of separation.

The Genealogy Narrative in Chinese Ethnic Affairs

China as a sovereign country continues to practice the genealogy narrative. The mainland Chinese people expect the overseas Chinese to share the moral duty of strengthening the motherland. Similarly, the Chinese state is responsible for the welfare of the overseas Chinese. In fact, such a Confucian argument is likewise present in the Korean government's overseas Korean policy. In China, one of the eight democratic co-ruling parties—the Zhigong Party—specialized in overseas Chinese affairs. Overseas Chinese are deeply involved in the political and economic development of China, but very few Chinese conceive this intervention as improper. In comparison, the Taiwanese constitution allows overseas Chinese to run for public office as long as they renounce their foreign citizenship before inauguration. In addition, there are quotas reserved for overseas Taiwanese representatives.

Ethnicity became a legal concept after 1956, the year the central government formally designated fifty-five ethnic minorities. The concept of the minority is meaningful only in the fixed and rigid territorial domain, so that the relative size of a particular community can be determined. While the government claims that their demarcation of ethnicity has many different reference points other than genealogy, it does not allow any legal room for those who want to change their ethnicity. This is despite evidence that these people have assimilated into a different ethnic culture. In fact, many incidents show that it is common for ethnic minorities to culturally disguise their identity to avoid discrimination.[19] Nevertheless, the legal status of the minority presupposes a deep-rooted genealogy assumption: once parents' ethnic identities are determined, so too are their children's identities. There cannot be another change of identity in the lineage, even for those accounting for changes in cultural habit. All the policy privileges provided to the ethnic communities promoting modernization, including birth control quota, extra points for minority students taking examinations, or negative discrimination to recruit minority cadres, reproduce the exclusive relevance of blood.

The presupposed goal of national strengthening is modernization. In a sense, this means Westernization, which incurs the anxiety toward the loss of Chinese-ness.[20] The prolonged debate between the Western and the Chinese school since the early twentieth century is still going on. For the Western school, the Chinese are Chinese despite their way of life, whether traditional or modern. The Western school thus implicitly adopts the genealogy narrative, asserting that changes in cultural style do not affect one's national identity. [21] The general trend toward modernization in the past hundred years suggests that the Western School has the upper hand.[22] Therefore, the genealogy narrative assumed by the Western school must also be more popular than the cultural narrative. Interestingly, along with modernization, there is another theory that the Chinese nation originally came from outside of China. Just as the Buyi scholars dispute the migrant theory of the Buyi people, there are also Chinese scholars who denounce the Chinese migration theory.[23]

The function of the cultural narrative should be evident by now. The cultural proposition asserts the formation of the Chinese nation to be a kind of cultural formation. Judging from the pervasive and ubiquitous genealogy narrative, the cultural argument cannot be serious. The cultural narrative is serviceable to the genealogy narrative in the sense that it helps those self-proclaimed Chinese, minorities, or those self-proclaimed non-Chinese, to identify who are and who are not Chinese. It is useful to the formation of both the Chinese nation and the ethnic identities to show that there is a Chinese nation while each ethnic identity remains authentic.[24] It is unlikely for people today to be certain about their lineage in the unknown past. Therefore, for the genealogy narrative to continue, there must be indicators suggesting where the scope of genealogy lies.[25] When people subscribe to the same culture, the Chinese narrators are more comfortable at assuming that those who appear culturally alike are part of the same Chinese genealogy. Moreover, if the people are certain about their origin, even though it may only be a matter of imagination, the loss of the shared cultural practice is no longer lethal. In the case of the overseas Chinese or the migrant minority in the city, their knowledge of their origin is sufficient to support their identity. There is no need for them to speak the ethnic language or dress in ethnic clothing. This is probably why the central government is always lukewarm toward the cultural revival of ethnic minorities. However, they remain active in providing policy exemptions to those carrying supposedly ethnic genes.

The Cultural Narratives in Huishui

Genealogy is not useful when trying to present ethnicity because it would involve no performance. Besides, genealogy cannot be easily proven, unless there are distinctive physical features such as the color of the eyes or skin. Moreover, it will be more natural to represent an ethnic group in some distinctive cultural narrative, in order to receive recognition. With its complex ethnic composition, the Guizhou Province consciously utilizes ethnicity as the theme to represent itself. One recent venture it has is the establishment of divisions of Museum of Cultural Ecology, which include both Buyi and Miao cultures.

In this "cultural" museum, ethnic culture is supposedly different from the mainstream culture to warrant the investment in its preservation. Local culture should be natural and should avoid external intervention. A local interviewee quoted a research team from the Guizhou Social Science Academy, saying that Buyi's cultural ecology has eroded quickly because of its fast cultural assimilation into the Han culture.[26] Nevertheless, the idea of cultural ecology aims at protecting ethnic culture as a natural evolution. The museum was established under the guidance of Norwegian experts; the government takes more responsibility in initiating each museum of cultural ecology. The County Bureau of Culture is in charge of the first stage. Then, a local committee is set up to gradually take over the responsibility. The idea is not to promote tourism, although there is no opposition to it. The rationale is that cultural museums of this sort can better record the process of assimilation from the past and into the future. The assumption is that ethnic ecology is a continuum, and not an abruption. In other words, it is about the cultural evolution of an originally authentic people. Consequently, the familiar line between the cultural and the natural becomes obscure in the cultural museums that preserve ethnicity as part of natural ecology.

In reality, however, young villagers sent to Norway to learn the management of cultural ecology no longer wanted to return to the mountains. They even encouraged other young people in the neighborhood to go with them. Suo Xiaoxia, a researcher at the Guizhou Social Science Academy observes:

> Guizhou has been the first in China to begin the protection of cultural ecology. In Guizhou, for example, the Miao people have the custom of saving the hair of their dead. The history of the cultural ecological zone shows on these hairs. For another example, the local panpipe melody is full of sorrow. . . . The most advanced management of cultural ecology could keep all these things significant unlike any tourist program in which authenticity could be lost. Nowadays, the young people strongly want to leave the mountains. Those who returned from Norway did not want to come back, in particular. Instead, they led local young females to leave the village. Even the ghost priest was reported to have left the mountain. Nonetheless, the cultural ecological zone is still good in the sense that the serious art will not suffer from the influence of pop music. The Buyi Museum of Cultural Ecology is in Huaxi Township, but the style of dressing there is no longer typical of Buyi. In order to further develop under the premise of preservation, there must be some theory to guide the people. Otherwise, the ecology could erode. Without the establishment of these museums, resources will not come, nor will history be clear. For the local people, the establishment of the museum means that there will be investments coming in. After all, the museum is not opposed to development.[27]

The preservation of culture is the key in Suo's analysis. She calls this "cultural self-consciousness."[28] To record the cultural traits as part of ecology grants the Buyi an ontological position that no one can question. It is not against development, as she emphasizes, but its focus is on the preservation of evolution. Between the lines is the assumption that there is an origin. A cultural origin exclusively for Buyi means that there is something about Buyi that other ethnic groups belonging to the Chinese nation cannot share. While cultural argument suggests that the Chinese nation is a cultural formation, in Guizhou, the cultural narrative purports to maintain a separate origin.

Both functions—fusion and separation—are serviceable to the imagination of common genealogy. Cultural fusion reproduces the sense of Han superiority and therefore soothes the potential anxiety among the Han population resulting from intermarriage between the Han and other groups. Cultural separation, on the other hand, reproduces a sense of Buyi distinction, and therefore soothes the potential anxiety in the Buyi community caused by fusion with the Han. The latter function is especially important, as the world is now preoccupied with globalization and self-representation. This process sensitizes local groups to their distinction, no matter how much imagination it takes. The need to present a different self is likely to damage inter-ethnic relations. The separation narrative has the ability to resolve the potential confrontation by giving each group ontological status. The fusion narrative enlarges the scope of common genealogy, so that all the different groups become connected while the separation narrative maintains an inner circle of common genealogy only those in the group can share.

In reality, the shared culture cannot really prove common genealogy and ancestry. The widely used cultural program—"Up on the Knife Mountain and Down to the Fire Sea"—is representative of Yao, Shui, and Miao ethnicities, respectively, in different research sites previously visited. In fact, Daoist priests in the Han area also perform the same program. No one would argue that these four groups share a common origin because this would almost certainly cause anxiety among the three minorities. The implication of different groups using the same cultural program to demonstrate distinctive ethnicity is that the cultural program which local populations share is no more than an indicator of common genealogy for them in the local environment. It is not an ethnic culture per se. Instead, it is but a convenient way for the local ethnic group to claim distinction from the Han or other neighboring ethnic groups.

In Huishui, the most commonly mentioned cultural program is ancestor worship, which takes place on the third of the Lunar March. An SSB publication chooses March 3 as the most important festival for the Buyi people. Interestingly, the award winning cultural program of the neighboring Baijin Township of the ethnic Miao, which also belongs to Huishui County, similarly holds its festival every March 3. In fact, in Dalong Township where Buyi and Miao reside, the two ethnic groups celebrate together. Therefore, this ethnic program in Huishui is not purely Buyi or purely Miao. Rather, it is clearly a claim of distinction from the Han people.

There are plenty of cultural activities that serve to highlight ethnic distinction in Huishui. This is true to Buyi as well as Miao. In Yarong Township, the teaching of the ethnic mountain song is an important component of the so-called "quality education" in school. The Miao school has Miao-styled clothes for its schoolchildren, while the Buyi school develops and teaches Buyi dancing to its pupils. The Bureau of Ethnic Affairs in Huishui has its own collection of ethnic clothes. It is also involved in promoting ethnic building style and ethnic athletic programs such as human wrestling, and chicken and bird wrestling. Unlike many other ethnic areas where the government actively promotes tourism by inventing ethnic programs, Huishui's cultural activities already exist, and the government is now interested in exploiting its economic values. The government officials believe that these activities in Huishui are truly cultural and ethnic.

An episode reveals the genealogy premise of the cultural narrative. As mentioned earlier, local officials were unanimously frustrated about the fact that the weather conditions killed the chance to see the Buyi people who are of "original taste." Indeed, the Buyi villagers are not unlike Han or Miao in the neighborhood. The officials repeatedly apologized for not arranging to see how real Buyi people dress up. Their worry suggests that if culture is insufficient to demonstrate the distinction, the Buyi people would lose their ontological status. In other words, something else, presumably genealogy, has already determined the Buyi identity. Yet, the interviewees cannot present this to the visitors. The imagination of Buyi authenticity can be sustained only through some sort of cultural distinction.

The Genealogy Narrative in Huishui

The cultural narrative is not fully dependable for the reproduction of ethnicity because culture evolves over time and is vulnerable to mingling. Relatively speaking, the culture of ancestor worship is an efficient way of maintaining ethnic identity because it involves a genealogy narrative. In Huishui, almost all homes show the five big characters on the wall facing the front door, designating heaven, earth, state, parent, and teacher. The same practice is very popular in many other minorities living in the southwestern Chinese mountains.[29] In the Wamiao village, old men like to talk about how their ancestors migrated from Jiangxi. Although the SSB scholars denounce the migration theory, the point is not where they were from originally but that they are similarly embedded in the narrative of origin in one way or another.

According to the local Buyi belief, the soul never dies with the body. Therefore, they believe that their ancestors' souls live among the contemporary. Ancestor worship is such an established custom for the Buyi people that all homes have shrines and ancestor plates. If there are common ancestors, there should be a ritual to worship them together. In fact, there are many surname groups each living in close habitation to one another. The kin habitation and ancestor worship enable one to develop one's ethnic identity in the living environment, so the sense of belonging to the group is prior to the ethnic name given to the person. This is different from the identity that the state legally gives to an individual first, subsequently to make him or her interested in finding other members with the same identity. Despite the fact that the ethnic consciousness is not strong in Huishui in general, people are ready to become sensitive again because the genealogy relationship is beyond challenge. Similarly, the cultural activities that constantly remind people of their genealogy through ancestor worship, love stories, birth and marriage rituals, etc. all serve to prepare one for the ethnic name calling when it comes.

The Buyi priest who is responsible for the worship ritual is called a Bible priest, ghost priest, or magic priest. They subscribe to the Daoist style of worship, which is blind to ethnicity. The significance does not lie in the style of ritual, but in the contents of the teaching, which invariably pertains to their ancestors' story. They also play the role of medical doctors because they are theoretically knowledgeable of the lower world where the dead have gone. In Wamiao village, an old villager explained the hanging of a piece of red cloth at the gate. According to him, a ghost priest uses it to dispel the ghosts when an old man's first son is very sick. Unfortunately, in this particular instance, the son still passed away, but the cloth has stayed since then. On the other side of the compound, his grandson attaches a shining silver-colored film diskette at the same place of his gate to dispel the ghosts. Interestingly, the film is about a folk hero—Huang Feihong, a popular Hong Kong movie subject.

Like elsewhere, any customs related to birth, marriage, and death receive serious attention.[30] In the old man's house, for example, a small hand-made "flower bridge" hangs on his daughter-in-law's bed. This "flower bridge" serves as the medium of the Emperor's Heavenly Mother in sending children to the couple. Indeed, the flower bridge is the same as what is portrayed in the book introducing the Buyi customs. Another practice that would also account for their customs is when a woman squats by a ditch, with her baby. She places a bowl of rice on her side as she "calls the soul." According to the book, this local custom is to help the sick child get well.

In addition to March 3, the sixth of Lunar June is another occasion for ancestor worship. With the government's promotion, these occasions also include the mountain song singing contest or lovers' gift giving. The traditional love song duet in Donglang Bridge expands to become a large-scale singing occasion in the renovated Donglang Humpback.

The lack of sensitivity to genealogy differences might cause serious policy problems. This applies to what happened in Huishui village where the hybrid of Han and Miao resides. When a Han won the previous election for the position of village director, the township government later designated another Han to be the party secretary. This caused dissatisfaction among Miao villagers. Later, the village director installed an electric generator, which was placed more closely to the Han habitation. Because of this, the Miao villagers refused to share the expense. Nevertheless, the director forced them to pay, thus the situation led to a confrontation. According to the cultural narrative, these Miao villagers have accepted cultural assimilation. They spoke the same local dialect and dressed themselves similarly. However, a simple analysis of the ethnic confrontation points to a deeper sense of identity that the cultural narrative is unable to reconcile.

For the central government, the contribution of the Buyi people to the Chinese nation should be evaluated based on economic terms. However, the SSB scholars have a different view. They came up with a list of Buyi people who contributed to the Chinese nation. To begin with, they listed martyrs in history, followed by many officials in the government, as well as retired officials and cadres. It might look like a wonderful show of loyalty to the state, but nothing like it was ever made. The contributions of those listed were more to the recognition of the Buyi people:

> In the long haul of history, the Buyi people in Huishui, who depend on their own ingenuity and industry as well as the selfless spirit of dedication to the motherland, together with all other ethnic people in the county, have made active contributions to the defense of the motherland, to the building of the motherland, to the advancement of the society for the sake of economic and cultural development of the motherland, and for the sake of achieving national unity. For the survival and development of our own nationality [author: Buyi], talented men and women have come out in large numbers over thousands of years.[31]

The Chinese Genealogy Nation

Even though there is usually no direct mention of genealogy or blood, the genealogy narrative is pervasive in the government's policy on recruiting minority cadres, giving extra credits to minority examinees, allowing a higher birth quota to a minority village, and investing in local ethnic schools. It is true that the experts sent by the government to study ethnic demarcation before 1956 had studied both culture and genealogy. The fact that the cultural assimilation cannot change a person's ethnic identity suggests that reference to the cultural narrative before 1956 was not more than an act of ensuring a common genealogy.

Similarly, the designation of Buyi ethnicity by the government makes it imperative that the Buyi people have an exclusive Buyi ancestry. The cultural narrative may be useful in demonstrating that the Buyi people and the Chinese have fused together. On the other hand, the cultural narrative embedded in ancestor worship is also serviceable to the demonstration of Buyi ethnicity being distinctive in terms of genealogy. Two cultural narratives camouflage two genealogy narratives. First, the Buyi people and the other ethnic groups in China have practiced intermarriage, and second, the Buyi people remain somewhat unique due to their origin from a separate historical route. The rich local Buyi cultural activities enable the Buyi people to claim distinction. However, because these activities are not exclusively Buyi but are simultaneously Miao, the claimed distinction is not a distinction per se in cultural terms, but a circular claim of distinctive genealogy.

The story about common ancestors or genealogy has to show as much imagination as the constructed shared culture. The point is not that both the genealogy and the cultural narratives remain narratives or figments of the imagination, but that the genealogy narrative is psychologically deeper than the cultural narrative. On the other hand, the cultural narrative is as similarly important because it is the cultural narrative that allows the people to identify those with whom they share common ancestors. The popular proposition that the Chinese nation is primarily a cultural formation is therefore questionable. Instrumentally speaking, though, the Chinese nation is a cultural nation at the same time. However, the legitimacy the Chinese nationalist demands of ethnic as well as separatist communities is invariably their imagined common ancestors. In this regard, the cultural narrative is indispensable in identifying the scope of people sharing common Chinese ancestors. The most useful cultural narrative is Confucianism, which is about ancestor worship, and is thus a hidden genealogy narrative. The idea that all the Chinese are the children of Emperors Yan and Huang still remains questionable but the idea of Confucianism has proven to be helpful in identifying the contemporary Chinese origin. This is why even though Yan and Huang knew no Confucianism, one can say that their children subscribed to Confucianism in order to feel being their children. On the other hand, the need to feel being a Buyi child has prompted the quest for Buyi cultural narratives that indirectly highlight a distinct Buyi genealogy, with which the Chinese nation has no share. While participation and contribution to Chinese multinationalism remain relevant to the representation of the Buyi ethnicity, backward mapping toward the Buyi origin might prevail over the teleology toward the reproduction of the Chinese nation. Moreover, unity becomes the discursive foundation of the Buyi people to create the distinctive origin with legitimacy. Contrary to the official discourse on unity, which grants the Buyi ethnicity an origin to evolve into the Chinese multi-nationalism, the emerging Buyi discourse reads into the Chinese multi-nationalism an irreplaceable Buyi origin.

CHAPTER 6

Cement or Excrement?
Autonomous Ecological Thinking in Xiaoxi's Poverty Discourse

Chapter 3 tells how cadres mediating between the state and the villagers might develop views or feelings of their own. In addition, villagers do not always accept the image of cultural backwardness passively. The notion of helping the poor ecologically has actually had some sense of local subjective feelings in ethnic Western Hunan. The villages are ready to take the state's ecological turn seriously and to reevaluate their relationship with the environment and the state. In fact, the state and its ecological Helping-the-Poor programs together constitute an important part of the nascent identity in a Western Hunan township. This is not unlike the situation in Chapters 4 and 5 in which the state contributes positively to the evolution of self-consciousness in the local ethnic communities. Here, the contrast is also present in that the state is both an initiator of the change in self-consciousness and a convenient "other" to differentiate the local identity.

The Emerging Agency of the Ethnic Poor

The Helping-the-Poor campaign in China started out as an attempt to transfer resources to poverty areas. The focus practically shifted away from this objective, and the intention to establish profitable business instead took over as the major element in the campaign. Renovating the local culture is what the campaigners believe to be the key to success, especially in areas where the campaign either failed or never began. The outright reference to cultural reformation transforms the quest of the Helping-the-Poor campaign into a crusade to "civilize" people, especially in the sphere of ethnicity. In fact, this "civilizing" aspect of the Helping-the-Poor campaign is nothing new—signs of it existed during the earlier stages, but it was not as obvious. Note that once placed on a national income and wealth scale, villagers living in the categorically poor areas immediately suffer from the image of cultural backwardness.

As the villagers whom the campaigners supposedly help also learn to focus their attention on poverty, these villagers are inclined to act dependently. The villagers' knowledge about the local conditions, their way of life, and their existing social relations are of no use or relevance, since they begin to learn the Helping-the-Poor language brought to them by the external campaigners who naturally conceive of these local perspectives as the reasons for their misery. As a result of this civilizing aspect, local perspectives that are irrelevant to the goal of the Helping-the-Poor campaign are not discursively meaningful. The villagers are no longer able to anticipate their own future and therefore appear dependent. In ethnic areas, campaigners might even regard ethnicity as a barrier against their task to ameliorate the situation. Periodical performance checks mostly portray villagers as incompetent, if not inferior citizens.

The situation begins to change toward the end of the last century, once the notion of ecological Helping-the-Poor attracts increasing attention. The ecological Helping-the-Poor campaign is a new way of thinking, a response to the abuse of the environment due to "overdevelopment." It is also a reflection of the aborted Helping-the-Poor campaign in many parts of China in the past. The thrust of this new thinking combines the preservation of ecological resources with the ability to raise the local wealth level.

While the essence of the "crusade to civilize" remains strong in this new way of thinking, its emphasis upon the local ecology nevertheless brings local villagers into the big picture. It would be logical to assume that the success of the ecological Helping-the-Poor campaign would rely on the immediate understanding of the environment. Supposedly, local residents are among those who best understand the local ecology. Moreover, if residents of a local district belong to a specific ethnic group, it is likely that their participation in an ecological Helping-the-Poor campaign might create an ethnic dimension. This is because local mountains and rivers are often sources of legends that produce ancestral consciousness. This type of consciousness is perhaps the most significant element when defining ethnicity in China.

The following pages are devoted to the story of nascent local consciousness resulting from ecological Helping-the-Poor campaigns. One will learn about cadres and villagers from the Xiaoxi Village of Xiaoxi Township as they relate their stories. All of them play two roles: the role of narrators in the tale of their lives, and the role of "backward villagers in need of rescue." Xioaxi Township is under the jurisdiction of Yongshun County of the ethnic Xiangxi Tujia and Miao Autonomous Prefecture. Hunan Province is responsible for the administration of this land.

Western Hunan's Participation in the Ecological Helping-the-Poor Campaign

Western Hunan is a heavily ethnic area that actively promotes the idea of ecological Helping-the-Poor initiatives. This shift of policy priority is in line with the review of past Helping-the-Poor policies of the provincial government of Hunan.

According to those who participated in the review work, the transfer of resources to poor areas hardly creates long-term effects. Businesses established with the help of external Helping-the-Poor campaigners are vulnerable to factors such as natural disasters, unexpected market fluctuations, and limited technical capability. Cases where subjects successfully proceed to a higher wealth level in a given year might suddenly regress, resulting in a phenomenon earlier discussed as a "return to poverty." Once individual cases "fall," few are able to make a comeback by themselves.

In general, the review is pessimistic about the attempts at improving local business culture and the cadres' efforts at relieving poverty. The officials interviewed commented that the current Helping-the-Poor campaign brought too many unfamiliar ideas from the outside. They believe that customized solutions, especially those that have the least impact upon the locals' lifestyles and conditions, are called for. This is why Hunan officials look to ecological Helping-the-Poor projects for answers.

Ecological Helping-the-Poor campaigns are not just "a different way of enhancing the wealth level." Poverty has always been defined in terms of per capita income in official documents. There is no fixed "poverty line," however, simply because the condition varies by year, region, and the level of governance. Hunan cadres at various levels of government are likely to quote different "poverty lines." While differences exist, most agree that the line is a quantifiable notion of income.

In general, the majority of Helping-the-Poor projects in Western Hunan involve road construction, electricity supply installation, and water reservoir building. Perhaps resulting from what they have seen as indicative of local backwardness, officials involved in Helping-the-Poor campaigns often say that they are not capable of cultural reformation. Provincial officials acknowledge that upgrading the local income level is a very difficult task.

On the other hand, the population of the targeted area often possesses a distorted view regarding the campaign personals and the campaign itself: their presence sends an unrealistic hope to the villagers, convincing them that the campaign work unit in charge can work miracles. Yet in most cases, the campaigning work unit cannot handle these unsolicited and unrealistic expectations, both economically and psychologically.

Ecological Helping-the-Poor initiatives redirect the attention of Helping-the-Poor campaign from profit making to the preservation of natural environment. This is the case in Western Hunan, where there are abundant natural resources and evidence of a rich cultural heritage. The past trend of Helping-the-Poor campaigns, characterized by the exploitation of natural resources to make a profit, has been completely reversed. Rather than using transferred capital to exploit the natural environment in poor areas, the new thinking has encouraged investing the funneled capital into areas of environmental preservation.

Underdevelopment is no longer the cause of poverty; it is now an important factor in relieving poverty. Production of natural gas is one of the nationally sponsored projects in the ecological Helping-the-Poor campaign. The project achieved favorable results in Western Hunan, where they have an "edge" in generating natural gas—pig excrement is the key; carbon oxygen produced in the process cycle is used to preserve oranges, which can be sold later during off-season; excrement can also be used in organic vegetable gardens; and organic "vegetable picking" tours attract city dwellers during weekends.

Local cadres in Western Hunan talk about these success stories with pride. However, it is unclear what all this means. In fact, much of the Helping-the-Poor literature comes from official sources.[1] Few of them even touch upon the subject of ecological Helping-the-Poor campaigns at all. At the national level, the party general secretary and the top government officials believe that this campaign has advanced to a new stage.[2] They call for a renewed effort by the whole country to "march into the middle class." While the official document notes the dwindling of the population reeling in poverty, the danger of poverty's return remains very real.

Ecological Helping-the-Poor projects carried out in the countryside need more research to appreciate the potential of the local villagers to rewrite the official success stories to express their own experience with what is thought to be just poverty. Official Helping-the-Poor campaigns as civilized projects do not involve the poor villagers in this regard. Now that the ecological version creates an opening for such response, stories told from local viewpoints would be useful to help judge just how efficient local agencies are at giving new meaning to the extensive Helping-the-Poor campaign. This can be seen in ethnic villages, such as Xiaoxi.

Xiaoxi Township is located in southeastern Yongshun. The town lies northwest of the Western Hunan Prefecture and borders Chongqing. It sits on Yongshun's border area next to Yuanling County. There are nineteen villages under the township jurisdiction with a population of approximately eight thousand, composed mostly of ethnic Tujia. About 90 percent of its sixty thousand acres are covered with forests.

Xiangxi Prefecture was the last to participate in the national project of the Grand Development of the West, and Yongshun is a nationally designated county of poverty. Running through Xiaoxi Township are six rivers: Hongxi, Daming, Yuquan, Xiaoxi, Chayuan, and Shanmu. In 1982, the provincial government designated the Xiaoxi forest as a natural reserve area. Fifteen years later, the first reserve office was established. Through the research efforts of a small group of villagers under the leadership of a forest guide named Ru Guicheng, along with the works of scientists from other regions, local inhabitants persuaded the central government to upgrade the Xiaoxi forest to a national reserve. Staff from the Western Hunan television station visited the village to make a documentary film once the upgrade was completed.

Scientific research data played an important role in determining Xiaoxi's upgrading, because results show that the Xiaoxi reserve is the only broad-leaved green forest left in its altitude, which dates back to the Ice Age. According to the findings of a local research crew,[3] the Xiaoxi forest features the following:

1. Uniqueness: Xiaoxi is the only sub-tropical forest at the same parallel that contains evergreen conifers, and deciduous and broad-leaved trees. The average temperature of Xiaoxi Township is roughly 6°C, which is lower in average than that of Yongshun County. It is also a tropical forest with rainfall of over 1,300 mm a year.

2. Variety: While new varieties of life continue to be discovered and added to the roster, as of the end of 2003, there have been 2,702 different plant species, belonging to 222 families, and 208 different vertebrates discovered in the forest. This includes the legendary spotted leopard, though no one has ever seen it. The species' excrement has been discovered, proving its existence. Even European experts understood the importance of Xiaoxi, calling it a "gene reservoir."

3. Rareness: The trees in Xiaoxi forest have a very long lifespan, forming a habitat that permits the survival of ancient and precious plants. Thirty-nine of the plants are exclusively local. Twenty-one plants found in the forest are named after Xiaoxi. Seven of these are ranked at level one for special protection. They are also classified at the national level, and a good number of others are ranked at level two.

4. Abnormality: Plants that belong to different climate zones thrive in the Xiaoxi forest. For example, there are eleven tropical plants growing in the sub-tropical forest terrain.

Ecological tourism forms the core of the township government's development plan. Abiding by the National Reserve Law, local cadres plan to relocate villagers dwelling in the forest to the plains. There are over one thousand emigrants that must leave, in compliance with the Reserve Law. The targeted township is Maoping. However, five years have passed and no relocation has taken place. This is due both to the fact that preparation at Maoping is way behind schedule, and that the funding needed for the plan has not arrived.[4] Natural disasters have frequented the area in recent years; this drained much of the funds that might have been kept for the use of moving the villagers. Caught between the aborted relocation plan and the ban on further construction in the forest (again, in compliance with the Reserve Law), no progress in the "tourism" plan could be achieved. No new lodgings can be legally built to accommodate tourists. Without further construction, these places lack bathing facilities, toilets, and even running water. The first (and only) paved road leading to Xiaoxi from the outside was finally completed in the spring of 2003. Unfortunately, a flood destroyed it immediately in the early summer. The area can now be accessed only by ferrying and rafting. However, one will not see any docking area after four hours on the ferry ride to Xiaoxi. The ferry stops always looked muddy, perhaps due to flooding. Sporadic tourists who visit the area are there to satisfy their curiosity of this rural location, not to escape city life. Having seen the situation, however, few will ever come back for a second visit.[5]

Two Narratives of Xiaoxi Ecology

The importance of ecology has gained wide acceptance in the world today. Xiaoxi's adoption of the ecological Helping-the-Poor campaign to preserve the natural forest can be seen as a part of this trend. However, having ecological consciousness does not lead to any definite conclusion regarding how the Helping-the-Poor campaign should proceed. To be specific, shared concern over the preservation of the natural forest results in divergent views regarding pollution. There is a noticeable gap between the opinion of outsiders and that of the villagers regarding what threatens local ecology. Consequently, both would come up with their own strategy to preserve the ecology and one plan could easily contradict the other.

Unfortunately, there seems to be no dialogue between the different narratives regarding the Xiaoxi reserve. Existing perspectives reflect very different lifestyles and worldviews. Without genuine interaction between the proponents of the different plans, those advocating their plans could not appreciate the relativity of their own positions. It is very possible that ecological strategy for one is seen as counterproductive (or even destructive) by another. The interview transcript shows two distinct narratives. One sees the villagers as the primary source of pollution, while the other proclaims that outsiders are the ones liable.

Contention about the ecological preservation in Xiaoxi is not the stereotypical one that centers on the contest of principles between modernist development and ecological reserve. This is not because China has bypassed the modern stage and immediately jumped into a postmodern stage to appreciate all the drawbacks associated with modernization but because modernization remains a remote destiny in a backward countryside, so to speak, such as Xiaoxi.

Companies interested in profit would probably not consider investing there, since it relies on ferry trips to get to and from the outside world, and it is located four hours away from the nearest railroad station. In addition, Xiaoxi villagers have shown no interest in modern forms of business, whatsoever. Yet, recent Helping-the-Poor campaigns nevertheless cause anxiety among the villagers, making them aware of their impoverished status. Limited access to public media has made the villagers aware of the force of the market and money economies, only to aggravate their sense of inferiority. Petty consumers emerge in the village, selling fast-food commodities such as instant noodles, Coke, chips, etc., and offering karaoke. These items, although not needed for basic survival, are among the favorites of the younger generations. The perceived "function" of these consumer products is very different as far as the population of Xiaoxi is concerned. For example, parents enticed in a conversation might give toddlers the spicy sauce found in the instant noodle pack not to free the working middle class from the chore and the time of cooking, but rather to taste the modern lifestyle.

These kinds of phenomenon can be considered as distortions to modern consumption culture.

The bizarre harmony between some modern consumption and backward lifestyle might lead outsiders to criticize the "Xiaoxi way." Criticism is inevitable, both because those who come to Xiaoxi are often ecologically sensitive, and because pollution caused by these petty consumer goods accumulates. For example, Xiaoxi villagers do not dispose of garbage properly. Instant noodles wrappers, chopsticks, and other food scatter with the wind, landing anywhere between the rivers and the mountains. Villagers are even surprised whenever they see visitors bringing empty bottles back to the hotel with them after a day's outing in the forests. This does not matter, since the villagers will eventually toss the bottles somewhere in the mountains even if tourists do not do so themselves. They wash clothes along the rivers with detergent, and answer the call of nature in the rivers where they bathe, and spit anywhere they like. For them, life in the mountains is being one with the natural environment. In their view, villagers see outsiders as fools who cannot grasp the concept that Mother Nature is able to digest almost anything. On the other hand, outsiders see villagers as a serious source of pollution to the cherished forest, which theoretically belongs to the whole nation and all peoples of this planet. Not surprisingly, government officials think they are well justified to demand that the villagers be relocated away from this precious forest reserve.

The villagers are unable to appreciate the importance of running water and bathrooms, which city dwellers view as necessities. They themselves jump into the rivers whenever they feel like it. The guide bathed three times in the water during the seven-hour trip and he was nude! It is a little surprising that these people feel little need for toilets. Yet, they spend all the time convincing outsiders that they are really strict with housekeeping. With a mop by her side, a maid appears ready to enter the three-square-meter room almost any minute, ready to clean even a tea drop on the floor. This is like a drama centering on their love for cleanliness. Still, urban tourists are generally unimpressed with local sanitation measures, primarily because there is no toilet for them to use. No matter how clean the room may be, outsiders continue to think that the villagers are unclean. Villagers do not understand the strong repulsiveness felt by outsiders, and think these visitors are fussy people.[6] In fact, to certain articulate villagers, the outsiders' criticism is insignificant, especially since they believe that the outsiders are the ones who bring the pollution.

While the outsiders (including the government officials) appear to "know their stuff" when it comes to modern technology and conceptualization of matters regarding environmental protection, their behavior and policy are not completely understood by the locals. For example, the government has a policy to revive the forest where trees were cut down for private use or for sale. For each tree the villagers grow in their cultivated land, there is both a monetary reward and some compensation in the form of rice. Villagers welcome the policy in general, since growing trees looks like an easy task.

The rationale behind the policy is not easily comprehensible to the locals, since they have lived in the mountains for thousands of years, so they cannot envision their lifestyle to be destructive to their habitat. In their experience, which is primarily hunting, cutting wood for periodic house renovation does not directly damage their environment. Even in recent years, processing and selling lumber occurred only on a limited scale. The forests and the mountains are too big for them to foresee any plausible limits. Besides, trees always grow back in time, as long as one cuts them wisely. Now that the Reserve Law has banned woodcutting, where do they expect the villagers to find material for house renovation, for making coffins, or to accommodate tourists? Without construction materials, how can any Helping-the-Poor campaign be sensible? Is lumbering for the purpose of constructing a get-away lodging house comparable to cutting down trees en masse for sale?

A more serious accusation is that which concerns the government as being the major polluter of the environment. One of the government's favorite ecological Helping-the-Poor projects is tourism. The government of Xiaoxi allocates a major portion of funds to the building of walking trails in the forest. In addition, low-interest loans are available for villagers who run get-away lodging facilities, and for renovating three-wheel vehicles used to bring visitors from the landing place to the forests. There are about two dozen of these three-wheels in Xiaoxi Village and they are visible sources of pollution.

The second component is the act of leading visitors into the forest. The government hires a construction team from a city and purchases needed cement and iron for building trails and bridges inside the forest area. These trails are normally made of cement. Along the beautiful waterfalls found within the forest, iron bridges have been installed to allow tourists to walk across. Cement and iron are part of the standard landscape of the city, but they are not typical features in Xiaoxi. The trails and bridges appear very awkward in the eyes of local residents.

Some suggest using dry wood in place of the cement and rocks for the steps of the stairs, which are really pieces of hard dry wood, although they might not look so at first glimpse. Moreover, if a flood destroys the trails or the foundations of a bridge, they will be much easier to repair if they were made of natural materials. The construction teams turned down the suggestion because tourists from the city might think that these wooden trails are not secure and so they will not dare step on them.

Ecology is obviously of no concern to the construction team. The family hotel owners call these iron bridges "monsters." Interestingly, there is no solid evidence that city dwellers actually feel comfortable with the so-called monsters. Local guides claim that they will still push for the building of future paths with rocks.

The two entities responsible for pollution have not yet really spoken to each other. From the government's point of view, villagers are the source of the problem. Perhaps the villagers are in no position to argue directly with the government, but this should not mean that the villagers will just sit by idly forever. In the following pages, this chapter will present different messages. The first is rather pessimistic, showing how villagers are discursively locked into certain identities that suffocate avenues for dialogue. The second message is a bit more optimistic. It discusses how some hidden avenues of change have empowered a few villagers. Finally, this chapter conceptualizes the link between the official ecological thinking and nascent localized subjectivities.

Agency Lost in the Ecological Helping-the-Poor Campaign

According to the National Reserve Law, human habitation is not allowed in a natural forest. Understandably, relocation that used to be a Helping-the-Poor policy instrument is now another a legal requirement in Xiaoxi. The villagers were not aware of the stipulation of the Reserve Law when they applied to upgrade their forest reserve to the national level. Many became bitter with the results afterwards, complaining that the upgrade was a trap. In the government's experience, it is expected that local residents generally dislike relocation. However, that does not stop this relocation policy from being enforced. For instance, the famous Sanxia relocation involved millions of residents. From the socialist point of view, it is a duty of the national government to relocate residents to curtail poverty. But since relocation calls for the cooperation of emigrants and receiving villagers, a tremendous amount of persuasion, coordination, and redistribution is inevitable.

Relocation of this sort dramatizes socialism, which sacrifices the few for the good of the majority. Socialism legitimizes relocation in return. There is not much room for citizens to articulate their private concerns in the face of such noble cause. The targets appear to be dependent and passive, which further strengthens the backward image expected of poor villagers. The only resistance they can offer to slow down the process is to raise pragmatic questions. Once the negotiations enter the pragmatic, relocation comes in only a matter of time.

For Xiaoxi residents, relocation became an issue in 1999, the year during which the forest reserve was upgraded to provincial level one. The Yongshun County government decided that relocation should be completed by the end of 2002. The prospect of relocation appeared inevitable by 2001. However, there was a lack of support from all government levels and its participation was needed to justify socialistic collectivism in the process. In fact, without government coordination, inhabitants of villages that serve as relocation destinations were less than enthusiastic in receiving their future neighbors. Xiaoxi Township director, Mr. Zhu Dazhou, had painstakingly accepted the idea of relocation and was the first one to formulate a plan. For him, the snail-paced process had prevented him from achieving anything. On one hand, he was to abide by the law and execute the policy of cordoning off the mountain for lumbering. However, because the relocation was halted for the last five years, his mountain closing-off policy was criticized as extremely rigid and unreasonable to local people. Villagers eventually restarted cutting trees for house renovation as well as the construction of hotels and lodges. In 2003, there had been over thirty houses renovated and over twenty were being built.

Zhu is actually quite reluctant about enforcing the closing-off policy. He describes this situation as an oil tank and he is the match that could set the whole thing on fire. Enforcing the closing-off policy could indeed have dire consequences. Another related problem is that some villagers demand to immigrate to the site currently occupied by the county office (which also sits in the forest and is a relocation target) in order to cash in on the benefits brought by tourism.

Zhu's relocation plan divides the villagers into three categories. The first category consists mostly of peasants who will receive lots and continue crop cultivation once they move to the destination. Those with some background related to staffing a forest maintenance company, patrolling forest areas, ticket selling, and cleaning, all belong to the second category. The third category refers to the small proportion of villagers who have already invested in tourism and should continue this kind of business. Yet, as of today, the third category cannot expand its business due to the Reserve Law Zhu has tried to persuade this group not to break the law as he has promised help with a "honey business." Villagers realize that both female and elderly tourists take a special interest in purchasing honey. However, the government has not hinted at supporting such an investment.

Zhu describes the attitude of the county government as unsupportive and not having enough understanding of the honey business. Yet, the local effort to overcome poverty or adapt to policy limitations is to find seasonal manual jobs in Guangzhou. However, due to lack of education, their capability level is so low that it is unlikely that any of them can send extra money back home to even build a brick house. The whole purpose of leaving the village is to control the family size in order for the rest to survive on a subsistence economy.

No one is actively prepared for relocation, despite talks at the county level. The township government of Maoping, for one, has guaranteed to provide every emigrant family a four-story house; but this is not enough for large families. Besides, the emigrant village would need space for an administrative office. Xiaoxi residents are equally uninterested in this. One Xiaoxi shop runner, whose shop is located deep within the mountains, confesses that she is not interested in relocation at all. She first said the reason is that the climate in the mountains is cooler. Then she said she has a better social network in the mountains, without which there could be no business. Then she began telling an interesting story. She criticized Xiaoxi Township for refusing to allocate land to a Taiwanese bridegroom married to her neighbor. She said that this was against the freedom of residence. She encouraged the bridegroom to go to court. Coincidentally, her story about freedom of residence occurred during our discussion on the relocation policy, although she did not connect the two subjects.

Xiaoxi residents as well as their governments at all levels are poor by any known standard. For instance, the doctor in the township stopped his practice because no one could afford medical treatment.[7] School children pay their tuition by giving crops; the schoolteachers are responsible for turning these into cash, if they like. With tourist arrivals, some villagers learned to make a living by selling snakes, although this is not exactly a safe business. Zhu estimates that less than 1 percent of the township population benefits from tourism. Cadres feel deprived when they see this small group make money. The finances of the local government used to depend heavily on fees collected from lumbering. As this is no longer allowed today, its finances totally rely on the county government's allocation.

In the past, there were Helping-the-Poor teams coming in to help. These were not strong teams, however. What they achieved was no more than building a few mountain trails. They could not even install facilities that will provide running water.

Cadres admitted that they gradually lost sight of the purpose of their work; their despair came from not knowing what they should do. In fact, they felt uncertain about their own future. Failure to execute government policy is likely to cost them their jobs. They once put hope on the seed money promised by the European Union. The associate county director of Yongshun claimed that the money had arrived and had been allocated to Xiaoxi Township. But in the field, cadres reported that they "did not even see the shadow of it."

The township is now in a very difficult financial situation. The monthly administrative allowance for the township director is not even sufficient for paying transportation for one to attend a county government meeting, and the director might need to go more than once during the month. The Yongshun County government itself is ranked high on the poverty scale. There have been no funds allocated to establish a forest bureau or any patrolling posts since the upgrade decision. Ironically, the neighboring county that failed the upgrading application has already set up a bureau-level office responsible for ecological preservation. Notably, the chances that Xiaoxi Township can overcome poverty are very slim, even in the eyes of the local cadres.

Both cadres and villagers have something in mind, but they cannot find the right occasion to voice their opinions. For example, Zhu has received an invitation to report Xiaoxi's situation to the National People's Congress, but he has no idea why he received such an invitation. He composed a short promotional report of roughly five hundred characters, which invited all social sectors to invest in Xiaoxi. Yet, there is no mention of the policy banning construction in Xiaoxi. The reason, according to him, is that the complaint is useless. Even if he did put it in, he believed that it would be tossed out anyway. He spoke from experience, because the last time he reported the per capita income of his township, his superior arbitrarily changed the number. Nonetheless, he concurred that perhaps the support for relocation could be an issue that he could use with the Beijing official.

Other interviewees point out that the government should reconceptualize the notion of ecology to include people who live in the forest. Even "the way we bite things" should be considered an ecological feature. A hotel owner who used to work in the sanitation bureau adds some new responsibilities to the aforementioned second category that Zhu has in mind. This category would now include the additional task of ethnic dancing and cultural performance. (He never spoke to Zhu about his idea.) He also believes that vegetable farming should be allowed in the mountains. An elderly party member told the interviewer that relocation is not going to work because people move in and out of the mountains freely.[8] This is not something that could be easily regulated.

Agency Created by the Helping-the-Poor Discourse

The aforementioned revelation regarding the villagers' thinking indicates that they have different views, while still embedded in the government's Helping-the-Poor discourse. There are also other views worth noting that are not embedded in the Helping-the-Poor discourse. This has to do with the emergence of local consciousness (sometimes even indirectly associated with ethnic consciousness), as mentioned earlier in this chapter. The opportunity for self-empowerment is a result of change in position facilitated by the Helping-the-Poor campaign. Note that under the circumstances created by the Helping-the-Poor campaign, the image of villagers has shifted from "someone to be civilized" to "someone who knows the ecology that is being cherished."

Initially the campaigners believed that the ecology of a poor village is a limitation of development when they design a development strategy. The strategy is invariably about profit making, although villagers are consulted during the process. The primary belief is that the villagers' opinions provide the best clues to their mindset; therefore, they are ultimately unimportant since they possess limited knowledge about the world of business. Once villagers accept the criterion of poverty and the value of development, they begin to see their way of living as a "miserable life". In short, a Helping-the-Poor campaign assumes passivity on the villagers' side. The challenge to individuals carrying out the campaign is to provide a different incentive to improve the villagers' way of life. Ironically, this might further alienate villagers from the state and the modernist value whereas villagers lose their sense of subjectivity.

Once the state classifies the Xiaoxi forest as a national treasure, those who know the forests become the know-it-all sages, the narrators, and subsequently the opinion leaders. Villagers can comfortably utilize their life experiences when talking ecology to the outsiders, which is something they know well. Ironically, this façade of confidence lures the outsiders into some sort of exotic imagination about the local lifestyle. This kind of acceptance provides legitimacy and reinforces the interpretation by the villagers. They show no hesitation about sharing their stories in their language, even in front of academics from respected scientific institutions in Beijing. In fact, these experts often need local help with identifying various plants.

Confidence resulting from a sense of selfhood that is both familiar and presentable supports the villagers in developing a language that does not directly correspond to Helping-the-Poor concerns. Not only do many villagers have their own views of how to protect the ecology, but also how to locate their own position in the ecology discourse. Ecology is a new concept in Xiaoxi, but the use of this new concept is full of possibilities. Once some of these possibilities are realized in their interaction with the outsiders, Xiaoxi villagers will no longer remain "just another group of people reeling in poverty."

The importance outsiders place upon the Xiaoxi forest nonetheless created a beneficial triggering effect. The first groups to visit included those from higher academies in Beijing as well as Western scientists. Villagers took them on a familiarization tour and spoke to them about plants. While they may be the passive dependents waiting to be rescued, they are also the transmitters of important knowledge.

Local guides are impressed with the ecological consciousness of American scientists who clean and bring back with them remnants of whatever they consumed. They are always fully equipped, appearing very different from the sandal-wearing guides. While guides praise visitors for walking even faster than they can on the trail, they still proudly mention how relatively faster the sandal-wearers can move once entering the deep mountains. At one point, the interviewer dove into the river late in the evening after a long dinner interview. Luckily, accompanying villagers were able to locate and rescue him in the dark. They found his sandals floating in the water nearby, and walked him ashore by letting his feet rest on theirs.

Villagers are not doing all this guide work in exchange for money. In fact, the most well known local guide earns only slightly over RMB700 a month. The reward for his daily effort is a meager RMB50. The villagers guide visitors for the purpose of showing off their forest to the outsiders. Within them, there is the sense of pride, confidence, and perhaps a deeper need of being represented.

The guide, Mr. Ru, once led the visitor to where a waterfall was located about an hour's climb to the mountains from the road. The chauffer driving the three-wheeler that carried them to the entry site into the forest (so to speak) refused to enter at first, for fear of being bitten by snakes. Mr. Ru, however, told him that he had the snakes all under control. The chauffer agreed to go with them, and saw the legendary waterfalls. The sight is something even locals would never get to see without Mr. Ru as the guide. The chauffer trusts Mr. Ru apparently because Mr. Ru explained that he knew prayers to control snakes, and he would release the snakes upon their leaving.

His prayers are said to be powerful because this power was handed down to him by his ancestors, according to Mr. Ru. Outsiders cannot learn the prayers, as they are a part of family tradition. He asked the interviewer to think why he was still all right after having been in the mountains for so many years, carrying out various activities, while so many others have died of snakebites. What else could explain the miracle, other than his knowledge of his ancestors' prayers? This kind of ancestor discourse is everywhere, although it is indirect and unintended.

In another case, while building mountain trails, the villagers warned the construction team not to move certain dying trees. The explanation was that those trees looked after the prosperity of the local people from generation to generation. Heeding warnings such as these, the construction teams usually built trails often blocked by a crossing trunk with two ends out of reach on either side. Trekkers would either have to cross over the trunks, or crawl underneath them.

Most people in today's society see ancestor consciousness as unrelated to modern state building, while others see it as an obstacle. Yet, it is often ancestor consciousness that defines one's ethnicity. Indeed, in Xiaoxi, with a large Tujia population, ancestor consciousness and local self-representation together lead the quest for the opportunity of the name of Xiaoxi to be known elsewhere.

Outsiders occupy a sensitive position in initiating action. The relocation project that will serve the villagers from their ancestor's ecology might cause some inexpressible sentiments. The rhetoric that involves ancestors is a challenge to the outsiders, who must judge if their knowledge of the local ecology is complete without knowing the ancestors of the local people. Both the Helping-the-Poor campaigners and scientists are unaware of the local reason behind naming and presenting Xiaoxi to the outsiders. For the campaigners, Xiaoxi is a township stricken by poverty. For the scientists, it is a forest reserve rich in flora and fauna to study.

Naming as a mode of self-representation has sensitized local villagers. Mr. Ru feels very frustrated whenever he spots a new plant in the region, then realizes that what he has discovered already has a regional name based on where it was first discovered. He will be most excited when he discovers anything that has never been found in any other place, because he can then give it a name carrying "Xiaoxi," "Yongshun," or "Western Hunan." Mr. Ru says that through the act of name giving, Xiaoxi obtains its own name. He understands that this name would spread with the new plant when it is discovered later somewhere else. He uses the term "mingfen" for a name, a term that Confucius used to designate everything under heaven with their own roles and duties. In the academic sense, Mr. Ru is searching for distinctive representation for his place in a world where identities have become increasingly obscure.

Mr. Ru is applying for a loan of RMB20000, in hope that funding could be secured to carry out a project he has had in mind for a long time. He wants to take photos of all the plants, bugs, and animals in his forest. He regrets that he does not know Latin, so much so he has to submit his newly discovered varieties to the Chinese Academy of Science each time for rectification. Having spent all these years as a guide, he realizes that he knows many more varieties than anyone else coming to him. A Ph.D. candidate knows about a thousand varieties, on the average. He told the interviewer that these scientists would need at least three years to learn what he already knows. He also wants to apply for funding to invite the central television station crew to come and report on the value and beauty of the Xiaoxi forest. This is probably beyond his influence, but his idea is indicative of a wish to be separately represented, outside the poverty discourse, and full of agency.

Conclusion

With few exceptions, the Helping-the-Poor campaign has not been very effective in raising the income and wealth level of the poor villagers. Western Hunan is among the least successful areas, due to the limitation of local conditions and the lack of business culture. Ecological Helping-the-Poor campaigns have created a new dimension in similar initiatives to Western Hunan, because these provide local residents a sense of subjectivity, since it is the villagers' ecology that is being protected. The continued emphasis on income and wealth by the campaigners is not necessarily incompatible with the emergence of local views that reflect the increasing need for self-representation.

Though the plan for natural gas tank manufacturing has been quite successful, it has not significantly changed local consciousness. In Xiaoxi, a different local subjectivity is being rediscovered. Like villagers elsewhere, Xiaoxi villagers do not find the idea of relocation attractive. However, Xiaoxi interviewees are able to develop reasons why they do not like relocation. Of course, the government would probably move them anyway, if not for the lack of anticipated support; nonetheless, Xiaoxi villagers are able to talk back. They do not necessarily want to disobey senior government officials or Helping-the-Poor campaigns, but there is a discursive string belonging exclusively to Xiaoxi villagers. They can form opinions regarding the Helping-the-Poor campaign or relocation plan, and evaluate their merits from a perspective not apparent or comprehensible to outsiders. Relocation is conceived as being inconsistent with the ecological policy. Ancestor consciousness emerges and makes the outsiders awkward participants. Some indirect resistance at the subconscious level may be forming in the process.[9]

The incompetent government has not been able to gear up sufficient resources to execute the relocation plan. This development has given the villagers time to form their own ideas. The expansion of tourist accommodations is accompanied by the loss of credit with the relocation plan. This type of dispute and divergence of interests also occurs everywhere in China. Xiaoxi villagers differentiate themselves based on their experience to the extent that they find ways of self-representation beyond the government Helping-the-Poor discourse.

It is not their actual capability to reverse the government policy that is worth noting. Their subjectivity does not rely on the government and the Helping-the-Poor campaigners. On the contrary, some of the villagers are already confident in telling their own story by using local sources and imagination. If not for the self-realization rising out of the ecological Helping-the-Poor programs of the state, the enhanced ancestor consciousness that reversed the formation of opinions about the state, now as an intruder, would not have matured.

PART 3

___

Out of Place

The official discourses on autonomy, ethnicity, and economics might fail to produce the expected responses. For example, the enforcement of regional autonomy, as discussed in Chapter 7, might lead to the loss of ethnic consciousness in areas where multiple minorities coexist. Other chapters similarly discuss that the system of autonomy is not sensitive to the differences among minorities because it comes from the mainstream Han's perspective. Similarly, ethnicity could be reduced to no more than a name, which provides no meaningful reference for ethnic villagers to understand the world. Chapter 8 discusses such a result of earlier decisions made by ancestors of diasporic Shui people to become indifferent to ethnic identities. Moreover, when Helping-the-Poor cadres arrive in the mountains, feelings of impotence and alienation might quickly register in their mind. The stories given by Western Hunan cadres in Chapter 9 reveal a kind of frustration previously inexpressible through the official discourse. None of these developments fit well in the state's quest for unity.

CHAPTER 7

3 + 1 + 1 = 1: Disempowerment in Multi-ethnic Autonomous Longsheng

Ethnicity Lost in Regional Autonomy

Granting local autonomy to ethnic communities has gained increasing support in China as a means of organizing a multi-ethnic state. Given the rigidity of the country's modern system of sovereignty, Chinese authorities believe that regional autonomy is the only viable option for reconciling assertions of sub-national ethnicity with national sovereignty. The thrust of China's policy is to create a sense of unity by recruiting minorities to work for the Party and the government; to give economic, educational, and demographic privileges to citizens with ethnic identification or those simply living in autonomous jurisdictions; and to provide exemptions from state mandates. In return, the state closely monitors all ethnic cultural, religious, and social activities, and demands political loyalty. The state treats minorities as individual citizens (who have special rights and privileges) rather than as groups. In other words, ethnicity is considered a component of citizenship, but not a component that legitimizes organizing groups outside of state control. This position was clearly evident at the first International Workshop on Regional Autonomy of Ethnic Minorities held in Beijing in 2001 (see Chapter 1). Almost all of the Chinese attendees supported the idea of national unity as the requisite foundation upon which the state could best promote the welfare of nationalities residing in relatively underdeveloped areas. They generally viewed regional autonomy as a mechanism to legitimize the unity required to channel economic subsidies into a region. Since many sub-nationalities live in China's western provinces, this line of thinking was particularly noticeable as part of the project "Grand Development of the West" that is now being promoted by the central government.

Regional autonomy gains more currency in terms of current trends toward globalization, and, since globalization must be carried out by individual localities, researchers have noted the concomitant trend of localization. Local agents support the movement of globalization across borders while at the same time reconfirming those movements. Accordingly, the processes of globalization tend to heighten the sensitivity of local agents toward regional identities, the existence of which consolidates borders. The forces of globalization require local identities to be transformed into global images. Globalization thus becomes a two-step process of translation that makes any local identity a potential item of consumption in other parts of the world (and vice versa). Thus, regions become capable of representing themselves in an imagined global sphere and of positioning themselves as consumers of images of other regions provided by the globalizers.

In addition to labeling, regional autonomy can alleviate the anxiety of those local groups which lose representation when their borders (both territorial and psycho-cultural) are opened up by the presumably more modern global forces represented by the state. Their autonomous status testifies to the existence of certain distinctions in their identity compared with the rest of the country, even though they represent top-down construction rather than indigenous spontaneity.

Regional nationalities are autonomous in two senses. On the one hand, regional governments enjoy a certain degree of administrative discretion that is specified and protected by the state. The degree to which nationalities can negotiate independently for their own interests varies on a case-to-case basis. In China, this is determined by the Communist Party's need to establish or maintain national unity.[1] On the other hand, local legislative discretion allows regional nationalities to reconsider, revise, or refuse legislation at higher levels. In recognition of this power, the central Chinese government shows some flexibility in its claim of sovereignty over nationality territories. The range of issues that can be decided on by local legislation is subject to negotiation. Generally speaking, however, the top-down approach favored in China refuses to grant any kind of veto power that might damage national unity.[2] In contrast, the bottom-up approach that prevails in Scandinavian countries views veto power as a means of protecting the human rights of nationalities.

At least in terms of name, regional title precedes nationality name, which precedes administrative level. The Chinese system favors region over nationality, for instance: Ningxia Hui Autonomous Region, Yanbian Korean Autonomous Prefecture, Jilin Province; Jinxiu Yao Autonomous County, Guangxi Zhuang Autonomous Region; and Sanren She Township,

Suichang County, Zhejiang Province. In areas where there is more than one nationality, multiple nationalities are combined into one autonomous body, for example: Xiangxi (Western Hunan) Tujia and Miao Autonomous Prefecture, Hunan Province; Puer Hani and Yi Autonomous County, Yunnan Province; and Fengshu Hui and Uygur Township, Changde City, Hunan Province.

Regarding the potential contradiction between ethnicity and autonomy in the prevailing discourse on ethnic autonomy, Zhou Yong is curious yet subversive.[3] He notes that the title of an ethnic autonomous region always places the regional title in front of the ethnic title so that China has Ningxia Hui Autonomy, not Hui Ningxia Autonomy, for example. Apparently, not all residents in one autonomous region belong to the major ethnic minority. Since the state law and policy are universally applied in the region regardless of ethnic identity, to put the regional title first seems reasonable. Zhou Yong is curious why it is necessary to have "ethnic" autonomy at all. He further questions the cases in which a region is multi-ethnic. For example, there is Western Hunan Tujia-Miao Autonomy. The question is whether or not autonomous power given to two ethnic groups at the same time deserves to be called ethnic. One extreme case he mentions is Longsheng Multi-ethnic Autonomous County, the subject of this current chapter. It is virtually unclear who is autonomous in this county. In these cases, neither Tujia and Miao nor those belonging to the "multi-ethnic" segregation are ethnic because the term "ethnic" in "ethnic autonomy" loses relevance if it means "two-ethnic" or "multi-ethnic." He circumvents that ethnic autonomy is only about autonomy, not about being ethnic.

Zhou Yong also raises a similarly deconstructive point from another angle. He finds that the ethnic population of a certain autonomous area is not even the majority. This means that ethnic autonomy, which might have the side effect of meeting the democratic principle, is not ethnic. One famous example is about the Guangxi Zhuang Autonomy in which ethnic Zhuang residents contribute to 40 percent of the total autonomous population in Guangxi. The rationale of not splitting Guangxi into one Zhuang autonomous region and another ordinary province was economic. Zhou argues that the initiation of the autonomous region in Guangxi was economic as well as regional, and not ethnic. To be ethnic, Zhou thinks it should have embodied "the formation of the collective will of the minority, the management of its own internal affairs, and the defense against the external society."[4] Moreover, in an autonomous region, a smaller ethnic group might establish a smaller autonomous government at lower levels such as that in a county, township, or even village. There are numerous cases in which such lower-level autonomous governments are not established. Zhou argues that the meaning of ethnic autonomy is practically confusing.

Examples of more than two nationalities in a single autonomous unit include Weining Yi, Hui, and Miao Autonomous County, Guizhou Province; Menglian Dai, Lahu, and Wa Autonomous County, Yunnan Province; Yuanjiang Hani, Yi, and Dai Autonomous County, Yunnan Province; Jinping Miao, Yao, and Dai Autonomous County, Yunnan Province; Zhenyuan Yi, Hani, and Lahu Autonomous County, Yunnan Province; Jishishan Baoan, Dongxiang, and Sala Autonomous County, Gansu Province; and Longsheng Multiethnic Autonomous County, Guangxi Zhuang Autonomous Region. Zhou Yong describes the Longsheng title as an extreme contradiction: the number of nationalities is too great to include all of their names. Clearly, the notions of "multiple" and "autonomy" do not coincide easily.

It is also important to note, however, that Zhou has never visited Longsheng,[5] which is the focus of this chapter. As an autonomous region without a dominant nationality, Longsheng might reflect a philosophy that does not exist in any other part of the world. Multi-ethnic autonomy makes more sense to the central government than it does to any specific ethnic group. This means that differences among these groups are lost to a certain degree. In a similar manner, ethnicity can lose its meaning in the regional autonomy of multiple nationalities that receive certain kinds of administrative treatment because of their uniqueness among surrounding Han communities—that is, when the autonomous designation discursively reproduces the quality of using the Han majority as a reference point. Multi-ethnic autonomy makes it possible to study how autonomy can reduce, rather than enhance, local agency. This was the focus of the research visit to Longsheng.

Longsheng's Multi-ethnic Conditions

In June 2002, an interview was held in Longsheng with some cadres and officials from the Office of United Front (and its subsection, the Bureau of Religious Affairs) in Heping and Jiangdi Townships. Also present were teachers from local primary and junior high schools. Most of the cadres were Han Chinese or members of the Zhuang and Dong nationalities; the non-cadres included many Miao teachers in Jiangdi, Yao teachers in the Heping primary school, the Miao chauffer, and a few Yao women peddlers during the one-day tour of the scenery site of the dragon backbone. There was no sign of any dissatisfaction among these Yao or Miao interviewees regarding the low percentages of their respective nationalities in government positions, even though the 2001 pamphlet celebrating the fiftieth anniversary of Longsheng County described the root cause of the problem as the low percentage of college-educated Yao and Miao. Because Longsheng includes significant populations of five major nationalities—Han, Zhuang, Dong, Yao, and Miao—giving a name to the political entity was a task requiring both sophistication and sensitivity.

Demographically, the Dong residents constitute the largest segment of the population, but administratively, Longsheng belongs to the Guangxi Zhuang Autonomous Region, which implies that the Zhuang and Han are the majority nationalities. In 1951, the central government decided that "multi-ethnic" (gezu) was the best designation for an area in which the Dong, Yao, and Miao now account for 57 percent of the total population. Over 70 percent of all township-level cadres come from these three minorities, and the county government has been led by an ethnic Dong for the past five decades.

There may be several reasons why the majority of cadre positions in the county are occupied by Dong families, but the most widely accepted is their educational attainment. Anecdotal evidence collected from teachers suggest that Dong children are the best academic achievers, a reputation that presents a challenge to the Communist Party's efforts to recruit more Yao or Miao cadres. The most visible Yao and Miao participation is in the more nominal local People's Congress and Political Consultative Conference. By its own account, the Longsheng County Commission on Ethnic Affairs is very concerned about the ratios of Yao and Miao children entering specially subsidized ethnic classes (particularly classes for girls), since it sees this as an avenue to gaining a larger percentage of cadre positions. Although in a Dong village, an entire family clan might support a child's education, many Yao and Miao parents are suspicious of school officials' motives, thus they use this as an excuse for not sending their children to school.

Some of the teachers claimed that many local families view formal education as serving the needs of teachers rather than those of children. A similar viewpoint is found in other remote ethnic villages, where the odds of entering college are close to zero. Many believe that if the main purpose of schooling is to empower children to eventually immigrate to China's coastal cities, college is the least likely channel. This attitude also discredits the usefulness of other levels of education; attendance rates stay close to 95 percent in primary school,[6] yet drop dramatically in junior high—the time when many children begin to learn what is considered useful manual trade. Most of the young people who leave their villages to find seasonal jobs in urban centers return to their villages within a few years. They then participate in a cycle of producing larger than average families (the one-child policy is less than effective in these mountains), poor land management practices, and prolonged poverty.

Several other factors contribute to school dropout rates. Those adolescents who return from the coastal cities wearing clothes like adults and telling stories of their urban experiences influence students to ignore their studies. The central government's official rules on child labor prohibit the hiring of children who have not completed junior high school; some parents see this as a reason to keep their children in school, because doing so increases their potential for finding relatively lucrative factory jobs in China's manufacturing centers. Still, junior high school dropout rates remain at over 50 percent in many villages; most of those who manage to extend their education beyond junior high school attend vocational schools. The very few residents of Longsheng who earn college degrees are predominantly Dong. Since the official central government policy requires that township cadres must have college education, the Yao and Miao populations are at a considerable disadvantage.

Longsheng has a very small education budget, but the teachers said that their salaries were paid on time. The central government has recently given junior high school teachers two salary increases so they now earn approximately US$80 a month; the top of the salary scale in many parts of the country is US$125 a month. While teacher salaries fall under township budgets, the county controls the disbursement of teachers' salaries in order to prevent embezzlement problems that plague townships in many other parts of the country. Except for salaries, educational budgets suffer from severe shortfalls. Financing from higher levels often demands a "relative fund" from the township—a demand unlikely to be met by the township government. Since 2001, the central government has banned the practice of collecting levies from parents, a measure which has eliminated a significant source of income for schools. Under a single-fee policy, parents pay a flat rate at the beginning of the school year according to a formula established by the local governments. The teachers complained that they now have only enough money to purchase chalk. Donations are considered a major source of income, but there was no mentioning of any formal fund-raising programs. Moreover, donations made come from government branches that are ordered to offer help or from charitable organizations that act on their own initiatives.

Multi-ethnicity as a Constructed Nationality

According to central government representatives, national unity is at the core of the country's nationality policy and its efforts to promote economic growth in ethnic regions. The policy refers exclusively to shared blood rather than cultural affiliations; blood relations are the bases from which the government allocates relaxed birth quotas, tax exemptions, school entrance preferences, and the like. While this form of legal discourse sometimes serves to alienate a nationality, ethnic identities in autonomous regions are clearly delineated even though the government is rarely involved in activities that reproduce them culturally or socially. In some ways, regional autonomy is sufficient by itself for maintaining identification at a level that is strong enough to provide agency.

It seems clear that the Chinese government is not concerned with providing the agency required to give meaning to ethnic identity, since it does not involve itself in activities that carry, produce, or revise such meanings unless they are clearly relevant to the execution of policy or the protection of national unity. For example, the government neither promotes nor dissuades the religious life of members of the Hui nationality as long as it does not affect government policy or ideology. On some occasions, ethnic identity carries a message that favors government policy. For instance, the majority of ethnic residents of Manchuria seem to hold great patriotic feelings for Chinese residents, in some ways even more than those carrying the Han identity. At other times, ethnic identity hinders policy, such as in the case of the Yi community. Described as having emerged only recently from a state of slavery, many Yi are alienated from institutionalized education because it provides few ethnically-related incentives for their participation. In short, governments at various levels tend to be inattentive to the function of local agency, which—based on the ethnic identity in question—occasionally reinterprets the meaning of those identities or alters the connotations of state policy.[7]

This appears to be the case among the Yi living in Meigu County of Liangshan Yi Autonomous Prefecture, Sichuan Province. Local teachers and cadres explain low school enrollments by citing the previous state designation of "slavery culture." It may be that the state prefers using this "backwardness" rationale to the more threatening interpretation that low enrollments reflect a tacit form of resistance associated with ethnic identity. In contrast, in Chapter 8, ethnic Shui villagers of Guangxi's Yizhou City have responded more positively to economic and educational mobilization, perhaps because of the city's greater diversity—a response that can also be viewed as a loss of ethnic consciousness and a loss of agency for the ethnic identities that remain. Many children from mixed Shui-Han families have consciously decided to take on an official Han designation, giving up certain privileges in order to become a member of the majority. Thus, both Yi and Shui are responding to state mobilization, one within the context of ethnic identity and the other outside of it. Perhaps maintaining a "backward" identity instead of an inactive one facilitates coping strategies.

Longsheng is distinctive in that it lacks an identity strategy. Lethargic county officials and township cadres have not fulfilled the mission to develop the local economy as mandated by the central government. This lack of enthusiasm at the county level is in contrast with at least thirty other previous research sites, where the lethargy was only apparent at the township level or below. Criticism of state policy in other counties reflects a strong sense of agency or will to adapt, even when the direction of adaptation is somewhat contradictory to government policy. In Longsheng, it appears that officials and cadres are very mindful of performance checks by their superiors—an impractical case of sensitivity, as these officials and cadres seem incapable of achieving their economic objectives in the first place. In this respect, ethnicity seems irrelevant to their superiors as well as to local communities.

The Lost Agency of a "Multi-ethnic" Nationality

Chengbu Miao Autonomous County in southwest Hunan is geographically close to Longsheng (in northeast Guangxi). According to the Chengbu Commission on Ethnic Affairs, in 2000, the Miao leadership manipulated economic figures to show that the county had successfully risen above the central government's official poverty line. Commission officials were very unhappy because the county was no longer qualified to receive a poverty subsidy, but the county leadership was pleased to receive good governance awards, which might lead to individual promotions. While officials were arguing over economic issues, the Miao chief of the Commission on Ethnic Affairs was engaged in a heated debate with other officials (especially the Miao chief of the Chengbu Commission on Education) over the issue of providing education *in* ethnic areas versus providing education *with* ethnic characteristics. The latter approach would stress a sense of ethnic uniqueness that would be irrelevant to performance measures. The debate spotlighted conflicts between personal and community interests. However, neither activity, falsifying statistics or promoting ethnic consciousness, may be said to be in line with state policy or local agency.[8]

Longsheng officials and cadres might differ in their perceived powers to act as agents of change, yet they share one thing in common: their use of the phrase, "We can do nothing about it" (*meiyou banfa*). Regardless of level, almost every official use this phrase at some point. When asked about a difficult situation or an unreasonable top-down decision, "*meiyou banfa*" seemed to end the discussion on the issue. In Sichuan Meigu County, Yi residents seem to comply passively with state decisions, but they are actually acting to protect themselves. For example, many Meigu Yi raise goats to provide security for themselves and their relatives in times of crisis or shortage. Meanwhile, Longsheng officials just like Chengbu officials want economic growth without the formality of performance checks. However, Longsheng interviewees never talked about taking action to change the top-down, unilateral style of policymaking, while Chengbu officials actively discussed alternative resources, wrote newspaper articles, and raised issues with the local People's Congress. In other words, some Chengbu officials were interested in formulating an ethnically meaningful policy, but Longsheng officials (who never failed to emphasize their ethnic identity in their interviews) seemed to have no interest in using their identity as a means of motivating political action. Furthermore, while Longsheng officials resorted to saying "*meiyou banfa*" and doing nothing, Chengbu officials seemed to always want to do something about a problem.

Using Zhou Yong's words, multi-ethnicity deprives officials and cadres of the agency from dealing directly with situations involving a single ethnicity, whether imagined or authentic. Cadres with certain ethnic backgrounds find it difficult to see meanings in a collective ("multi" or *ge*) identity. This difficulty puts multi-ethnicity on the same level as Han "ethnicity," whose members do not bring an ethnic perspective to their political participation. Governing Longsheng requires a sense of unity of various ethnicities in addition to a clear understanding of its relationship with its surrounding Zhuang and Han nationalities. If Longsheng officials would start with the unity question, "How is it possible for individual residents to take on a meaningful ethnic perspective?" even though the state continues to provide policy privileges and to nominate ethnic officials for leadership positions, these measures will not lead to creating an autonomous mindset based on a specific nationality.

According to Edward Said's critique in *Orientalism*, hybrid identities should be recognized as such without requiring conformity to either of the pure identifications they are borne from.[9] émigrés such as Said and his colleagues would want to shun finger pointing from both the motherland and the host society. Orientalists disavow this new representation of identity and discursively lock such hybrids into geographical spaces having exotic and frequently inferior designations. Said not only showed that this imagined Orient does not exist, but also traced the hybridity back to the two originating cultures. The lesson here is that no one should be considered "pure." The Longsheng situation, however, casts a shadow over Said's solution by suggesting that an administratively hybrid county is insufficient for providing agency. In other words, denied purity might lead to inaction. Said might have been overly optimistic about the capability of a hybrid community to respond, adapt, or improvise.

On the other hand, Longsheng might not stand as a good case of true hybridity, but of hybridity in name, making Said's solution inapplicable. Moreover, the simultaneous designation of multi-ethnicity and a single Longsheng identity results in an Orientalist fallacy because residents are torn between two fixed titles; this serves as a disincentive for member communities to develop a hybrid consciousness. Thus, multi-ethnicity is no more than a discursive device, aimed at creating unity but serving as a reminder of a community's non-existence. Making Longsheng a non-autonomous county might serve as a solution to this dilemma. Motivation for political participation might increase if emphasis were placed on single-ethnic townships rather than on a multi-ethnic county.

The Policy-driven Temperament of Multi-ethnicity

While there exists some ethnic mingling in Longsheng, this cross-culture contact does not necessarily benefit the development of agency for individual ethnic groups. For instance, children from various mountain communities must use Mandarin Chinese in their township primary schools, and teachers are not supposed to favor one group over another. Still, the reduced emphasis on ethnic consciousness in schools does not mean that communities outside of schools do not take their ethnic identities seriously. There were many examples of ethnic discourse in Longsheng during the visit—in contrast to Yizhou, where there are few reminders of ethnic identity among the Shui (Chapter 8). The practice of multi-ethnicity might diminish the utility of a single ethnic identity as a motivating factor but, depending on the population, residents maintain some degree of consciousness regarding their demobilized identities. The purpose of establishing Longsheng as a multi-ethnic political unit was to avoid alienating any of the resident nationalities, yet the result seems to be a passive attitude on the part of cadres and teachers.

Many interviewees expressed a strong dislike for performance measures, but there was plenty of evidence to show that they had made an effort to fulfill the goals that had been imposed on them. "Performance projects" constitute a major part of bureaucratic life in Longsheng; office walls contained numerous certificates in recognition of "vanguard township" or "civilized township" status. One interviewee sarcastically described these awards as supporting the only project of any true consequence: dabiao gongcheng, the "criterion-passing project," by which their superiors gain recognition from *shang shangji* ("top superiors") through the efforts of unrewarded teachers and low-level cadres. Some of the township cadres complained about the gift culture they are forced to participate in, meaning the wining and dining of higher officials that must be held in order to gain access to funding that has been officially designated for township use. However, instead of doing something to resist this practice, the governing attitude that exists is *"meiyou banfa."*

In a few cases, interviewees added some detail to the *"meiyou banfa"* perspective. As one might expect, common responses included the lack of funds required to make meaningful change and restrictions on employee responsibilities. A Longsheng County official at the Commission on Ethnic Affairs described his role as controlling a small step in the overall "administrative process," which means issuing identity proofs, application forms, or policy guidelines. He had no grasp of a larger plan for preserving cultural traits, supporting the continuation of ethnic languages, or of creating educational materials with local characteristics. From what its official reported, the most meaningful work being performed by the commission was the "Helping-the-Poor" project, which was only indirectly related to ethnic issues. In another area, passivity and skepticism were both clearly evident among Jiangdi Township schoolteachers, none of whom were willing to seek help from the county's Commission on Education or Ethnic Affairs. Officials at the Commission on Ethnic Affairs acknowledged having little contact with schoolteachers who lack outside donations to make up their personal financial donations. Instead of making an effort to engage in fundraising activities, commission members wait for donations from the Guangxi regional government somehow to float in their direction.

To describe how the education policy lacks sensitivity to special needs (ethnic or otherwise), some teachers used the common idiom *"yi dao qie"* ("a single cut with a knife"), meaning that high-level administrators prefer policies that are too broad to be effective, similar to someone who uses a knife to cut across an entire side of meat without separating the various sections. The teachers were particularly angry about the use of primary school attendance rates as a performance measure, complaining that they were forced to sacrifice the overall quality of education to meet imposed goals. They were not surprised that many parents refused to spend the money required to send their children to junior high school or higher levels, when it was clear that local teachers felt pressured to make sharp distinctions in terms of student potential to score high. Knowing this, some parents do not even bother to send their children to primary school. In light of these constraints, it seems strange to discuss whether ethnic relevance might serve as an educational incentive.

The probable reason why teachers put much effort into improving attendance rates is that their salary raises are tied to these rates. Furthermore, poor attendance or maintenance rates are also viewed as good reasons for cutting back on the number of teaching positions in a township center, therefore giving teachers some pressure to maintain their posts to avoid being assigned in more remote mountain communities, or being reassigned to positions such as cooks or sanitary workers if they fail their performance checks. An important result of these administrative measures and threats is the pervasiveness of the "*meiyou banfa*" attitude in Longsheng. One official at the Commission on Ethnic Affairs complained that the questions they hear and requests they receive often go beyond the commission's capabilities. For example, when elderly villagers complain about the loss of traditional culture, officials would tell them that no money is available to invest on cultural preservation. On the other hand, the commission has made no effort to coordinate its activities with the Commission on Education even though doing so is considered part of its mandate.

In an interview with an official at the Commission on Ethnic Affairs, the visitor told a story about how some Longsheng teachers were required to invest six hundred *yuan* per person (two hundred *yuan* on tuition and four hundred *yuan* on room and board) to learn basic computer skills,[10] even though their schools have no money to purchase computers. It was clear that he never considered the issue as something that could be brought up to the Commission on Education. During this exchange, an official from the Department of United Front cut in and promised that he would ask the Commission on Education about its policy rationale. In conclusion, the "*meiyou banfa*" attitude found in Longsheng County is not limited to township-level initiatives and politics; county level officials can be equally submissive. The only local initiative heard during the entire visit was an effort by a single teacher to write a newspaper article. It was never published, though, and the writer cited her lack of good connections to a publisher or editor as the reason.

Non-ethnic Multi-ethnicity

To the teachers, one major concern that poses a question is why county leaders never visit their schools or villages to investigate on problems. One township cadre questioned the need for such a large number of county-level officials, why they never bother to travel and observe the townships' situation. He had clearly given up trying to persuade them to visit his jurisdiction. From the point of view of an outsider, this puzzle also leads to the question "Why have the teachers or township cadres never reported the problems they encounter?" Leaders in Jiangdi, whose annual education budget in addition to personnel salaries is meagerly 30,000 *yuan*, decided to take out a loan in order to remodel the township's rundown classrooms. The cadres acknowledged that they had no payment plan. The school has no playground or library (with the latter serving as the teachers' collective sleeping room). The teachers are so close to the problem, however, that they fail to notice that their superiors do not know about their plight. At the same time, teachers are also disillusioned over dealing with parents. As one interviewee expressed, his effort to shape students' development and behavior in a five-day lesson was often wasted easily by one weekend of a parent's negative inluence. This is only one of the many complaints about negative role models at home, especially in terms of etiquette and failure to reinforce school rules. Again, however, the response to such a problem was "*meiyou banfa.*"

The role of the central government is to give special subsidies, exemptions, releases, and permissions to autonomous counties, without distinguishing among them or their resident nationalities. This purported the attempt that to establish a nationality-blind policy is understandable in light of the large number of ethnic groups (fifty-five) in China. However, Longsheng County officials also fail to distinguish among the various nationalities within its jurisdiction, even though one might expect them to have a more precise understanding of their constituents' needs. Achieving such an understanding seems to be a challenging task in an administrative unit with so many nationalities competing for attention. It appears that the achievements in the area of ethnicity that Longsheng leaders point to as signs of success are not about ethnicity at all; the only possible argument they could make to the contrary is that their achievements are "ethnic" because they take place in an ethnic area (yet one with no dominant ethnicity).

The special pamphlet, which the Longsheng government published for its fiftieth anniversary, contains language that attests to how irrelevant ethnicity can be to ethnic policy. Rough translations of the headings of different chapters include "Citizens' Economy Develops Continuously, Fast, and Healthily; Economic Structures Have Evidently Improved"; "Infrastructure Construction Appears to Have Speeded up, and the Economic Environment Has Witnessed Further Amelioration"; "The Third Sector, Headed by the Tourist Industry, Shows Strength"; "The Final, Hardest Stage of Helping-the-Poor Has Achieved Great Victory"; and "Various Social Projects Thrive in Bloom." In the entire pamphlet, only one sentence has anything to do with nationalities: ethnic athletic activities.[11]

Administratively, the definitions of nationality are exclusively focused on kinship or blood relations. From the central government's viewpoint, the only method of treating Longsheng as an ethnic region is to support the distribution of policy privileges to county residents. Yet, looking for ethnic meaning from a local perspective is equally frustrating because Longsheng officials are required to represent multi-ethnicity, with nothing to truly distinguish that designation from a non-autonomous, Han-dominated area. When ethnic officials are restrained from taking positions that represent a specific nationality, the concept of nationality is lost—and this might explain the lack of motivation among Longsheng cadres and officials to encourage or change their view of political participation.

Economics and education are the two sectors that both the central and local governments emphasize in their performance checks. Specifically, Longsheng officials file reports on how many kilometers of roads are built or maintained in one year, as well as other infrastructure projects. In terms of the economy, they stress their "Helping-the-Poor" efforts. All county bureaus have special "Helping-the-Poor" assignments. Ethnic policy of this kind is more of a reflection of national policy in an ethnic area than of regional policy with ethnic considerations. Longsheng officals at the Longsheng Commission on Ethnic Affairs are much more passive than their counterparts in other autonomous counties, who acknowledge their responsibility to promote, preserve, or develop ethnic culture.

Their passivity has led to the evolution of an education policy whose major concern is to acquire resources to remodel classrooms and support children from low-income families. In some cases, teachers and cadres are the primary donors, since they want to improve their performance evaluations even though they do not have the knowledge or connections to get outside help. This situation is less damaging in terms of overall educational goals than some other adaptation, for example, closing schools in remote mountain villages because those students' scores bring down the average for the entire district. Those few students who are motivated to continue their education are generally ill-prepared to pay extra for room and board. In some cases, teachers do not only accept the burden of providing for those students, but also serve as full-time surrogate parents.

While local education in Longsheng contains very little ethnic content, there is plenty of national ideological indoctrination. The focus of political education in county schools is the "Three Represent" theory; that is, the Communist Party represents a historical vanguard, means of advanced production, and the interests of the Chinese people. Most officials who have earned college degrees did so at schools that were especially created to teach Communist Party principles. One result is the widespread suspicion of religious practices among party cadres and officials. Daoist preachers who offer prayers at funerals in many ethnic areas are regularly described as representatives of feudal superstitions, and their activities are restricted to the houses of the deceased. No organized private Daoist studies are permitted. Similarly, Christians are allowed only to perform rituals and to express their religious beliefs within the walls of officially sanctioned churches, the closest of which is at least a two-hour bus ride away from Longsheng. Although the Longsheng Commissions on Ethnic and Religious Affairs are administratively one unit, connections between ethnic and religious affairs were never discussed in any of the interviews.

Multi-ethnicity as Policy Construction

According to the previous discussion, multi-ethnic autonomy differs considerably from single-ethnic autonomy. The former is similar to a Han administrative area in which certain officials have the specific responsibility of dealing with ethnic affairs among the multiple nationalities within their jurisdictions. In such cases, Han officials operate from an external position from which they distribute special policy privileges, but feel no obligation to promote either ethnic characteristics or any sense of crisis regarding the loss of cultural practices and values. In contrast, ethnic officials in autonomous regions are more conscious of their identities and cultural conventions, and more willing to participate in the coordinated efforts required to carry out central government policy in a manner that considers ethnic sensibilities. In other words, the orientation of Longsheng officials seems more akin to that of a Han administration than to that of a single-ethnicity autonomous region.

This is not to say that all ethnic officials in single-ethnicity autonomous areas are conscious of and active in promoting cultural conventions. For example, a significant number of ethnic officials work for their own self-interests, for instance, to receive promotions that might allow them to leave their underdeveloped hometowns. However, officials in other single-ethnicity regions can be very devoted to the welfare of their communities, the preservation of ethnic culture, and the creative use of ethnic policy to benefit local residents. Unfortunately, morale in Longsheng seems so low that the motivation to define local problems and to look for solutions is very difficult to generate.

In conclusion, the multi-ethnic identity of Longsheng undermines the formation of a strong bottom-up voice. Representation requires a unified voice, but the creation of such a voice in Longsheng is blocked by the number of nationalities involved. This is true regardless of expectations that individuals will act in the interest of a shared multi-ethnic nationality, which is perhaps best described as a "policy-constructed nationality." For reasons that go beyond the scope of this book, the human rights approach to ethnic autonomy, discussed in Chapter 1, is not applicable to China. One might accept the official position that national unity is the guiding principle of ethnic affairs in that country. By giving ethnic identities to different communities, the state ensures political loyalty over independent regional interests, which allows it to take a more relaxed position on interpretations of ethnicity at the local level. This should be acceptable to human rights proponents as long as ethnic identities provide some agency for local communities to identify, preserve, promote, and create economic, political, social, and religious opportunities. Only when ethnic identities meaningfully contribute to people's lives can the state expect the loyalty that is required for an operational state. Accordingly, the multi-ethnic character of Longsheng County is not beneficial for enhancing or maintaining that sense of loyalty.

CHAPTER 8

Lost Agency for Change: The Diasporic Identity in Yizhou's Shui Villages

Diasporic Identity

In his *Culture and Imperialism*, the late Edward Said argued for a method that allows an ethnic community to assert itself in a non-threatening way, so that the larger surrounding community could remain peaceful.[1] However, this is not an easy task, as the politics of diaspora has plagued world politics since the end of the Cold War. Ethnic violence, terrorism, and even war-scaled conflict all appear to be related to the politics of diaspora. To resolve the conflict around it is to deal with diasporic identities and the identities of the larger community at the same time. Said did not offer a definite solution, but he nonetheless pointed his readers in a direction. Specifically, Said was looking for a discourse that acknowledged those identities that originated from multiple sources. He believed that such identities always happen to be one of a kind by itself, a hybrid by nature. Said's position is not identical with multi-culturalism. The latter advocates a liberal solution and stresses that all cultures are equal. Yet, multi-culturalism assumes that everyone belongs to some known culture.[2] Said's "problematiqué" addresses the identity issue of those diasporic communities that run into problems with readily defined cultural categories. Said actually spoke from his peculiar position, being a Christian Palestinian living in the United States. Said believed every hybrid community was in itself a kind, and had no need to find expression from the vantage point of any known culture.[3] In fact, postcolonial writers, many of whom Said's writings inspire, tend to be skeptical of any claim to cultural purity.

Although diasporas often suffer from the inexpressible cultural conditions, Said's analysis suggests that the real world is running rampant with possibilities for diasporas to resolve their identification. In fact, many postcolonial writers painstakingly read agency into hybrid communities' ability to adapt to external pressure. While being critical of the treatment being received by diasporas residing within the larger community, postcolonial writers are generally optimistic about diasporas, resisting arbitrary construction of their identity by the larger community.[4] The ability to take advantage of cultural hybridity is of particular interest to postcolonial writers. The capacity of diasporas to strategically adapt to, and make the most of, each specific circumstance deconstructs the politics of identity that is taken for granted in the larger community.

Postmodern writings often stress the importance of agencies. Most writers praise agencies of subaltern origins for creating new possibilities under the pretentious control of the hegemonic cultural forces. The diasporas' agency to deconstruct cultural hegemony is one such important point of departure for many writers.[5] However, this optimism toward agency for deconstruction is questionable from the vantage point of the critical writers, especially for those who worry that stressing hybridity plays into the hands of the ruling class, which manipulates the atmosphere of liberation by incorporating hybridity into its political narrative. Consequently, the deconstruction becomes a part of the existing relations of production, as the will for revolution becomes significantly weakened.[6] Another serious pitfall is the fall of postcolonial resistance to violence. In brief, post colonialism might commit the same fallacy of believing in some fixed identity, granted that it is hybrid and less suppressive. Nevertheless, the concern for agency of the subaltern classes is common to all—postcolonial writers' belief in the subaltern classes to resist cultural hegemonies, critical Neo-Marxian writers' belief in the masses to overthrow the owners of the means of production, and postmodern writers' belief in the narrator's creativity to escape control.

The question addressed in this chapter approaches the issue from another direction. Instead of lauding the agency of the subaltern class, one might ask how the agency for change/resistance/escape might diminish to the extent that the ability to escape fixation, the motivation to assert difference, or the interest in revolution may be lost. In other words, among all the options that students of cultural studies can find, there is one that is missing. The missing choice is the claim that identity fails to generate agency for self-empowerment, but is detrimental to the ability to take advantage of coincidence or to adapt creatively to contingency. This is about the story of the Shui people living in the suburban countryside of Yizhou, which is under the jurisdiction of Guangxi Zhuang Autonomous Region.

The Shui Villages in Yizhou

The Shui people living in the city of Yizhou do not politically have an autonomous administration because the ethnic population is small in number and scattered throughout the area. This is not unlike ethnic diasporas in many other areas concerning their politics of representation. These locations include the Uygurs residents in Changde, Hunan; She villages in Lishui, Zhejiang; and Man villages in Beining, Liaoning.[7] In these places, one always experiences various ways of self-assertion, which more or less correspond with the official line of the central government, but are nonetheless embedded with certain claims of difference, straightforwardly as well as implicitly. These claims are creative. For example, an Uygur village party secretary sets apart the spheres of religion, custom, and ethnicity so that he/she could practice Islamic custom without violating atheism; a Man teacher resorts to the scene of Manchurian Palace Museum to express his patriotism toward the Chinese state; and a She senior citizen dresses school children in ethnic clothes to celebrate the return of Hong Kong to the motherland. In other words, autonomous administrative statute is not a necessary condition for a diasporic identity to generate agency for self-empowerment.

The purpose of going to Yizhou was to learn from the Shui people their creative strategies of self-empowerment; the result, instead, was to learn something entirely different. There are only a couple of villages that contain a sizable Shui population. Their economic conditions are backward, compared with the larger Han and Zhuang communities. There does not seem to be any mundane incentives left to encourage practicing the Shui identity in religious or cultural ways. Less than two thousand Shui villagers are scattered around sixteen different townships. These locations include Longtou and Beiya, where there was a relatively dense gathering of Shui villagers. Longtou has over nine hundred Shui villagers while Beiya has about two hundred. The local cadres arranged the visits to Longpan village, its primary school, Peng family's ancestor's place, and the township office in Longtou. The majority of the villagers in Longtou are Shui. Out of 200 students, 105 are Shui. In Beiya, the visits included Ermei village, its primary school, and its township office. In Ermei, there are eleven Shui families and ten Shui students. Few Shui students attend the junior high school and there is only one college student from the two villages.

Legend has it that the Shui people emigrated to Yizhou from Guangdong, which is east of Guangxi. These ancestors first moved to Guizhou, which is north of Guangdong and Guangxi before settling down in Guangxi. There is a Shui autonomous county in Guizhou, which once sent a delegation to Yizhou to investigate the conditions of the Shui people there. This is not unlike the Xinjiang Uygur autonomous areas, sending delegations to call on the sporadic Uygurs in Changde. However, the Shui people are small in number, compared with over eight thousand Uygurs in Changde. They are insignificant in light of the much larger surrounding communities. In the case of Shui, these are Han and Zhuang communities. To further complicate matters, the Zhuang people are highly acculturated to the mainstream Han culture. The accompanying officials could not even mention at least one Shui feature to their visitors throughout the trip. The interviewees themselves did not think there is anything about Shui in their beliefs, customs, or language that is extraordinary. The Shui in Yizhou seem to be no more than a forgotten name.

The Difference Portrayed in Self-narratives

Like all the other ethnic groups, ancestor worship and consciousness is fundamental to maintaining ethnic identity in Longpan. In fact, many of the customs and rituals are primarily serviceable to the imagination of common ancestry. The theory of common ancestry assumes the existence of an exclusive "blood origin" for each particular ethnic group. Beyond this string, one would belong to a different ethnic group. If no shared customs or rituals exist, the ethnic group in question cannot be identified. Consequently, the common ancestry would be unidentifiable. On the other hand, the increased acceptance of social customs would also increase the acceptance of a concept regarding a common ancestry. In this case, the group would be a much larger one. For example, a huge populace has accepted Confucianism. People subscribing to Confucianism believe that indeed, they share the common ancestry of Emperors Yan and Huang. Unfortunately, for the Shui people in Yizhou, the loss of Shui custom makes it increasingly more difficult to identify themselves as the Shui people. To be identified as Shui, one has to exclusively resort to ancestor worship.

The Shui people in Yizhou try to trace their common ancestry to a rather remote point in time. In the ancestors' place of the Peng family that lives in Longpan village, the calligraphy on the wall encourages the children of the Pengs to practice the gentleman's virtue of the Shang Dynasty (of 1000 BC), and to cherish the family fame recorded in the history of Song Dynasty (of 1000 AD). Senior villagers do not know why there should be mention of the two dynasties from the far ends of time. Their ancestors carried these words with them to Yizhou, so these words were already there during the Guangdong period. Another piece of calligraphy was the work of a son-in-law from a very long time ago. The said calligrapher passed the dynastic examination during the Qing Dynasty. His work was renovated in 1999 by the eighteenth generation of the Peng family. Another Peng from Ermei Village confirms that his family also has a long list of family names, currently kept by the ninety-year-old head of his family.

The Shui community celebrates most Han festivals. At least one of the Shui customs remains effective in Longpan—the celebration of the Duan Festival on lunar August 30. This is directly related to ancestor worship. On the day of the celebration, all villagers get together to worship their own ancestors. The ritual itself is not for the common ancestor of all Shui people, since there is no such knowledge of common ancestry. Nonetheless, the ritual of ancestral worship can still serve as a reminder of one's ethnic identity, as it is an exclusively Shui festival. Those married into Shui families are considered Shui, and so their children would be Shui, too. On the other hand, those married to Han or Zhuang families might retain their identity, so that their children would still have the option to be Shui. The only advantage of an ethnic Shui involves policy privilege in terms of either subsidy or exemption.

In Ermei village, when a relative passes away, the family conducts a religious ritual. Only a limited number of priests can recite certain biblical texts that are available today. One of the priests, whose formal job is to promote birth control, speaks of these rituals as he comments on birth control. He feels much at ease alternating between the concepts of death and birth during his sermons. His father used to be a priest. He says that no one really understands the biblical texts today and accuses priests' work as sheer superstition. According to his analysis, villagers worry that if they do not invite a priest to recite the biblical texts, the ancestors would not protect them. His involvement in a priest's work is ambivalent. He learned it from his father, and quit the practice later because he did not believe it. But recently, he chose to continue the practice because he could not manage with his meager salary of RMB90 monthly as a birth control worker. Before his return, he worked as a veterinary surgeon. One other reason that he is willing to be a priest is because his involvement with birth control makes him unpopular among villagers. He finds that villagers continue to practice some kind of misogyny by wanting to have a son. This makes his job difficult. On the other hand, serving as a priest wins him popularity. Indeed the priest's work is functional in the maintenance of ancestor worship. In fact, in both villages, five big Chinese characters—heaven, earth, emperor, parents, and teacher—are written on the wall in every household, facing the door. The priest comments that heaven means father and earth means mother, so parents are the most important figures in the world. It is natural that when parents pass away, the family members must call the priest to conduct the necessary rituals.

The tradition of priesthood is related to Daoism. The Shui priests do not study Daoist texts in order to learn their practice. They simply follow the tradition. Major contents involve choosing the right day for ritual and the right place for burial. The party secretary of Erya actually suggests only villagers of higher cultural levels would invite a priest to conduct a ritual. In his domain, he confirms that every family depends on the priest to pray over the dead and to comfort the family. He calls the priest "ghost priest" and sees the work as a market demand. This makes the Shui priest much more a priest than a Shui member. The priest serves all the people, not just Shui villagers. It is not the ritual that is about Shui. Rather, it is ancestor worship embedded in the ritual that recreates the Shui consciousness. According to the secretary, many priests are actually the head of a surname group. Their priest work and their social status complement each other.

Another minor custom in the Shui community is fish worship. During the lunar New Year (January 1), Shui villagers prepare vegetarian food. While most other Chinese communities would want to have many fish dishes because the words 'fish' and 'surplus' share the same pronunciation in Chinese, the Shui villagers in Longpan and Erya worship fish on the first and fifteenth of lunar January. One Shui villager jokes about this custom, saying that the custom might have something to do with the word Shui, which literally means water. However difficult it is to substantiate this joke, the joke nonetheless assumes authenticity of the Shui ethnicity, and is a way to confirm that Shui is a meaningful ethnic category. In addition, the distinct style of preparing New Year dishes is indicative of a difference, even though it is insignificant in comparison to many other signs of acculturation of the Shui community.

Many other ethnicities face similar difficulties in keeping their cultural traits, but as long as they receive autonomous administrative status, ethnic identities translate into policy privileges. The Shui community in Yizhou has yet to be qualified to receive autonomous status. The only privileges available include a permit allowing two children per household, and some extra points for students from the Shui villages who will take entrance examinations for high school. These privileges contribute to a minor increase in the Shui population in Yizhou. Basically, the increase in population comes from two sources—the newly born, and the families returning to Shui ethnicity for their children to take advantage of the examination points.

On the whole, there is not much left for the Shui community to claim an authentic difference as compared to the other ethnic groups. Even a common ancestor is not in the self-narratives. Consequently, the name of Shui increases in importance. When asked if it is possible that Shui and Han would eventually become one category, a senior villager responds that one cannot change ethnicity because one ultimately belongs to an ethnic group. This is not the same with losing the Shui language or culture. He mentions that the Shui community in Guizhou, which once called on Longpan, brought with them a few books on the history of the Shui people. Senior villagers in the site then began to discuss where these books went, and surely, no one knew where the books were kept. Similarly, in the Longpan school, teachers have never consulted these books or gathered legends from them for class discussion. Another senior villager explains this passive attitude toward the Shui identity. He believes that the larger environment has evolved and there is no way they can keep the Shui culture intact. The maximal attempt is to bear in mind one's Shui identity, as if it is one's name. After all, one needs no reason in keeping his or her name.

Negative Construction of the Shui Identity

In the eyes of government officials, the Shui community in Yizhou is completely acculturated; there is no need for policy privileges except for those applied to individuals. No research material on the Shui community is available in Yizhou's Bureau of Ethnic Affairs. Bureau officials have very little to say about the Shui people in their jurisdiction. They do know, though, that the Shui people share with the Han and the Zhuang neighbors similarities in their style of building construction, the way they make rice wine, or even the way they prepare their daily meals. The only research done on Shui people in Yizhou was by the Office of Taiwan Affairs, on how many Shui villagers joined the Kuomintang troops in Taiwan before 1949. What the Bureau officials care about most is the unity among the different ethnic groups. In this regard, the Shui community obviously poses no threat at all. At the township level, cadres likewise have little to say about the Shui villagers. The general impression is that their villages have good public security records. No differences in policy have been worth noting. There is no special treatment in government investments, nor are there any school texts prepared for the ethnic students.

The characteristic of education stressed by the central government allows each school much leeway in developing local characteristics. Accordingly, it means music and art techniques for the Erwen school and athletics and literature for Longpan. The local characteristic of education does not include the teaching of folk songs or mountain songs, which Yizhou is nationally famous for. Reconnection with the Shui community in Guizhou does not include any follow-up cultural activities. For the cadres, the policy priority is to recruit as many children into school as possible. Shui students reach an entrance rate of 100 percent at the primary level. The principal of Longpan School only has a simple wish—to have a basketball court. What the principal considers to be the biggest achievement would be a new class building. The problem facing the school, according to the teachers, is that the school can no longer charge parents fees for the services the school provides. The new nationwide policy is to enforce the so-called policy of one flat rate at the beginning of each academic semester. As a result, the school cannot afford any renovation of its teaching facilities. For the teachers, the ethnicity of their students means little, if anything.

Longpan School is officially an ethnic school and more than half of the students are Shui descendents. This status should receive special treatment and schoolteachers should be mindful of the ethnic status of the school. As an ethnic school, the teachers have extra channels to express their concerns, namely, the Office of United Front as well as the Bureau of Ethnic Affairs, in addition to the Bureau of Education. However, there is no such sensitivity—no effort to provide ethnic clothing for school children as many other ethnic schools have done. In addition, there are no attempts to teach mountain songs, nor signing agreements with a sister school in a richer area. Their first priority is to meet the national criteria set by the central and the Guangxi governments. One of the criteria is to make sure that all schoolteachers pass the Mandarin exam. In Guangxi, it is required that all teachers participate in the preparation for the test regardless of whether a teacher is already fluent in Mandarin. Each must pay a tuition of RMB180, excluding transportation. The monthly salary of a teacher ranges from RMB500 to RMB600. When asked why the teachers do not seek help through the Bureau of Ethnic Affairs to perhaps get a discount, the teachers replied that they did not even know where to find the Bureau. The same question was posed to the Bureau official while in Yizhou. One official acknowledged that the Shui community is not a priority because their number is insignificant and they have been acculturated.

In fact, the City Bureau of Ethnic Affairs has a number of limitations in executing ethnic policies. These limitations have to do with the passive attitude of superior officials at the regional level. The party secretary of the Bureau realistically tells of its difficulties:

> We face two constraints: when there is room to make policy, the region often fails to make the necessary legislation to enforce the policy. For example, there is the policy given by the central government that, in the autonomous region, the basic administrative level can keep a higher ratio of tax revenue. However, Regional People's Congress has not turned this policy into legislation, so we cannot allow the lower governments to keep more revenue. Secondly, Yizhou is not an autonomous administration like the neighboring Yao autonomous county. This means Yizhou must rely on the region to legislate for it.[8]

The reason that the Regional People's Congress gave up on this policy privilege for the basic government has to do with the low status of the Bureau of Ethnic Affairs compared with other profession bureaus. When the officials of ethnic affairs sent the draft of the legislation to other bureaus, the respective bureaus each had their own departmental concerns and crossed out those draft clauses that might run contrary to their interests. The few clauses left were too minor to make any difference. As a result, the legislation process ceased to continue. Another bureau official comments that Guangxi ethnic people are too mild to attract attention. He feels that the Tibetans and Xinjiang Uygurs are good examples of how to negotiate for policy concession by raising their voice. He traces the mild Guanxi style to the high level of acculturation; the comment is likewise applicable to the Shui community. Neither Zhuang nor Shui are used to approaching any issue from an ethnic point of view.

The mild attitude also contributes to the lax nature of top-down mobilization, as well as political indoctrination. The first person who came out to receive the visitor in the Longtou Township office was not a township official, a village cadre, nor a Helping-the-Poor team member, but a county official who was sent to the township to promote the Three Represents theory. He had been there for three months. All the campaign papers written by township cadres are posted on the room's wall. At the time of the visit, the campaign was being extended to the schoolteachers. In fact, the school principal reported that his meeting with officials and teachers from other areas was primarily about the theory of the Three Represents. In the future, this learning campaign would include all the villagers, he said. The same thing was true in the Erya Township office. A township cadre confessed to me that he did not really understand what he wrote. In Longpan village, the campaign was conducted through some kind of quiz competition. Since

Yizhou is well known for its long tradition of mountain songs, the campaign also takes the form of a mountain song contest. Longtou Township is creative enough to cash in on the campaign in the same way. According to the theory, the communist party represents the interests of the majority, thus the township party asks the villagers to raise their demands. The party then reports the demands to the superiors to get approval to use the campaign money to meet their demands. In fact, the paved road that leads the village to a township road was under construction when the visit to Longpan village took place. The cement was bought with the budget allocated for political campaign, in the name of fulfilling one of the Three Represents—the people's interest.

Chances for a Different Politics of Identity

For an immigrant community that has a smaller population, is economically backward, and politically unrecognized, acculturation is among the most likely developments. However, there are cases in which there is no such disadvantage in either number or level of development. Nonetheless, it succumbs to the pressure of acculturation. The Tujia people living in density in Western Hunan and the Zhuang people in Guangxi are two similar cases. One cannot deny that living in high population density areas composed of members of the same group provides a sense of belonging. This can serve as a social foundation for the revival of ethnic consciousness when other conditions for such a development are ripe. On the other hand, if immigrant communities are socially differentiated in the larger communities, the number is not always important. This is especially true, when the motherland is discursively available to support the diasporas in searching for a secured identity. For the Shui community in Yizhou, Guizhou's Shui people play such a role, but obviously this has not been a strong connection. As a result, there are no social or economic incentives for the Shui people in Yizhou to remain sensitive to their own ethnic identity, nor is there discrimination in the larger communities that reminds them of their specific ethnicity.

Other cases suggest that deliberate construction can be conducive to ethnic consciousness. The She people in Lishui, Zhejiang are an example, where a senior villager has pushed for ethnic education in the village school and has successfully turned the school into a base for a cultural renaissance. Another case is in the Uygur community in Changde, Hunan, where the villagers are different in appearance, religiously practice Islam, and administratively incorporate "Uygur" in the name of the township. In Yizhou, there is no such attempt except the establishment of an ethnic school. However, teachers are not ethnically sensitive, and the curriculum is far from being ethnically oriented. This is very different from the She case in Lshui. Another ethnic school was unsuccessful in characterizing the curriculum. But there was an effort to try anyhow. In this Miao ethnic school in Chengbu Autonomous County, Hunan teachers tried to introduce ethnic clothing. Likewise, in an ethnic Dong village in Chengbu's suburban mountain area, the village council members installed ethnic clothing for themselves as a self-reminder. Although these efforts may be no more than psychological compensation for the loss of ethnic traits in the long haul of history, the attempt nonetheless signals a kind of reorientation for some sort of revival. In Yizhou, no such thinking is registered.

This brings up another possibility. It is a matter of choice concerning whether or not the ancestors of today's diasporas had wanted to be mindful of their being different from the larger society. Another case features the Yao community in Nandan Autonomous County, also in Guangxi. In Nandan, the community, which often falls victim to natural disaster, refused donations of clothing from the outside world, lest these clothes eventually replaced the traditional dressing style. Currently, they are known as White-Pants Yao, for all men wear white pants. While clothing has become a political issue in many places, so has been the language. In Erchahe village, which is an ethnic Qiang community belonging to Wadi Township of Ahba Tibetan Autonomous County in Sichuan, villagers returning from the city are obliged to speak Qiang to avoid the criticism of being disrespectful toward the community.[9] In contrast, the spoken Shui is no longer available in both townships in question. However, the villagers report that in the Desheng township of Yizhou, the Magai tone of the Shui people is still spoken.

A quick glance at these cases suggests that acculturation involves decisions, whether deliberate or by chance. The central officials of ethnic affairs are sensitive toward the issue of acculturation, because many ethnic communities are against it. This rising ethnic consciousness warns the officials to refrain from employing the once praised notion of acculturation. When used in rhetoric, they say "natural" acculturation. A more appropriate substitute is perhaps "willing" acculturation, as opposed to the "unwilling" version. The Erya secretary uses "natural" to describe the Shui community's acculturation. However, to be unable to use the Magai tone or to give up cultural customs involved decisions, and no matter how insignificant they might appear to be at the time of the decisions, these decisions transform how a diasporic community looks. These were strategic decisions concerning how the Shui ancestors wanted to be seen by the larger communities. In the same vein, if diasporas of a few generations later become sensitive to the politics of identity, there will be strategic decisions to use whatever historical memory is functional for the reconstruction of difference. One Ermei teacher literally comments that "the cause of acculturation" of the Shui community is that the Shui "ancestors failed to insist practicing cultural customs."

There is always the possibility of revival, as long as diasporas still carry official ethnic status. Legends could be invented and customs could be reconstructed. In the ancestors' place of the Pengs, visitors sees two huge trunks of wood lying diagonally across the room, extending from the top of the door to the floor in the middle of the room. Villagers say the pieces are used for carrying coffins. When carrying a coffin, they need two long pieces of wood and four short ones. The family members will fetch the short ones from anywhere in the mountain, but the two big trunks already have been used for over one hundred years. The inquiry has been the subject of interesting conversation. One senior villager explained that the use of old trunks was to show respect for the dead old man. Another senior villager added that when a middle-aged person passes away, the same two trunks were used, so the respect was for every dead person, not just the older ones. Another senior villager tried to clarify by saying that it was not easy to find such huge trunks and this was the only reason they were still being used after so many years.

The meaning of keeping these two trunks in Peng's ancestors' place varies depending on the time and situation. The old trunks have meant different things to different senior villagers. A historical practice begins to acquire meaning due to the unexpected intrusion of curious outsiders. It is not unlikely that the two old trunks would eventually become the basis of some kind of legend when the time is ripe for the revival of ethnic consciousness in the future. However, if there is no such need to join the politics of identity, they will have to be left lying there until they rot.

Another example also suggests how easily cultural customs can be reconstructed; this happened at Ermei. The Ermei village won an athletic contest in the Ethnic Games in 1996 with a program called "Grabbing the Flower Lamp." In the following year, the team was invited to perform in Hong Kong to celebrate its return to the motherland. The program is now called "The Shui People Grabbing the Flower Lamp," because the designer and the leading performer is ethnically Shui. The program was developed from the popular program called "Up on the Knife Mountain and Down to the Fire Sea." In Chapter 2, the same program is shown in the Guilin Municipal

Museum of Folk Ethnicities as an ethnic Yao traditional program, and in suburban Guiyang as an ethnic Miao traditional program. The program itself is actually a stereotyped ethnic program, and Han tourists care very little about which group it actually belongs to. However, the program is used in Yizhou to highlight the Shui ethnicity. In fact, when the township cadre introduced the program to the visitor, he said this was "an award-winning activity for the Shui people."

The Shui designer confirms that he thought that his son should learn to perform in the program. His son eventually did so. The Yizhou Art Team offered him RMB300 a month to join the team, but his son turned down the offer. He moved to a different city for good, temporarily leaving his son and daughter to be brought up by the grandfather. The degree of Shui ethnicity of this program is not felt at the current time. The possibility cannot be ruled out, however, that if the program can profit in the market some day, it could become a carrier of Shui ethnicity into the future.

Whether or not cultural customs can be invented or reconstructed depends on the micro-decision made by everyone, whether they are in the community or outside of it. Every move to keep, claim, or replace a cultural custom involves a decision, which is at the same time a political statement of one's identity. How strong the need of a particular diasporic community is to distinguish itself from the larger community is both a psychological and mundane calculation. In this sense, the cause of acculturation is not that the ancestors fail to practice their customs. The loss of custom or the language is the behavioral product of the declining need for feeling different from the larger communities. With such a need, one would expect the school teachers would easily think of the officials of a united front or ethnic affairs in order to lobby for exemption or discount for their Mandarin class. Whether or not one needs to feel different is not something social scientists can definitely determine.

Non-ethnic Agency for Change in the Shui Community

What is left in the Shui identity in Longpan and Ermei is no more than the privilege of having two children and getting extra credits in examinations. This is hardly the kind of thing that generates the sense of self-respect or confidence. If ethnicity is represented exclusively by policy privilege, ethnicity indicates the protection of the weak, and implies backwardness. Under this assumption, ethnic identity does not motivate people to look for signs of their being different. On the contrary, people might want to hide it. As a result, the Shui people lose the ethnic perspective that allows them to judge things outside of the role granted to them by the state. As a result, their responses to the state's top-down mobilization, in terms of education curriculum, political indoctrination, as well as anti-poverty campaigns, generally lack innovation and are often filled with passivity. On the matter that they are entitled to articulating opinion, namely the ethnic-related affairs, they remain quiet. The Shui experience makes the postcolonial and postmodern celebration of a diasporic avenue for change obsolete.

The loss of agency for change and willing acculturation does not necessarily confirm the modernization theory's linear historiography. What the Shui example confirms is that the agency for change cannot be taken for granted. Although the hybrid component in the Shui ethnicity is not felt today, the chances that some revived ethnic consciousness can reinvent cultural customs should not be ruled out, as long as the Shui community continues to carry the name of Shui. The invention of "The Shui People Grabbing the Flower Lamp" and the interpretation of keeping the old trunks in the ancestors' place are two such possible sources for a reawakened consciousness. However, hybridity of this sort is reinvented from, and not embedded in, their identity. Nevertheless, the quest for being different from the larger community is both a matter of internal need and an external construction. This is why the simple name of Shui cannot guarantee itself as a basis for revival. The problem with postcolonialism and postmodernism is that these writers too readily read resistance or subversion into the hybrid identity.

The key to the ethnic revival lies in the inherent need to be different. This has to be a decision made by the Shui community—just as the loss of agency for change and the acculturation have also been results of earlier decisions. In addition, the lost agency for change in the Shui identity does not preclude the survival of avenues for change in other identities. To use the "Three Represents" for the sake of paving a village road illustrates this possibility, except that this hidden agency in good citizenship has little to do with Shui ethnicity.

CHAPTER 9

Feeling Poverty: On the Same Side of the Poor in Baise's Zhuang Villages

Between the State and the Poor

"Helping the poor" has been a long-term policy concern in China. In the twenty-first century, the government has created a new slogan stating that China will enter the stage in which all households will live in sufficiency. Amidst the triumphant atmosphere of overcoming poverty, there are still problems that the government has left unresolved, as noted in Chapter 3. First, there is a portion of the population that fails to respond to the call of helping the poor. Second, a significant portion of those who seem to have overcome poverty in the recent past has fallen back to a subsistence economy. Third, another portion of those nascent sufficient communities has developed strong and continuous dependency on the aids provided by the decade-long Helping-the-Poor campaign.

The central government's knowledge on poverty comes from statistics, which is based primarily on per capita income. Therefore, its Helping-the-Poor programs center on the management of statistics to target primarily the ability of the poor to achieve economic growth. This preoccupation with growth statistics misses other aspects of poverty.

In fact, as reported in Chapter 3, a number of mid-level officials responsible for Helping-the-Poor campaigns have made the observation that many non-economic factors have shaped Helping-the-Poor campaigns in several communities differently—how close the poor villages are geographically to the paved road, socially to the county leadership, and electronically to the mass media. If the poor villages can narrow the geographical, social, and electronic distance to the affluent world, they believe, their chances of upgrading their status would be better. Furthermore, if one includes the perspective of those living in the poor villages, the levels of understanding of poverty can be much more diverse. These levels of understanding are not expressible because once they face the issue of poverty, poor villages have no proper language to use so as not to expose their stupidity and ignorance. Trapped in the campaign against poverty, other needs and various different feelings generated during the campaign fail to become legitimate topics. Perhaps only local cadres working in villages or townships can empathize with the poor villagers.

Continuing the discussion of poverty with the provincial officials in Chapter 3, this chapter goes to the street level to meet with the county and township cadres and shows that, between the central government dedicated to raising per capita income in poor areas and the poor villagers trying to enhance their income, the local cadres are the points of compromise.[1] Indeed, many county officials have decided that the focus of the Helping-the-Poor campaign should concentrate on ameliorating poor living conditions such by supplying running water, electricity, and paved roads. One cannot expect that running water will bring in investments. However, many Helping-the-Poor campaigners find the supply of running water as the most direct and useful way to help the villagers. Though changes in the living conditions do not respond to the central government's concern over statistics directly, it does not alter the importance of statistics, either. Nonetheless, local adjustment should imply a kind of subjectivity that is outside the central government. Ethnicity might play a role. Accordingly, under what circumstances a local cadre would feel confident to make such adjustment toward living conditions, away from profiting capacity, is worth discussing. Note that their subjectivity incorporates the inexpressible feelings of the poor. One Helping-the-Poor campaigner reflects upon his own changes: "While we were studying at the agricultural school, our teacher had told us that, when we arrived at a village, we should not only introduce the new science and technology, but more importantly, we had to reform the thought of the peasants. However, once we arrived at a village, sometimes we found that we could not change the way peasants thought. Furthermore, under their influence, our way of thinking adapted to theirs."[2]

This chapter reports the thoughts of selected local Helping-the-Poor cadres as if they could talk about poverty from a different perspective. Usually, the central government dominates the formulation of the discourse on poverty and the subsequent resource allocation in accordance with its definition of the problem. This chapter will examine the likelihood that those who carry out Helping-the-Poor policies can learn from the inexpressible needs and feelings of poor villagers and develop different concepts of poverty. If local cadres can develop their own perspective on poverty through their interaction with villagers, they can feel comfortable in forming opinions about the central government's stand on poverty. This means that villagers indirectly affect the knowledge of the central government, which is initially the exclusive source of knowledge on poverty and is now reduced to just one source among many—although it is still the most powerful source. Nonetheless, once affected by villagers, the top-down discourse on poverty, to which Helping-the-Poor campaigners refer, turns into the bottom-up feelings of dependency and impotence.

Background of the Research Site

The research plan presented in this chapter is to see how cadres might differ in their approach to poverty so that together they compose a potential field of reflections, allowing different perspectives on poverty to emerge. For the study of local perspectives on poverty, those visited include poor villagers, township and county cadres, and prefecture and provincial officials in ethnic Tujia and Miao Western Hunan. The city of Baise in the ethnic Zhuang Autonomous Guangxi was selected to study the local cadres' approach to the divergence of the villagers and the central government. The research site was not selected for any theoretical reason because there should be no theoretical underpinnings guiding one in what to look for. Notice that the basic assumption here is that the local cadres are the "knowers." There should be no universal framework to determine what general tendencies exist among cadres of different places. It is therefore only proper to learn what any of them have to say about poverty.

The research sites included the following administrative places. One is Pingban Village of the Banshui Township, under the administration of the Youjiang region. (Youjiang is a specially designated administrative unit between agricultural township and urban city.) Others include Yian Village and Yongchang Village of the Nabo Township in Tianyang County, and Liulian Village of Bayu Township, also located in Tianyang. In the last village, there is the sacred mountain of the ethnic Zhuang people, which has become, through tourism, an important point in helping the poor. Baise is located near the west of Guangxi within the vicinity of the nationally designated poor province of Guizhou to its north, Yunnan to its west, Vietnam to the south, and the capital city of Guangxi, Nanning to the east. The total territory covered is about 36,000 square kilometers. The city has twelve counties with 90 percent of its population (or 3,300,000 residents) in the agricultural villages. The city comprises seven different ethnic groups.

Mountain ranges account for 95 percent of its territory, of which 33 percent is limestone mountains. Baise, both socially and economically disadvantaged, owns all five characteristics that warrant some special treatment by the central government—old revolutionary areas, ethnic areas, border areas, mountain areas, and poor areas. Baise is one of eighteen nationally designated poor areas, and ten of its counties are designated as poor counties by the central government. As of the summer of 2004, there were 1,015 subsistent villages with a total population of 900,000.

Youjiang, whose territory includes the capital of Baise, is at the west end of Baise on the borders of Yunnan, Guizhou, and Guangxi. There are twelve counties in Youjiang, covering 3,700 square kilometers. Eight of them are agricultural, with 116 villages and 900,000 residents. There are paved roads leading to each village center. However, in Banshui Township, the road maintenance has been problematic, preventing the export of fruits. Pingban Village lacks intra-village roads. The 331 households with 1,500 villagers depend on anise as the major source of income, which also suffers from fluctuating market prices. As a result, the per capita income stays at around US$130. Of about one hundred schoolchildren, twenty-two will not be able to afford tuition in the near future.

Tianyang is located toward the east of Youjiang in Ganzhuang Mountain and is under the jurisdiction of Liulian Village. This is the sacred mountain of the Zhuang people. Ganzhuang Mountain is the location of the legendary Nurser Stone, where Buluotuo, the legendary primogenitor of Zhuang, and the legendary figure Muliujia, who nursed and bred Buluotuo, presumably lived.

Recently, archaeologists discovered frog-shaped drawings on the bottom of a few stone plates, a style widely held as the totem of Zhuang over four thousand years ago. They also found eight remnants, all within fifteen kilometers of Nurser Stone, dating back to as early as 803,000 years. Since Buluotuo worship exists in domestic Guangdong and overseas Thailand, Vietnam, and Myanmar, the location has become a site of interest appointed by the Tianyang Bureau of Tourism.[3]

There is a festival here every March 7 of the lunar year. The Zhuang people gather to sing. This custom allegedly began in the Sui Dynasty (roughly 600 BCE). The festival continues for three days. The festival was once terminated during the Cultural Revolution, but resumed during the early 1980s. At the festival, the Zhuang people sing praise in honor of the birth of their common ancestor.

Yongchang Village became a model of helping the poor in Tianyang in recent years. Both Jiang Zemin and Hu Jintao visited the village several times. Many Helping-the-Poor benefactors provided substantial help. During the early 1990s, the place experienced shortage of water, electricity, and paved roads, and it recorded a per capita income of US$27. In 2004, the per capita income was US$160. In addition, 40 percent of the graduates from middle school went on to enter high school. A few miles up from Yongchang, Yian is located in the stone mountain. The only crops left in the village were corn, bamboo, and sugarcane. Little improvement was made in the past decade.

Yian once received Hu Jintao but the Helping-the-Poor program only began in 2003. No collective investment by the village council was ever attempted. The per capita income is currently US$75. Three of its natural villages lack water or electricity. Yian Villagers depended on the stone pit for income. When the government imposed a levy on the license two years ago, the stone pit was no longer active.

The Helping-the-Poor campaign in Baise invariably begins with water supply and road paving. Hopefully this will link the stone mountain residents with the world outside. Another effort is to install electricity so that villagers can watch television. In the twenty-first century, the campaign has focused on installing household biogas supply. However, since the plan requires each household to come up with a relative fund and to own two pigs or cows, its recipients are limited. The villagers prefer another program that "refunds" the cost of each tree planted in the mountain. However, the policy is advantageous only to those residing along the provincial highway because the county government is more interested in making the results visible to the public.[4]

Whether or not a poor community is able to sustain its growth is contingent on various factors, including some Helping-the-Poor campaigners cannot control. The hardest part of the Helping-the-Poor campaign is to identify an investment that can move and keep the villagers above subsistence levels. Both Youjiang and Tianyang encourage growing vegetables, for example. The Regional Office of United Front and its Office of Taiwan Affairs use their connections in Hong Kong and Taiwan to get grade-A seeds.[5] Supported by the local People's Liberation Army, Yongchang receives preferential treatment due to its media exposure. Pingban is not so privileged since the helpers are three Taiwan Affairs officials. Compared with the neighboring county of Pingguo, a nationally designated poor county, Tianyang receives much less support. Tianyang officials have complained that Pingguo had in reality achieved the goal of the campaign.[6] Significantly, the resource Pingguo received cut into Tianyang's share.

Perspectives of the Local Cadres

Local cadres sit between the central government and the villagers.[7] Their Helping-the-Poor mission should be simple and clear, namely, to increase the per capita income through all possible means. Perhaps the first goal includes ameliorating the living conditions and the infrastructure. However, each village has its unique cultural and natural ecology. Any Helping-the-Poor campaigner needs to understand the basic situation upon entering the village, as the situation is often different from what is expected.

The villagers also want to learn what they can expect from the campaign team. Gradually, through extensive consultation and engagement, it is clear to any serious campaigner that the mission cannot be limited to executing certain Helping-the-Poor programs. Enormous social interactions thus ensue, involving the villagers and the campaign cadres in a kind of mutually constituted experience, so that the cadres begin to adjust their perspectives on poverty.

The cadres would first like to know how the villagers see the world in order to change them. This exercise brings the cadres into the inner world of the village and the villagers. Their superior institutional position, which enables them to take an intensive approach, is no longer enough. When the cadres introduce the standard of sufficiency, the villagers can only negotiate a destiny they know little about. Their inability for creative participation puts the villagers in a passive and dependent position. This wins them only an image of cultural backwardness. Only by living in the village for a prolonged period could the cadres begin to understand. If the campaign team is sent by a big bureaucracy such as the People's Liberation Army, individual cadres living in the village have very little room in which to adapt. They do not need to do so, since the big bureaucracy is too resourceful to be interested in the senselessness of local sentiments. They send in resources and change the outlook of the village in a few months. However, small teams and individual campaigners lack full support from their home institution. Their frustration over their inability to make changes effectively forces them to take up the villagers' perspective. Unlike villagers who have little education, the cadres can enlist rhetoric to reflect the villagers' feelings once they allow these feelings to sink in.

The first change is often emotional in nature. The villagers feel unsatisfied with many things, but they do not know how to formulate intelligent opinions. After a few evenings of drinking together, their frustration could reach the campaigners. It does not take too long for the campaigners to realize that it is indeed difficult to generate any sustainable growth. Although the government might have all sorts of reasons why things do not go the way the villagers like it, or blame the villagers for being ignorant of the bigger picture, the campaign cadres in the village become more sympathetic to the villagers' frustration or inaction.

The watershed of the change in mood is when the cadres begin to feel that villagers should not be held responsible for their own poverty, and place the responsibility on the living environment as well as the higher government's policy failures. After all, if villagers were stupid, the campaigners who fail would be, too. The reversal of sentiment toward the once assumed stupidity of the villagers makes them more accessible to the inner world of the village. Consciously or not, some of the cadres become the spokespersons for local interest. They become critical of those phenomena that the villagers dislike. Some of them would even argue against the stereotyping of the poor villagers being culturally backward, lazy, or stupid.

Officials responsible for helping the poor at different levels might face their work with different attitudes. Street-level campaigners who experience increasing empathy toward the local villagers might at the same time experience a role conflict. When discussing work with the home institution or the county officials, they take into consideration the policy language that seeks to drive the villagers toward higher income. However, once back in the village, their feelings are again with the villagers who hold a suspicious attitude toward the Helping-the-Poor rhetoric.

Unlike the township cadres who grow up with the villagers, the campaign cadres who will eventually return to their home institution at the end of the term must face the superior who demands results. This role conflict is not easy to understand from the home institution's or the higher government's perspectives. Township officials have been passive all along, since they would not be the ones to be blamed when there is a persistently poor village in their jurisdiction. They are supposedly the ones to be helped. That is why there is a theory that to eliminate poverty, the local leadership must go through some reshuffling.

In comparison, higher government officials at the prefecture or the county level have the support from the central government. Therefore, it is almost certain that some achievement will show somewhere in their jurisdiction. This is especially true in ethnic autonomous areas where achievement in helping the poor revises the pride of being an ethnic minority.

Between Two Emotions

There can be four different types of responses when caught between the central government and the villagers. First, campaign cadres could brag about the Helping-the-Poor policy on one hand, while complaining about the policy failure on the other. One of these cadres sent to Nabo Township by the Tianyang County government, Mr. NH, demonstrated this kind of ambivalence. He was very critical of the village culture for being lethargic. He defended an obviously failed investment by the government, citing it as a way to establish a scale of economy that could attract private investment. He was referring to the investment in certain crops that failed. The failure, according to his analysis, had made possible subsequent investment in growing a different crop by an outside investor. He argued that it was necessary that the government force the village cadres to try out the new crop so that there could be a model of success that might win the confidence of the villagers in the following year. He believed that the intensive mobilization style of work was what brought the villagers into the market:

> Now, the strategy is to use market forces to change their habits that are given to lethargy, and to change their customs. In the past, the villagers did nothing except drink and chat. A bunch of people gather in one place to drink and then go home to sleep drunk. I tried to persuade them to work, but they said the prices were too cheap to make any money. Even if one had worked, one would not make money. How about today? See, they are all busy carrying tomatoes. If I called on them to drink together, they would all deny me the invitation. They are now busy counting their money. Thought reform is not going to make them move. Giving them real benefit through the market is what has changed them.[8]

He quickly adjusted his position when discussing the investment in a stone pit in Yian Village. He analyzed the problem Yian had faced. The problem was that the government would not issue them a license. Without the license, there could be no bank investment. He said, "Our only hope left was to wait for some big company to notice us." Without trying, he rejected the suggestion made by the visitor that the Bureau of Ethnic Affairs might assume some responsibility to ask the Bureau of Finance to mediate with a local bank on behalf of the villagers. The same strategy worked elsewhere.

At Yian Village, after explaining the government's levy on the license for the stone pit, which virtually terminated the business, he became so frustrated that he accused the government of not caring about people's lives. What he did not explain was the overall policy to stop the stone pit for both environmental and public security reasons. His attitude turned surprisingly passive, in comparison with his attitude toward introducing new crops. He concluded, "Since there was no big company interested in us, we could not receive advanced technology."

Mr. TH, an official from the Office of Helping-the-Poor of Tianyang County, was on the spot. He immediately reported a government loan of as high as RMB500,000 for any good investment project. However, it is the potential applicant's responsibility to submit a good proposal. The money has been there for almost a year but no application has been submitted. He then observed that Helping-the-Poor programs usually lacked substantial accomplishment. For example, the local government is ready to introduce new agricultural technology. However, no agricultural companies respond to the initiative, despite the fact that officials are more than ready to make all kinds of concessions.

Another example involved the terrain of stone mountains, which is only good for bamboo cultivation; however, there is no communal cooperative to protect the sale price, so the peasants are not serious about the bamboo. Biogas technology is another example. The have-not households cannot afford the relative fund or the pig breeding, so they gave up the government subsidy. Finally, even though the government is ready to fund relocation, they find that no land is available. Mr. TH recognized the government's input in terms of providing the seeds or paving the road, if individual peasants could find opportunities for relocation and serve as tenants in the plains area. However, he criticized the rigidity in the official designation of poverty status. He believed that the sufficiency status of Tianyang had distracted the central government's attention from the extreme poverty in its villages.

On the other hand, Mr. TH did not say anything negative about the peasants throughout his interview. He was very sympathetic, but his sympathy came from an outsider's perspective. For example, his sympathy went to the old lady who walked barefoot on snow; the forty male villagers who were too poor to marry and raise families; and the highland peasants who cannot find a place where they can relocate. All this was outsider's sympathy because the sympathy did not come from practicing the local way of life, but from the comparison with his own experiences.

The solution in his mind to transfer more resources to these villagers was not possible. Gradually, he adopted the local custom of exchanging drinking glasses to show goodwill, instead of persuading the peasants to stop drinking, as he initially wanted, for reasons that involved personal hygiene. His frustration comes from a Helping-the-Poor policy that borders on helplessness: "After working for such a long time, I now feel that I cannot help. The only thing that I can do now is to donate some winter clothes. I once saw an old woman selling vegetables in the market; I decided to buy a huge bunch, believing that I could help a little bit. When I went home, my wife thought

I was going to have a big party. How much can I really help? I want to do more, but I cannot."[9]

A campaign team member sent to Pingban Township by the Youjiang regional government, Mr. PY, also had reservations about the effect of the Helping-the-Poor policy. He believed that the cultural quality of the peasants should not have been the real issue. The issue was the poor environment for investment that could not attract big investors. The key was the need for paved roads that could transport the fruits to the outside market. The reason that paved roads had been ignored, according to Mr. PY, was social in nature. The problem is that there were no leaders in the Youjiang region that originally came from Pingban.

There is also the possibility that a cadre is able to see through the eyes of the peasant yet acknowledge the limitation of the Helping-the-Poor policy at the same time. Mr. BC, party secretary assigned to Banshui village to deal specifically with resolving poverty problem, pointed out one root of the problem being the overly high agricultural tax, to the extent that Banshui had only slightly over RMB100,000 a year. He criticized the tuition policy that the school could only charge one flat fee at the beginning of the school year. This policy left the school with only enough revenue to cover expenses for chalk.

He further criticized the electricity policy, which used the village land to build two power plants without any feedback, and still charged each household for fees. In this last incident, he arranged for a settlement in which the plants agreed to offer a monetary return of RMB5,000 to the Pingban Township government. Helping-the-Poor programs could ameliorate the living conditions, but they do not resolve the problem of the poverty, according to him. The village he is responsible for had a standing loan of RMB40,000, which he used to maintain the school building and the village office. The village business he established yielded no profit, so the bank filed a lawsuit against the village for payment overdue. However, the most urgent task for him was not to repay the loan but to find another loan to maintain the school's earth closet. He was frustrated about the tree-planting subsidy that was given to those villages along the road. This came as a sacrifice for extremely poor villages in the mountains, such as Banshui.

Mr. BC was particularly sensitive with the school enrollment problem. Twenty-two students depended on the teacher's donation to be able to attend school. Teachers also paid for the travel expenses of a student team that participated in contests elsewhere. The problem is that the parents would not pay. Mr. BC understood well that these schoolchildren could not escape poverty even after finishing school. If they would remain in perpetual poverty, why would anyone invest in education (other than teachers), in which the chances of being plucked out of the rut were slim due to the low enrollment at a higher level?

He defied the impression that peasants are by nature against education. Instead, they are simply rational beings. Moreover, he found that the one-child policy cut the size of the student body to the extent that it was financially impossible for townships to maintain remote teaching sites (i.e., a partial school) to educate youngsters. Without teaching sites (where one teacher teaches a few children of lower grades in combination) for the nine-year-old or younger, an older child would not be ready for schooling in the village school.

This is not about passivity and inaction. Mr. BC actually praised the Banshui villagers for being very active and supportive. Whenever there was a policy promulgation session, the villagers attended it. While the central government issued specific orders that the government at all levels was not to impose compulsory work on the peasants, the Banshui peasants always voluntarily provided manual work for the government. Embedded deeply in plain and modest Confucianism, they are anything but backward, lazy, or stupid, Mr. BC insisted.

However, there were cadres who embraced government rhetoric, to the point that they always reiterated government perspectives, and lacked sensitivity toward the peasants' feelings. In Tianyang, a campaign team member, Mr. TZ, blamed the peasants for always being satisfied with the status quo. In addition, these were ethnic minorities whom Mr. TZ felt were too conservative. In this situation, the government policy was the critical factor to facilitate changes. He praised the government for paving certain roads. However, local villagers did not maintain the roads well, so these fell apart after only a few years. He said that even if government introduced good crops or projects, the villagers would simply eat the seeds given to them. Another team member, Mr. UX, agreed with Mr. TZ and believed that the problem was that peasants did not know what was going on outside the mountains. Their only strategy was to "wait, depend, and beg."

Table I summarizes the four types of cadres that have come out of these interviews, depending on whether or not their view incorporates the villagers' feelings toward poverty and the Helping-the-Poor policy, and whether or not their views espouse the central government's Helping-the-Poor discourse: Mr. NH used the government's perspective even as he sometimes sympathized with the villagers' feelings; Mr. TH and Mr. PY criticized the Helping-the-Poor policy without taking the peasants' perspective; Mr. BC was able to empathize with the villagers' attitude, yet at the same time remain reserved about the Helping-the-Poor policy; and finally, Mr. TZ and Mr. UX took the government's Helping-the-Poor discourse and supported its policy.

The Subjectivity up from Poverty

The first thing one usually does after arriving in Tianyang is not to do business (for example, seeing a Helping-the-Poor program in the village) but to see the sacred Ganzhuang Mountain, which had become the focus of the Helping-the-Poor campaign due to its potential to increasingly attract tourists. For a long time, the dominant impression has been that the highly assimilated Zhuang people have a weak ethnic identity. Therefore, they would not actively seek policy resources in the name of ethnicity. Those with previous research experiences in Guangxi rarely came across discussion on Zhuang ethnicity.[10]

However, the county officials seemed to have developed some kind of ethnic consciousness from the Helping-the-Poor program of Ganzhuang Mountain. In order to develop tourism in Ganzhuang, a discourse on genealogy is made present in all sorts of Buluotuo narratives. Some, in the form of the mountain song contests, appear to attract tourists' attention. The county and township officials also spoke of a contrasting period during the Cultural Revolution when ancient plates in the Ganzhuang Mountain were either destroyed for being feudalistic or sunk to the bottom of the water to make a dam. It was not until 2002 that the government decided Ganzhuang Mountain was going to be part of the Helping-the-Poor campaign.[11]

The development of Ganzhuang led to the revival of the local ethnic consciousness. Implicitly in the Bureau of Tourism's brief was a sense of achievement in relation to ethnic consciousness. The brief introduces the process of applying for status of cultural reserve, the design of the route, the singing of mountain songs, the collection of copies of the Bible, and the decision to promote the Zhuang people as the indigenous people of the Zhujiang Delta plain, a land widely considered as the hinterland of Guangzhou (Canton).

Table I. Four Approaches Relating to Poverty

		Bottom-up	
		Empathize with the villagers	
Top-down		*Yes*	*No*
Support the Helping-	*Yes*	NH	TH and PY
the-Poor policy	*No*	BC	TZ and UX

The researchers discovered a total of eighteen old mountain songs that presumably portrayed a scene close to that of Ganzhuang.[12] The researchers also suggested that the Zhuang language overlapped with many ethnic languages in Southeast Asia. Bangkok, for example, means "my home country" in the Zhuang language. This discovery prompts the claim that the Zhuang people are an open-minded lot. Furthermore, this open-mindedness had allegedly prepared the success of Deng Xiaoping's revolutionary strike in Baise in 1929. This strike is well known as "Baise Uprising."[13]

One associate county director explained how to combine the development of Ganzhuang Mountain with the Helping-the-Poor program as if he were promoting the Buluotuo spirit:

> From the economic tourism point of view, this is a point of significance. From the humanity point of view, there is the Old Stone Age culture of 800,000 years old. The smokeless industry of room and board will lead the growth of the local service sector. In addition, this area is the nationally designated site of agricultural demonstration. All these point to tourism. The first mission is to encourage the academic work on the Buluotuo culture. The second mission is to identify the Zhuang people with the Buluotuo culture, which includes Na culture. This is the most venerable and established base of humanism. It involves worship of the human culture, celestial culture, and rice culture, especially wild rice. This further leads to the worship for wild birds, which eat wild rice and due to widespread digestion problems produce excrement processed as fertilizer. The additional Paleolithic culture can be used to apply for status of the first grade reserve and the Neolithic culture can. . . . In modern times, there are other customs to show, to arrange, and to categorize. We did too little in the past because the Zhuang people are very unpretentious.[14]

Moreover, an ethnic interpretation emerges in the gender discourse. Explaining that the Zhuang people always value gender equality, the chief of the Bureau of Tourism talked about a female governor who led the Zhuang troops to fight the Japanese during the Ming Dynasty. Legend has it that the governor was Cenwa, originally from Jingxi (which belongs to Baise). Allegedly, this was the source of the legends of Hua Mulan. She emphasized that Cenwa was regarded as the Secondary Madame of the Dynasty. Unexpectedly, this remark encountered serious opposition from an associate county director. The director believed that there were too many women to be recognized as Secondary Madame, which was not a status the Zhuang people should feel proud about. He contended that this was a tactic used by the Han court to co-opt the ethnic minorities. He urged the

Bureau of Tourism to concentrate on the gathering of mountain songs, and not to interfere in cultural affairs.

Economic development promotes other aspects of identity consciousness. An official of Baise's Office of United Front points to many distinctive features of Baise including the exploitation of world-level alumina by the most advanced company in the world. Furthermore, the discovery of twenty-eight 100-meter deep earth pits, the largest of which is 600 meters deep, has led to the idea of a new tourist program called "heavenly pit." Scientists have found living organisms in the pits that have never been discovered elsewhere. With increasing confidence and pride in being a Baise resident, he denounced the outside world, which saw Baise as a backward place:

> If you say Baise is economically poor, I take it. However, this is not the same as being backward. Remember Deng Xiaoping's Baise uprising. How can a revolutionary place be backward? Economic underdevelopment is the result of natural, historical, and other objective factors. Those who were born in Beijing or Shanghai would be much more backward than I am if they came to live in Baise. Experts always describe those under poverty as foolish or stupid. We just don't have the opportunities to study in school. To develop economically takes time. During the Cultural Revolution, no one in the country could develop but this does not mean all the Chinese are fools. Baise has a lot of advantages so even (if) it is a poor area, other people still come. For example, we have the best alumina in the world. The whole world wants to invest in alumina exploitation. Who can compare with us?[15]

How county level officials have developed such a strong local identity out of their Helping-the-Poor activity seems beyond the comprehension of the street-level campaigners. This is probably because these officials have had to deal with the superior government or outside observers and their opinion that Baise residents are culturally inferior and economically impoverished. In other parts of the country, there is a different approach. In this strategy, the county officials would use the outsiders' tone to deride the poverty of the villagers as if the officials were outsiders. Note that the Baise officials change sides. Some of them take the side of the local residents and talk back to those outsiders who only analyze the local situation according to their own life experiences.

The thing is, there is a difference between the associate county director's aforementioned ethnic consciousness and the United Front official's local consciousness. They share the strategic use of a discourse that allows them to look up or look out. They creatively use either Buluotuo culture or the alumina and heavenly pit as the point of reference. From the central government's point of view, this is perhaps by far the most unexpected development of the Helping-the-Poor program.

Acknowledging New Knowledge on Poverty

The purpose of this chapter is to expose the top-down perspective hidden within current discussions on helping the poor. The focus is invariably on per capita income or external investment that can save the poor villagers from poverty. The interviews show that poor villagers do not idly accept whatever is imposed by the central government. Equally important is the role of the Helping-the-Poor cadres who may be affected by the poor villagers, to the extent that the inexpressible emotion of the poor villagers can become a source of knowledge, allowing the cadres to formulate perspectives beyond those of the central government's poverty discourse.

Different types of cadres might lead to different combinations between their empathy with the villagers' feelings and their role as Helping-the-Poor campaigners. The resulting subjectivity, which emerges either in the mind of the lower-level township and team cadres or the higher-level county officials might present themselves in different ways. In brief, the issue is not just what poverty objectively means or how to eliminate poverty defined by per capita income. It is also how poverty can become a component of identity that affects the knowledge about poverty for those who once interpreted poverty literally and saw it in its raw state. Among these perspectives, there is even a feeling that the responsibility of unsuccessful development programs lies on the shoulders of the government. Empathetically, the external helpers learn to be dependent and passive.

PART 4

———

Riding the Citizenship

This section depicts more realistic pictures for the state, whose obsession with unity mostly results in mixed outcomes. Strong self-awareness in ethnic Mulao communities, discussed in Chapter 10, and their acquiring of the autonomous status reinforce each other to enhance the participatory rigor in political economic reform, even though the reform is not always successful. The system of ethnic autonomy described in Chapter 11 demonstrates that ethnic Yao villagers might have their own agendas unintended by the system of autonomy. Autonomy affects but does not determines the local responses. Chapter 12 describes how, in addition, moral peasants can learn to be rational as the Helping-the-Poor campaign in ethnic Miao mountains in Chapter 12 introduces the market mechanism. While the state could lack sensitivity toward the local conditions, local communities comply anyway, most of the time. However, they are able to actively use the state agenda for their own purpose and yet remain alerted to some other aspects of the state's intervention. In other words, the drive for unity creates new dimensions in the ethnic communities' self-understanding. Accordingly, the relationship between the ethnic communities and the state is constantly under negotiation.

CHAPTER 10

Assimilation into Mulao Consciousness: The Rise of Participatory Rigor in Luocheng

Introduction

This chapter presents the possibility in which the acquiring of ethninc autonomous status enhances the participatory rigor of the local communities in reform that is embedded in a seemingly unrelated property rights arrangement and marketization. Property rights reform is a popular subject in Chinese studies, but this topic will not be addressed in this book. Instead, given the property rights reform, this chapter attends to the cultural capability of the ethnic Mulao community to adapt to it. This cultural capability to adapt to political economic changes is noticeably lacking in most other ethnic communities.

In the study of Chinese political economy, as well as reform, the institutional approach that emphasizes property rights appears most popular. According to the property rights analysis, different property rights arrangements provide different incentives, resulting in different behavioral choices.[1] There are still debates within the field of institutional studies concerning how much institution can constrain rationality.[2] Some stress the rationality of people to follow market reform, where the wise man directs behavior by redesigning the incentive mechanism according to his purpose;[3] others contend that historical paths constrain the evolution of private property, and the room for maneuvering the incentive mechanism is rather limited.[4] Whether reform is an intervening variable (subject to the wise man's restructuring efforts) or an independent variable that has its own path is what separates the rational approach from the historicist approach. While the role of the wise man is critical in resolving the debate, people do not have any doubt about the constraint of reform on human behavior. This means that behavior motivated by purposes outside of property rights arrangement is not considered theoretically relevant.[5]

The problem with the current property rights approach is that it pays no attention to the change of self-knowledge that takes place along with reform. In fact, merging into reform is often the cause of nostalgia toward any previous social network that was destroyed during the process of "marketization." This means that participation in reform also reflects a change (albeit indirectly) in identity strategy, since it produces a different self-other relationship through the regulation and appropriation of property rights. On the other hand, a change in self-knowledge likewise affects how a particular reform setting is to be acted upon. In short, whether rationalism or historicism is a better approach depends on how well the members of a community feel comfortable with a particular type of reform. This is not something that reform can choose for itself. Once one understands that participation in reform is indirectly a matter of choosing identities, one can legitimately attend to the alternative identities that compete with reform in defining the purpose of a community life. Since mainstream society by large ignores the identity issue, an ethnic community would be a much better place to uncover the interaction between reform and identity.

This chapter thus discusses how change in identity might affect how current political economic reform is acted upon in an ethnic local community. Specifically, this chapter investigates how a seemingly "assimilating" autonomy system might enhance the participatory rigor in political economy even though the result of participation is not successful. The community selected for this study is the Mulao nationality of the autonomous Luocheng County, which falls under the jurisdiction of the Guangxi Zhuang Autonomous Region. The chapter begins with a brief discussion on several pieces of previous research that point to the possibility of opening reform to various local interpretations pertaining, in particular, to how different identity strategies result in different practices under the same political economic circumstance. Then, Luocheng's practice demonstrates how change in the autonomous status of the county has prompted the strengthening of identity consciousness. Enhanced identity consciousness generates stronger motivation in using the existing political economic setting for self-actualization, despite both the installation of regional ethnic autonomy and market reform assimilate, and not distinguishing it from, the Mulao community.

This chapter does not deal with specific reform policy. Instead, it serves to move the literature on reform away from property rights, and closer to the self-knowledge of the local community under study. When the term "reform" is used hereafter, it is generally referred to as "marketization" as a substitute for planning, privatization to expand the scope of the market and market incentive, and the state's transfer to subsidize an underdeveloped region. This evolution theoretically serves the function of dissolving ethnic self-consciousness by individualizing as well as materializing one's identity. Due to the indecisiveness of identity, however, one must refrain from trying to draw a universal conclusion from these top-down maneuverings of incentive or representation.

The Identity Condition

The state-initiated system of regional autonomy is of particular relevance in the formation of ethnic identity. The Chinese government divided its citizens into fifty-five nationalities. As such, administrative jurisdictions, where there are particular nationalities in residence, can receive autonomous status. The acquisition of this status often involves an intensive process of application, investigation, discussion, and consultation, as well as an overall political consideration. Clearly, elements of arbitration and luck are present in any decision to grant autonomous status to a local administration. The level of autonomy varies in each case, from region (parallel to Province), to county. The level of an autonomous prefecture is located somewhere in between. Below the county level, those townships with residents with nationalities different from those of the county or municipality can become ethnic townships, thereby enjoying certain autonomous privileges. Three possibilities might result from this institutional arrangement: non-autonomous nationalities living sporadically, autonomous single nationalities living in density, and autonomous multiple nationalities living in density.

Once autonomous status is set, there are different incentive mechanisms available for the state to solicit and mobilize support from the local ethnic community. Policy privileges, exemptions from regulation, and affirmative actions are among these instruments. For individuals of Han backgrounds living in the autonomous region, there can still be applicable privileges such as extra points in the college entrance examination. Nevertheless, an incentive of this sort is weak in urban areas, to the extent that some might choose to disguise their ethnicities, either to avoid social discrimination or to conceal a sense of inferiority. Similarly, multi-ethnic areas lack clear identity to motivate the administration to work actively for its residents. Consequently, as discussed in Chapter 7, granting privilege to multi-ethnic autonomous areas is like granting privilege to nationalities in the non-autonomous areas. In comparison, only under single-nationality autonomy can the autonomous administration advocate higher ethnic consciousness. The interaction between identity and the participation strategy in reform generates a variety of possibilities in single-nationality autonomy.

Given the operation of autonomy as a state-initiated institution, both non-autonomous nationalities living sporadically and autonomous residents living in density are, by definition, practicing some sort of identity politics. Comparing how they react to the state gives the outsider a clue to what differences the system of ethnic autonomy might or might not make in one's identity consciousness.[6] A typical case of sporadic, non-autonomous nationality is Hui whose people's self-consciousness relies heavily on practicing religious belief and customs, rather than state-granted autonomous identity. Economic reform stressing individual rights does not necessarily threaten the Hui people's identity. In the non-autonomous areas, there is no report regarding the distinctive features of the Hui people's participation in the market. Another non-autonomous example is the She people in Lishui, Zhejiang. There is a very strong ethnic consciousness in Lishui. The township communist party has decided to dedicate itself to the work of extricating the disappearing ethnic characteristics. However, their participation in the market economy is weak in comparison with the surrounding Han community. Ethnic-related activities center upon school activities. The local community decided to hire a Han village director to explore economic opportunities. The third case, mentioned in Chapter 8, is the sporadic Shui in Yizhou, Guangxi.[7] There are no ethnic-related activities reported in the villages, nor is the participation in the market active or successful. In short, in the non-autonomous areas, one runs into a variety of possibilities—Hui's high consciousness unrelated to the level of participation in the market, Lishui She's high consciousness with low participation, and Yizhou Shui's low consciousness with low participation.

In autonomous multi-ethnic jurisdictions, there is no single identity to provide identity-generated motivation. Likewise in the aforementioned case of autonomous multi-ethnic Longshen, Guangxi, where there are five nationalities, each living in density within the county, the formal ethnic title is the administrative term of "multi-ethnic." However, the use of this autonomous status is not associated with a detectable incentive to either enhance ethnic consciousness or encourage participation in market activities. In double-ethnic areas where both nationalities appear in the title of the administrative jurisdiction, there can be ethnically related incentives. In Xiangxi Tujia and Miao Autonomous Prefecture, for example, the Tujia-led Yongshun County consciously takes advantage of its ethnic status to demand policy privileges, even though there is no noticeable effort to engage in cultural activities. In contrast, the level of development is quite low in Yongshun, whose case suggests that even if multi-ethnicity as an autonomous identity might not motivate economic participation, it does not necessarily block the active use of policy incentives exclusively associated with the autonomous status for the sake of economic gains.

A wide range of possibilities appears in the single-ethnic jurisdiction. The state is highly concerned with economic development and political loyalty under this type of ethnic autonomy. For the state, ethnic identity is an important channel through which the state engages in political economic mobilization. Cultural activities that might preserve or enhance self-dignity of the nationality is tolerated, but never encouraged by the high level administrations. As a result, ethnic consciousness that continues outside the state co-exists with the economically oriented autonomous status. In the example of the Litong area in Ningxia Autonomous Hui Region, a unique identity-economic style appears whereby Hui villagers forty years old or less spend most of their time in economic activities, while those over sixty are committed to Islamic discipleship,. The activities in the Mosque include the teaching of both the state policies and the Koran. Party secretaries have no need to visit the Mosque and they do not do so. There seems to be a tacit negotiation between the identity and reform to divide one's life into two periods with a ten-year transition period between forty and fifty. In Changede, Hunan, a more extreme case is worth researching. Local cadres in the ethnic villages conceptually separate religion, customs, and identity to accommodate the situation that some Uygurs in the areas actually consume pork while others raise swine sold in the market. Furthermore, the party cadre can legitimately practice Hui customs without the risk of violating proletarian antitheism. Here, the state's ethnic autonomy and the style of harmonizing ethnicity in the state are not in contradiction.

Another style of harmonizing ethnicity in the state is completely opposite to Litong Hui's case. An example of this is the Korean nationality in Shenyang. In Litong, a Hui begins as a citizen who becomes an ethnic Hui later on. By contrast, the Koreans in Shenyang begin as Koreans who then take on the identity of Chinese citizens. The state avoids contradiction between identities outside and inside the state. They do so by officially supporting the reproduction of the local Korean identity economically as well as culturally, in exchange for their loyalty to the Chinese identity. In comparison with the harmonized ethnicity into the state, Chengbu Miao Autonomous County in Hunan witnesses strong ethnic consciousness taking on a confrontational stance. The county ethnic commission officials run into tremendous pressure from the education officials who dissuade the former's effort to enhance ethnic consciousness in ethnic schools. In particular, a Miao education official is in the mood of de-emphasizing his own ethnicity, therefore reflecting the state's reluctance to sensitize ethnicity in the identity institution. Although this attitude exists among education officials, the atmosphere of resistance is still felt amongst a few Miao cadres who promote ethnic awareness.

Within regional autonomy, a complying ethnic citizen has at least the options of adhering to proletarian antitheism as young Litong Huis or Changde's Uygur party secretary have done; exchanging utilities for loyalty to the state, as Shenyang Koreans did; or de-emphasizing one's own ethnicity, as Chengbu Miao's education official did. On the outside, one might remain religious like the older Litong Huis and the Changde's Uygur secretary, or witness strong ethnic consciousness as Shenyang Koreans or the Chengbu ethnic commission officials. Resolving potential contradiction between ethnic consciousness inside and outside of the system of autonomy is not a relevant issue in other areas. For example, in the Man autonomous villages in Beining, Liaoning, there are no cultural activities to promote Man's features, yet the people in this area are noticeably patriotic. This patriotism does not seem to threaten the Man identity at all because the Man people have historically ruled China. This guarantees that no one would question the existence of the Man identity, whose villages in Beining consciously want to join in the market, although they have not successfully done so to date. Given this, one might say that success in reform is not related to the type of regional autonomy.

It is also possible for cases of harmonious coexistence of the inside and outside identities to become detrimental to economic mobilization due to the lack of consistency between the identity and reform. One evident example is the ethnic Yi villages in Meigu Liangshan Yi Autonomous Prefecture. Some Meigu children indulge in primitive pasturage and do not attend school. Training into reform is unsuccessful. According to official discourse, Yi is not far away from its slave economy. There is no positive image of Yi in the system of regional autonomy. Ironically, local cadres use this backward image as an excuse for not participating in market opportunities. In response, the state officials consider this alienation a facade of backward culture; hence, no urgent sense of reform is considered in addition to reallocating some extra resources to the area.

The relevance of identity to reform is clear in many areas but never fixed in a direction. It depends on the type of autonomy system at work in particular areas, the nature of the identity formation outside the autonomy system, and the level of consistency among various identities inside and outside of ethnic autonomy, as well as between the ethnic identity and reform.

Mulao Cadres in Autonomous Luocheng

What characterizes the Luocheng case is its non-assertive style of self-identity, which is conciliatory, assimilable, indistinct, yet self-conscious, confident, and aggressive. A missing example in the aforementioned possibilities is exactly a case where the practice of identity institution effectively contributes to the participation in reform. The Western Hunan case comes close but the result of the active quest for policy privileges is not successful, since Yongshun continues to rank among the poorest counties of the country. Besides, in Yongshun, the residents, with the exception of intellectuals, express very low Tujia ethnic consciousness. This missing case directs attention to the Luocheng Mulao Autonomous County. Local Mulao cadres reveal a strong ethnic identity in their interviews but they do not resemble the She people in Lishui, as the latter are not administratively autonomous. Neither do they resemble the case of the Koreans because the state actively supports the Korean identity for political reasons, nor the Hui people in Litong since the Mulao people experience no double identities between the state and the religion. Another close case, perhaps, is Chengbu, where factors of ethnic consciousness, self-empowering agency, and loyalty to the state all exist. However, there is no such confrontational mood in Luocheng as in Chengbu. One particular feature of Luocheng is that its autonomous status was newly granted in 1983 and it is the only Mulao autonomous jurisdiction in the whole country. The atmosphere of celebration and gratitude lingers even today.

The Mulao population totals about 160,000, while Luocheng has 30,000. The Mulao people are not mountain-living ethnic communities as many other nationalities are. They typically live in suburban areas, with intensive contacts with the Han community. Psychologically, the most important and recent institutional reformation for the Mulao community is not marketization or privatization. Rather, it is the installation of the autonomous jurisdiction in Luocheng. There was a large-scale celebration of its ascension to autonomous status on its tenth yearly anniversary in 1993. The first historical text on Mulao was published in the same year. The author, Hu Xiqiong, passed away in 2001, two years before the time he originally planned to publish the succeeding volume, The Long Cultural Corridor of Mulao. To complete and finish this publication eventually became the most important mission for a group of young Mulao cadres.

While all the cadres interviewed are highly involved in their work, they are not all ethnically sensitive in rhetorics. The newly installed party secretary, Mr. Yang, is such an example. He unprecedentedly opened his first township party secretary meeting to non-partisan outsiders. In the meeting, he impressively demonstrated his depth of knowledge regarding the chronic problems of the township. In order to resolve the financial and social difficulties inherited from his predecessors, he began by warning all the village party secretaries not to forget the principle that there was only a people's government, and there is no such thing as a government's people. Then he turned his position around to speak for his township by claiming that in the eyes of county government, townships are the people. With this principle in mind, the new township secretary declared his confidence in resolving all historical problems, especially the property rights issues concerning the woods. Attending village party secretaries explained their understanding of Yang's remark, that they should actively participate in any dispute involving property rights issues. In fact, the township secretary received instruction on the appropriate approach to resolve the controversial ownership of woods—always consulting with all relevant parties, including the country attorney general, the impartial neighboring villages, the senior villagers, and the parties in dispute. He declared that history had prepared a way out of the problems left by history itself and that he was ready to take a position.

Director Yu of the Office of Out-reaching (in charge of affairs dealing with other counties or provinces) shows similar confidence. She feels that there could be nothing too difficult for her to handle. She said she always prepares herself before undertaking any particular task. However, she has no intention of moving to a higher post because she dislikes work pressure. This was the reason why she left her previous teaching position to start a new career in the government, where life is much easier. Yu describes herself as someone who never listens to rumors or follows any trend. She shows a sense of pride concerning her ethnicity, and believes that Mulao culture is most attentive to gender equality, compared with other nationalities in China. In addition, she finds that the Mulao culture is very open and flexible—a very important point that comes up repeatedly in various encounters with the local people. Yu also pointed out that Mulao people have no interest in resisting assimilation into the mainstream Han culture. Assimilation does not threaten Mulao consciousness. According to her, the reason is that knowledge of Mulao ethnicity does not come from a distinctive language, habit, or costume; it comes from self-confidence, tautologically from somewhere inside the Mulao consciousness.

Yet, this self-consciousness does not help in soliciting subsidies for culturally related activities. For example, the ethnic elementary school is unable to raise the Regional stipend for each student to above RMB12 a month, a level decidedly drawn from 1988 living standards. A decision reached in 2000 would have raised it to RMB50 but this did not happen. Moreover, the County Bureau of Ethnic Affairs has repeatedly failed to pursue this issue with the superior Regional Commission, which is an ethnic Zhuang administration. School Principal Wu once wanted to raise funds so he could provide a set of Mulao costumes for the school band. Unlike what happened in Chengbu, Luocheng education officials supported the idea, but no funds ever arrived. Also, Luocheng lost to Yizhou in a competition to host the legendary "Sister Liu" who, as the legend says, was from Luocheng. The superior Zhuang government suggested that a Mulao area does not host a Zhuang legend, despite the fact that the Zhuang population accounts for the majority of Luocheng's jurisdiction. Overall, on the cultural front, Luocheng shows mediocre results when soliciting support from the superior Zhuang government.

The school principal kept expressing how much he loved his job. He stressed the fact that Mulao parents had been very active in pursuing opportunities for higher education for their children, when compared to Zhuang, Miao, and Yao parents in the same school. The only education-related problem Mulao people have is the recruitment of girls from remote mountain sites. The county education director even goes up to the mountains in an effort to persuade the girls' parents. In other areas, only teachers enter the mountains to carry out this strenuous task. At one time, local television station made a report about Director Lo's unusual dedication. Mulao teachers do not teach Mulao history in class, but their efforts to raise the high school enrollment is an important criterion that the superior government uses to judge the performance of ethnic policy. The County Bureau of Ethnic Affairs is given the task of promoting ethnic-sensitive activities. Thus, it promotes such activities on its own, without any project fund granted by the state.

In brief, the Mulao cadres actively operate within the institutional frame to resolve the problems at hand. They seem to have a clear orientation, experiencing no significant difficulties in adapting to "marketization" or privatization despite technical disputes. Furthermore, no sense of alienation, lack of confidence, inferiority or incapacity was noted throughout the interviews as in the case of Chapter 8 where these factors were noticeable.

The following section of this chapter attempts to put forth that Mulao consciousness actually plays a role in facilitating the participatory rigor of the Mulao community in Luocheng. It is also conducive to current reform despite that participation does not guarantee good results. Finally, the recent upgrade to autonomous jurisdiction enhances self-confidence.

Mulao Consciousness and the Identity Institution

The granting of autonomous status to Luocheng coincided with the end of the Cultural Revolution and the beginning of the Four Modernizations. The combining effects of institutional reform on both property rights and identity fronts might ironically remind Luocheng cadres of such contradiction. The Four Modernizations campaign reinforces the merge of the already highly assimilated Mulao community with the Han community. However, Mulao consciousness and the activities to enhance such consciousness have clearly been on the rise. Part of the reason is that Luocheng, once an average agricultural county belonging to the ethnically Zhuang Autonomous Region, but now the only autonomous Mulao jurisdiction in the country, officially represents all the Mulao population. This representative image became increasingly justified when the central government consulted with Luocheng officials regarding the application of a Guizhou Township for ethnic Mulao status. The Luocheng delegation investigated the application and recommended rejecting it, on the grounds that neither the language nor custom of the township resembled Luocheng's. The central government agreed with this recommendation, further strengthening the impression that Luocheng represents authentic Mulao ethnicity. This incident is more than just a simple reproduction of the Mulao identity; it also granted the Luocheng Mulao community the power to distinguish Mulao from other similar communities. They now had the knowledge to decide who is and who is not a Mulao.[8] Attaining this "othering" capability made up for the loss of ethnic distinction at a time of rapid fusion with the Han community.

Assimilation into the Han culture catches the attention of the officials at the Bureau of Ethnic Affairs in Luocheng, who work to retrieve the Mulao culture. In recent years, the bureau has spent much time extricating over twenty local customs that have disappeared. These customs are primarily athletic games, some of which are also shared by other ethnic communities. Older cadres used to play these games when they were young. In order to participate in the regional as well as national ethnic games, the bureau has invited experts to modernize a selected number of games such as "rice-cake grabbing," "torch balls," and "Ox Horn chess." The item, however, that earned the Luocheng team a national award is called "bamboo ball playing." However, these games are easily learned. Throughout the country, it is common that different ethnic teams feature similar performing athletics. Authenticity claimed through athletic items is hardly sustainable. Yet, the worry of losing authenticity is recognized among bureau officials; one of them has raised suspicion over a Cultural Bureau's program to translate Mulao mountain songs into Mandarin. The suspicion is justified on the grounds that Mulao mountain songs, once translated, will lose their authenticity. A sense of urgency exists, nonetheless. In response, the ethnic bureau now has a documentary project, filming a conventional local ritual called Yifan, which is still practiced during funerals in the Mulao community. The Yifan ritual, however, is already slowly disappearing. Yifan preachers are no longer among the popular marriage choices for girls, leading to a drop in their numbers.

Secretary You of the Bureau of Ethnic Affairs points out the contradiction between economic development and the preservation of ethnic culture. He has interviewed a number of senior scholars about Mulao culture, and has reported his interviewees' concern about the lack of cultural characteristics in the Mulao community. Ironically, the Mulao spoken language is the only characteristic that allows the highly assimilated Mulao community to sensually remain as Mulao. The award-winning Mulao drama, for example, must be spoken in Mandarin just to attract an audience. Moreover, emigrant workers feel no ethnic distinction in the coastal cities since few city dwellers are aware of Mulao; it is also difficult to distinguish between Mulao workers and their Han counterparts in their appearance. Sadly, for high-level government officials, their work in the ethnic area is to promote economic growth. Even in Luocheng, ethnicity seems to mean nothing more than dusty ethnic costumes stored in the office.

However, You is not really worried. He agrees with Director Li of the Office of Out-reaching that Mulao is an open-minded culture, one that effectively adapts to changes. This suggests that intrinsically, the Mulao community has a strong attachment to the Mulao identity, and these behavioral adjustments pose no threat to their Mulao identity. Therefore, looking for ethnic characteristics from the outlook of the Mulao community will result in nothing. According to You, the common characteristic of their people is the shared confidence in the Mulao identity. Note that the ethnic characteristics regarded by others to be disappearing are the indicator of strength to them.

A secure identity reinforced by the autonomous status affects the style of conflict resolution involving more than one ethnic group. The aforementioned property rights dispute concerning ownership of a particular piece of wood, for example, took place between a Han and a Mulao village. A dispute of this sort concerns ethnic affairs and is actually an important aspect of it. However, the Luocheng government decided that a property rights dispute should not be treated as an ethnic issue. The Mulao community does not need to involve Mulao consciousness when resolving a property rights dispute. In contrast, sensitivity to the differences among ethnic groups is often praised in other areas. In the neighboring Nandan County, where unique clothing is employed as a local ethnic feature, the ethnic Yao identity is so protected that the community even refuses donations of clothes in times of natural disasters. They fear that clothes from other groups would obscure their local identity and convert their ethnicity away from the easily presentable "White Pants Nationality" [*bai ku zu*].

Also according to You, a group of Mulao writers who hold the same belief in Mulao's intrinsic attachment now meet regularly. These writers work for different divisions of the county government, and they write while off work. Although they respect Hu Xiqiong's work, they feel that it is mainly a collection of data, and deeper analyses are still necessary to make the data mean something relevant. As there is not much time left for county officials to work on Mulao ethnic culture—even officials at the Bureau of Ethnic Affairs spend most of their time on Helping-the-Poor programs— these writers systematically search for senior villagers in an effort to gather more data or to extract meaning from the available data. They do not feel like discussing cultural issues with Helping-the-Poor officials, believing that the latter do not care. They would rather meet with people who share their thoughts and beliefs regarding the Mulao nationality.

Moreover, You is serious about his comment regarding the inner quality of Mulao. He considers himself a successor of Hu Xiqiong, although he lacks the discourse to present the deeper meaning of being a Mulao. Director Li supports You's feelings by citing the Mulao emigrant workers' practice of going home with their wives after marriage in coastal cities, instead of bringing wives back home as most husbands of other nationalities do. Director Li believes that this is the evidence that the Mulao identity is so deeply embedded and so secure that there is no need for any protective effort. Hu Xiqiong wrote about the Mulao psychology in the preface of his 1993 book:

> [C]ertain ethnic characteristics are deeply embedded. These included those feelings, attitudes, aesthetics, moral principles and identities, which reflect, as well as reproduce psychological features of the [Mulao] nationality that are not obvious. These characteristics need deep investigation, extrication and understanding in order to learn and appreciate them. Due to the limitation of certain historical factors and practical difficulties in the past . . . knowledge about the history, culture and present situation of this nationality and even its existence in the present time are hardly known.[9]

Perhaps the same feeling revealed in this quote prompted You to take the job offered at the Bureau of Ethnic Affairs. Although economic work is unfamiliar to him, and though it claims much of his time, he is nonetheless glad to have the opportunity to work on ethnic affairs. He describes his dedication to his work:

> Personally, if not for the love for home, I will not return. I graduated from the Central-South Nationalities College. The school asked me to stay. I turned it down. I remember I was full of rigor. My career did not develop according to my wish so I am now without achievement. Man's way of thinking is constantly changing, so I do not want to talk about the past. I have been working on ethnic affairs for ten years. I have never blindly followed my superior, but I try to work something out so I can be accountable to my conscience. The party organization has negative opinions about me. The party wanted to assign me to a village post. I refused. I want to do things that I love doing. The village post is like the eye of a needle with thousands of strings going through it. This is why I want to stay where I am. I can contribute to my community in a more substantive way. After all, I am not interested in being promoted to other posts.[10]

The hypothesis that could be derived from field interviews is that the autonomous status of the jurisdiction provides both the motivation of the cadres to work hard on the Mulao affairs and the ethnic incentive to allow intellectuals to work for the hometown government. It is granted that intrinsic attachment to the Mulao identity is strong even without the help of autonomous status. But without the political change, intellectuals would not come to the government to work out cultural activities that enhance Mulao self-dignity. Hu Xiqiong might not have had his work done. The theory of the intrinsic Mulao identity would not have emerged in publication. Furthermore, the quest for authenticity would not have felt as real. Consequently, it is possible that assimilation into the Han culture had reversely generated a sense of pride. The attachment must also be more secure with Luocheng being the only administrative representative of the nationality.

Economic Incentives Qualified

With a sense of stability provided by the Mulao consciousness, the Mulao people are able to take an active attitude toward their work. Still, this attitude could result in a very different behavior. On one hand, an active attitude toward work and life might motivate one to acknowledge the current "marketization" and privatization process. This pertains to the preparedness to grab opportunities that emerge. On the other hand, the willingness to make sacrifices for the sake of the Mulao community would be equally attractive to someone dedicated to the collective interests. This means being able to consciously forego the opportunity under certain circumstances. In the latter's case, the difference between the identity incentive and the economic incentive is not as great as it might seem. Note that the individual sacrifice for the benefit of the Mulao community is to contribute to the Mulao collective interests, while current economic reform primarily attends to individualized incentives. In other words, it is a kind of sacrifice aimed at enhancing the capacity of the Mulao community as a whole, to take advantage of the market opportunities that emerge. The identity and economic incentives are not in contradiction at the collective level. Interviews held at the Luocheng First High School bring out this point.

The school principal, Mr. Huang, introduced the campus construction and talked about his philosophy of management. He mentioned that education must begin with one's environment, thus he wanted to renovate the campus into a more natural environment. Taking advantage of First High's sixtieth anniversary, which was celebrated in 1998, he made the school's renovation possible by raising funds through the help of the alumni and without support from the government. Instead of renovating the school's building like most other schools, Principal Huang concentrated on changing the campus scenery. Indeed, First High School today looks entirely different from other high schools that exist anywhere in the world. The campus design has influenced neighboring schools to seriously consider following its initiatives of transforming their campuses into a green park type of campus. The first thing visitors will experience upon entering the main gate is the impression of entering a huge garden. Behind two rows of classrooms sits a small mountain, where there is an arbor and a stream. At the foot of the mountain are a corridor and a very long stone tablet recording Mulao history and its cultural features, making sure that both students and tourists will be engrossed in an atmosphere of Mulao humanity. It has also been hoped that students will thrive in such a relaxed environment and possibly have a strong and stable identity.

The renovation was unlikely without the donations from the alumni. Economics was still far behind during the late 1990s, but most of the alumni were able to donate RMB200 each. This was equivalent to their monthly salary at the time. In addition to the donations, Secretary You personally composed the text that was inscribed on the tablet. All graduating classes each donated a piece of the stone tablet. Still, in preparation for the sixtieth anniversary celebration, the principal reallocated part of the money he had raised to compensate for the losses of the peasants who had yielded the back mountain they used to cultivate. The renovation of the campus was completed in the same year. Today, anyone who tours Luocheng often comes to the First High School.

Passing through the corridor and seeing the Mulao history tablet, students are reminded of Mulao history whenever they visit the mountain during early mornings and evenings to study. Consequently, the principal reports a noteworthy change in students' behavior patterns. Fighting has significantly been reduced, and the college acceptance rate based on entrance examinations has steadily improved since 1998. More impressive is that every year, approximately half of the students who qualify for enrollment at the Hechi Regional First High school, which is considered the most competitive in the five-county area that encompasses Luocheng, decide to enroll at the Luocheng First High instead. The principal of the higher-ranking First High at neighboring Duan County, a Yao community, reportedly once showed disbelief at the choice made by those students.

However, Principal Huang at the Luocheng First High has to cope with various kinds of pressure. The strongest pressure pertains to the college entrance rate, while fund raising comes next. For example, he went to Beijing for a call on the head of the National Commission of Ethnic Affairs at home in order to raise funds for a building reserved for science classes. The immediate pressure is the outflow of top teachers to coastal schools. The living conditions and compensation for teachers in a place like Luocheng is obviously far behind those in coastal areas. With the school's improving reputation over the years, coastal schools' attempts to recruit the best teachers has intensified. As of 2004, teachers' salaries at the First High in the amount of RMB800 were much lower compared to the RMB3,000 in Zhejiang Province. Even salaries at other major regional high schools in Guangxi are higher. Some offer as much as three times the pay of teachers in Luocheng. Therefore, Luocheng teachers who want to support their children through college must begin saving money early in their careers. This is the incentive for them to leave for better offers. Although the county government has improved the salary scale, the rate of increase is still far behind the market rate.

Experienced teachers who have a market value decide to stay for reasons such as their special attachment to the school and their wanting to contribute to the development of the Mulao community. The Director of the Department of Teaching has stayed exactly for these reasons. Principal Huang himself must be resisting similar temptations. He has received an offer from a college to be a professor. He graduated from First High in 1977 and returned as a teacher in 1982. He expressed, though, that he is not sure of how long he can resist the offer being made to him:

> [L]ooking into the future, we as a national minority, and as part of the under-developed West, face the major problem of human resource—How to breed Mulao students into talented, high-quality timber, patriotic toward both the country and our Mulao people, home-loving, and capable of contributing to the economic development of the hometown? From the economic point of view, however, the regional development is losing balance. This definitely leads the local talents to have a second thought about their career . . . I once planned to leave for good before the school's anniversary this year, but the county government persuaded me to stay. This is not going to work for me in the long run, though.

The Mulao community, in general, sees education as an important factor. A famous "Scholar Village" in suburban Luocheng has trained over one hundred college graduates. The population of the village is not even one thousand. Amidst the narrow mud walls of village households is a village school made of cement. All the names of the villagers who have donated money to put up the school are inscribed on a tablet. This footnotes the participatory rigor that prepares the local community to meet competitive marketization.

The Relevance of Identity

Bureau Secretary You's anti-poverty campaign, Principal Huang's fund raising, Director Yu and Director Li's welcoming attitude towards the township's visitors, Party Secretary Yang's display of confidence in his people, and many teachers' dedication to hometown education all evidenty point to the Mulao cadres' active attitude toward participating in contemporary political and economic reform. Granted that enthusiasm cannot be measured objectively, the impression from interviews at Luocheng was certainly very different from the reservation, alienation, and even superficiality seen at other ethnic mountain sites. The interviewees' attitudinal characteristics should have something to do with the installation of the autonomous jurisdiction.

Both the representative identity the Luocheng community achieves through their autonomous status, and the psychological reflection on deeper identification with the Mulao community are conducive to these attitudinal characteristics. Unlike intellectuals of other mountain nationalities (such as Tujia in Western Hunan and She in Lishui), Mulao intellectuals do not really worry about the waning of cultural features as much.

This puts the Mulao closer to the Man identity, whose carriers show little self-doubt in front of the near-total assimilation of Man into the Han culture. Mulao is different from Man in the sense that Mulao consciousness is strong and on the rise. While the Man in Beining are losing autonomous status due to urbanization, the Mulao are enjoying their gain. Mulao cadres work to extricate and define Mulao authenticity while Man intellectuals do not.

The autonomous status that has been applied in a top-down, or wise-man fashion to Luocheng County affects the reproduction of identity, but it does not monopolize local response. The deep feeling about being Mulao allows its cadres to read positive elements out of the wise man's granting. Both rationalism and historicism are valid to the extent that the system of autonomy can affect the local's way of life, but only within the existing frame of self-understanding. The ethnic identity further affects the property rights reform in such a way that the identity consciousness prepares the individual Mulao community members either to take advantage of the new market opportunities while remaining conscious of the Mulao identity, or to make a personal sacrifice in order to enhance the whole community's competitive capacity in the market. The autonomous status in Luocheng successfully accommodates the Mulao identity, so that there is no potential conflict between double identities, as in the case of Hui in Litong or the Korean in Shenyang. The installation of autonomous jurisdiction also mobilizes the local Mulao community to participate positively. This is unlike the case of Yi in Meigu, where alienation marks the local identity. The Mulao way of interpreting assimilation into the Han culture, i.e., conciliatory assimilation as a proof of deep-seated Mulao identity, shows a unique way of adjustment and self-empowerment. In short, the property rights reform does not exclusively determine behavior through the setting up of incentives. Instead, how a property rights reform is taken or practiced should in itself be something to be explained.

CHAPTER 11

Living with the State: Multiplying Ethnic Yao Narratives in Jinxiu

A Bottom-up Perspective on Ethnic Autonomy

The relationship between the state and the ethnic minority is an interdisciplinary subject of political science and anthropology. For political science, which is the science of state, issues involving the ethnic minority are primarily concerned with participation and social welfare. This pertains to a top-down perspective; the political science literature is generally uninterested in how ethnic minorities view the state,[1] or the bottom-up perspective. On the other hand, anthropologists who often stay empathetic and close to an ethnic community are typically inattentive to the issues of the state. As a result, both disciplines leave out from their respective research agenda subjects such as how and what ethnicity means to the state and how and what the state means to each ethnic community. In practice, the tasks of identifying, mobilizing, and governing of ethnic communities belong to the state. It is assumed that the state has the knowledge regarding these ethnic practices. Ironically, however, the state rarely develops an effective mechanism to communicate with its ethnic citizens, and is therefore unable to appreciate the responses each ethnic community has to the intervention of the state in its daily life. In short, neither political scientists nor anthropologists have developed any systematic way of looking at the state from the minority points of view.

In political economy, the difference between the state-centered and the society-centered approaches is widely noted. There is no such noted discussion on the difference between the state-centered and the ethnic-centered approaches, though. The emergence of political anthropology as a nascent "inter-" disciplinary field presumably attends to this sort of reflection, which should promise to re-examine the ethnic community as a knower vis-à-vis the state as a knower. Comparing the knowledge of ethnicity held by the state and the knowledge of the state held by ethnic community members could provide useful clues to the state, especially about why the state cannot exercise a monopoly and how ethnic community members can empower their own communities despite the policy and discursive dominance of the state.

This chapter argues that indeed, the state is influential in constraining the range of options available for the local ethnic community to understand its own identities as well as its fate. However, the ethnic community has the creativity to, consciously or not, reinterpret its identities and indirectly revise what the state means. The chapter bases its argument upon a number of in-depth interviews that were held in Jinxiu Yao Autunomous County in the Guangxi Zhuang Autonomous Region. The purpose of these interviews was to find out if it is possible for a policy that is not based upon ethnic characteristics to remain ethnic in a sense because the practice of the policy reflects the view that is not articulated or even expressible in the language familiar to the state. Jinxiu is a nationally designated county of poverty. The Helping-the-Poor office that was first set up in 1985 is responsible for raising funds for infrastructure, investment, and policy privileges. Before the reformation of the bureaucracy, the ethnic commission once belonged to the Office of United Front, which simultaneously included the Office Overseas Chinese Affairs and the Office of Taiwan Affairs. To highlight the ethnic status of the county, the district government decided to separate the ethnic commission from the others. The reformation reduced the size of the ethnic commission to only three key personnel, but its duty extended to include the Helping-the-Poor program. In addition to the ethnic commission, this chapter reports on visits to ethnic schools from where most future local cadres are recruited. In fact, local government workers as well as communist cadres typically come from the normative system of education. They are chiefly transferred from a teacher's job or an educational official.

Policy Issues in the Eyes of State Officials

Into the twenty-first century, the greatest concern of the government about Jinxiu is its poverty situation, which further leads to a worsened educational situation. From the government's point of view, there is nothing ethnic about poverty. Hence, poverty only either constrains the capacity to execute the policy of the central government, or it disables the people to comply with the government's policy. To illustrate, the legal duty of parents is to support their children to complete nine years of education. However, most parents are not even able to support their children's primary education. Thus, when a child reaches adolescence, he or she is asked to help in the field. The same educational predicament appears in other nationalities, noticeably in the case of Sichuan Yi communities in Meigu, Hunan Dong communities in Chengbu, as well Yunnan Dai communities in Xishuangbanna.[2] The disincentive for education is the lack of opportunities for higher education after finishing middle school. Since there is little chance for a prospective college education, more years of education will not help the child leave the mountain village. Why would any parent invest in the child's education in the first place? One parent puts it straightforwardly—that he did not receive any formal education but lives fine nonetheless, so why cannot his child do the same? This attitude applies particularly strongly in the case of daughters.

The education policy of nine-year compulsory schooling is hardly enforceable in mountains where children live far away from one another. To allow a teacher to teach in the remote mountains, 183 teaching sites are set up in these areas. Ninety-eight of them have enrollments of less than ten students. The cost of teaching sites is twice as high as in the plain areas. Thus, there are a limited number of eligible teachers. Moreover, local townships cannot afford to pay many trained teachers. Substitute teachers are therefore common in Jinxiu, and each of them receives a meager salary of US$16 a month. To survive, they must cultivate in the field in addition to teaching. Thus, there seems to be less opportunity for these substitute teachers to grow professionally. Furthermore, children beyond the fourth grade should go to the township where there is an ethnic school for the fifth and sixth grades. Although the school is subsidized by the county government, many students understandably give up due to the sheer distance that has to be traveled to get to school.

The educational sector also lacks resources. Many of the school buildings are nearly in a condemned state if not otherwise already so; there are also no laboratory facilities in middle schools. Currently, the most important policy goal for the Bureau of Education in Jinsxiu is to raise the rate of school entrance at the primary and middle school levels. The main thrust is to improve the quality of teachers and their willingness to stay in the mountains. Good teachers can develop a curriculum appropriate for the students and help students in their career planning. Another way to attract students is to teach useful techniques in school. For example, in general, especially in the urban areas, the officially promoted "quality education" is often associated with arts and music education, but in Jinxiu, it is associated with techniques in swine raising, vegetable growing, top dressing, pruning, and the like.

While hunting and woodcutting are outlawed today, the view of the mountains is not at all that pretty. There are noticeably bare mountaintops everywhere in the county. The scenery itself is a warning of ecological erosion. The mountain villagers had already attended to the problem even before the government had legislated the closing-off policy. The government only seriously enforced the closing-off policy following the national flood of 1998. Although those areas that have benefited from this preservation policy have given some monetary feedback to Jinxiu, the bigger part of the feedback, along with the subsidy from the government, was used to finance the installation of patrolling teams and a regulation agency in the woods. In recent years, land that was once available for cultivation in the administrative township has mostly been taken to erect modern buildings. Unfortunately, the mountain villagers have not been given access to any land.

According to the interviewees, the major causes of extreme poverty are the underdevelopment of infrastructure and the lack of food production.[3] In the past, local residents depended on woodcutting for a living, but the highly sensitive ecological preservation problem led to the policy of closing off the mountains. The central government invested more in the recovery of the woods. The major agricultural activities allowed are now limited to those areas outside the mountains, and the crop left for the mountain area is anise. Moreover, the economic crops were of little help to the local economy because transportation was primitive. At the time of the interview in 2002 there were only a total of five administrative villages that sat within the jurisdiction of the village council office, and 214 natural villages were out of reach by road. No investor wanted to put up a business in the mountains due to the unavailability of transportation, not to mention the low skill levels of the villagers. Moreover, before the state could relocate the villagers, each of them must be supplied with a minimal amount of foodstuff. Furthermore, the official Helping-the-Poor program has remained very basic, concentrating on the teaching of critical living technique. For these villages, the closing-off of the mountains was tantamount to starving to death.

Loan opportunities were almost nonexistent because there was no sufficient guarantee to repay the loans. The County Bureau of Enterprise considered the cheap labor in the mountains as an attraction to potential investors.[4] There was only limited success, however, and mostly in the plains areas. The Bureau was nevertheless in a weak position because it was not eligible for participation in trading events, which were open only to companies. Fortunately, the Bureau managed to find a company that generously lent its name to the Bureau. This act of generosity enabled the Bureau to find investors and trading companies for the economic crops. However, a natural disaster struck the mountains in 2000; thus, a total of forty thousand peasants returned to the poverty level overnight. In the mountain area, the Helping-the-Poor campaign was vulnerable to the fluctuating market price of anise. Thus, anise actually made the return to poverty inevitable despite its advantage of being spotted at any possible place in the mountains.

Taking the State Seriously

When the state is looked at, it appears fragmented. Three factors contribute to the discursive fragmentation of the state. First of all, state officials at different levels have different styles of executing policy to give the state as many faces as there are officials.

Different villagers respond to each different face differently to the extent that unity cannot meaningfully exist. Most importantly, both villagers and officials alternate among multiple identities embedded in the ever-evolving social and political discourses. This is even true in what one might consider to be the most backward, dependent community. The Yao community in Jinxiu, Guangxi is one such community of poverty and dependency. In actuality, however, local cadres and villagers together are able to present a view of the state that cannot be expressed by any language familiar to the state. This is because their self-knowledge does not always operate within the scope of the state. The state's top-down designation of the Yao identity lacks respect toward the variety of dimensions of the Yao people's self-knowledge as being ethnically Yao.

Jinxiu has attracted outsiders since the late 1980s, and many anthropologists have arrived in Jinxiu from all over the world. However, the literature that treats the state's intervention in Jinxiu's Yao community is very limited, though highly impactful. Ralph A. Litzinger is the pioneer in this area.[5] He tackles the interaction between politics and culture directly and shows how the local Jinxiu community has read different meanings into their history as well as political revolution. He also shows how modernization, which the state promotes, ends up with practices that in reality denies the so-called unified state. On the other hand, stories of how unity has existed among several divisions of Yao ironically contradict the state discourse on their exploitation. Pertaining to Yao's self-knowledge, Litzinger is particularly sensitive toward the change and contradiction over time and across roles and positions. Yao is both homogeneous and heterogeneous depending on the timing of the speech and the role of the speaker. Many of his informants work for the state in one way or another to the effect of denying the state as either a reality or a force.

The following discussion supports Litzinger's argument with some revisions. While it does not treat the state as an internally homogenous reality, it nonetheless recognizes the state as a force, since acting in the name, or capacity, of the state usually leads to the pretension of universalism. Township as well as village cadres are villagers and state agents at the same time. They do not represent the state at all times. It is important to conceptually maintain the state as an actor to allow the development of self-criticism of those who participate in the administration of state policy and ideology. There would be a lack of target reflection if one purges the state as a meaningful concept completely. In fact, the force of the state often exists in the mind of cadres and affects the enactment of the Yao identities. To perform the top-down responsibility prepares the development of the bottom-up strategy, which deconstructs the state. Cadres speaking in the universal tone understand its pretension much better. It might appear that they practice the top-down policy in the same way, but their other identities will prepare their responses to the state very differently.

Accordingly, this book is about more than the interaction between the top-down and bottom-up perspectives. It attends to the irony of multiple identities. Litzinger describes different representation strategies of actors in different social positions, which are an ethnic division, a priest, a scholar, a member of a class, and so on. This research does the same. However, an outsider would be additionally intrigued by how a specific person shifts among various positions and roles, especially anyone who shoulders the policy and ideological responsibility given by the state. It is important not to attribute a perspective to a social position in order to avoid the misperception that this position determines the person's choices. The notion of multiple identities is useful because it places the person in an undecidable situation so that the person's decision on which identity to incur is above the constraint of social positions.

The phenomenon of multiple identities does not imply self-contradiction or a split personality at all. Rather, it suggests the coexistence of the top-down and bottom-up perspectives inside one mind. From the state's point of view, this composes contradiction, but for the person in question, it makes sense to be both in and out of the state capacity at the same time. The state is just another social role for lower-level officials, to be enacted alternatively, albeit most frequently in comparison with their other roles.

Take the example of a scholar/priest. The scholar responds to state ideology, while the priest adheres to the revival of Daoist customs. Take another example of a teacher/son. The teacher teaches Marxism and national unity, while the son cares about family tradition. There is no self-contradiction for either of the two examples. Multiple identities enable a person to face the state or act in the name of the state creatively, since there is no rule of how to alternate.

To appreciate the phenomenon of multiple identities, this chapter depends heavily on interviews with those who have some official responsibility. It does not quote specific names due to the unavoidability of the interviewer's misreading of the interviewees and hence violation of their integrity. Interviewing officials is not the same as interviewing ordinary villagers. The former are eloquent in comparison but usually allow no more than one visit, while the latter may be available for a much longer period of time, which accommodates multiple visits. The first visit to Nanning in 2001 was to prepare for a later trip, which involved the conducting of interviews in Jinxiu in 2002. Subsequent visits were shorter and were made as side trips on visits to neighboring Luocheng, Yizhou, Liuzhou, or Longsheng. To arrange these visits, both local officials of Taiwan Affairs and the Guangxi Social Science Academy came to help out.

The Negative Construction of the Yao Image

From the point of view of the state, Yao as an ethnicity is not much different from any other nationalities, sometimes not even from the majority Han ethnicity. This is because the central government is preoccupied with economic growth. The state would like to see growth anywhere in the country. Because of this, ethnicity requires special treatment only because ethnicity and poverty are in many cases symbiotic. There is the implicit assumption that increased wealth leads to assimilation into the dominant culture. The state subsidizes poor areas regardless of ethnicity. Even though there is an emphasis on ethnicity, it is not about any specific ethnicity. In short, Yao means ethnicity in general terms to the state, not specifically to the ethnic Yao. Therefore, any place that has woods must execute the closing-off policy, any place that has a low school entrance rate must receive support to recruit good teachers, and any area that is poor must launch a Helping-the-Poor campaign. The features of a Helping-the-Poor campaign invariably include road and bridge building, investments, policy privileges, cultural transformation, and so on. The state is used to a universally comprehensive development policy regardless of ethnicity.

However, the universalist style of policy making brings different results to different communities. In Xishuangbanna of neighboring Yunnan Province, for example, development policy reified in tourism has led to the killing of precious lives such as the pangolin for food and butterflies for decorative purposes. As the state bans hunting for a humble living, illegal hunting for business has spread. The closing-off policy in Xishuangbana intervened in the thousand-year-old practice of taungya (inter-cropping) that usually follows a long ecological cycle. To accompany the closing-off policy was ironically the exploitive plantation set-up by the People's Liberation Army. Similarly, the state had to be responsible for the bare mountain tops and the worsened water conditions of the surrounding twenty-five rivers in Jinxiu, according to a county official in private. It was the state during the Great Leap Forward campaign that encouraged the woodcutting to no limit. It was also the state in the early 1980s that exaggerated the desirability of quick earning ability that promoted the woodcutting. Only after the problem of woodcutting had already become a reality of life did the state decide that it was harmful.[6]

Not only did the state inappropriately handle the environmental issue, but it also ignored the contribution that the local Yao communities had been making to the state. Note that the local communities turned environmentally conscious before the state did. The Jinxiu residents organized and articulated their concern over the abuse of mountain resources because they believed that the mountains existed as elements for the worship of ancestors. This was long before the State Council ordered the closing-off policy. The communities' voluntary coordination with one another even prevented the outbreak of dispute among different ethnic groups over water resources.[7] The interviewees complained that the state never realized how much the Yao community had contributed to the harmony of inter-ethnic relations in the greater Guilin area, to which Jinxiu belongs. According to the interviewees, the ignorance lies in the central government's unawareness of the life experience of the local ethnic communities. As another example, a Chashan cadre stated that Chashan, a Yao division, was particularly unhappy with the sacrifices it had made to keep the society in harmony. In 1958, when the people's communes were being first set up, Pan, another division of Yao, migrated to the Chashan areas. After the commune was completely dissolved during the reform, the state never thought of having the Pan return the land to Chashan. In addition, in the mingling of the Yao, Han, and Zhuang people, the Chashan Yao cadre felt that his people always conceded to the interest of either the Han or the Zhuang to keep the harmonious relationship with them. Thus, as the informant complained, the Chashan Yao have always been taken for granted.[8]

The state is guilty at least to the extent that it has manipulated the meaning of poverty.[9] The state praised poverty to mean purity in the beginning because poor people were exempted from the bourgeois characteristics and were more compliant to communism. After 1979, poverty began to mean something bad: first, to mean having no food, then to mean having no money, later to having no infrastructure, no possibility for development, and finally, to even having no culture. Chashan Yao, not unlike Black Yi in Liangshan Prefecture, Sichuan, who were considered more culturally developed, were made poor because of the Great Leap Forward. Since then, they have been designated as culturally inferior.[10] This experience of being victimized by history partially explains the lukewarm response of Yao communities toward the school recruitment drive. There is no positive portrayal or reference to local communities in any of these centrally planned textbooks, not to mention the overall irrelevance of the subjects contained in them.

Granting that the state is more prone to the development of the material aspect in opposition to the cultural aspect, the state is often self-contradictive because different government branches simply do not cooperate with one another. For example, even if the official of Ethnic Affairs comes up with a new fund to support development, the financial branches would usually refer back to the existing criteria for loans and deny the applications in those areas that have standing loans. This would exclude, say Jinxiu, from accessing the newly available investment opportunities.[11] Another flaw of the system is that the officials of Ethnic Affairs are usually different from the agents of the Helping-the-Poor campaign.[12] The officials of Ethnic Affairs are much more accessible than those in other branches. If a policy is to be executed through the Council of Science, for example, the council members necessarily take into account their own interests in some specific scientific projects at the time, which is not primarily to the benefit of the ethnic communities. Consequently, Yao communities have no channels to articulate their needs, nor do they have the appropriate discourse to express what they want to say.

The discursive inability of the nationalities often results in the arrogant attitudes of higher-ranking government officials. It takes a movement from the state to the local community to realize how arbitrary the transition from the Great Leap Forward to the current reform has been and how the backward image of Yao communities has grown. The state, which claims order inside the borders and causes anarchy outside, naturally takes a universalist approach to local development, but it is unaware of the differences in history and culture that prepare the local communities into an inexpressible yet distinctive perspective. Under the universal education and development policy, the state does not know the environmental consciousness that emerged much earlier locally, the sense of alienation that the education system ironically generates, or the sacrifices that the local communities take. The state does not know, either, that the killing of precious species is the joint result of the closing-off of the mountains and the growth through tourism. In Jinxiu, Yao villagers in the mountains suffer from the state's development policy that is being carried out in their name. This means that the benefits they reap in the eyes of the state officials are different from what they actually need. If this is the case, universalism cannot apply. Therefore, the state has a problem, but ironically, the state is unaware of it.

Local Agency for Social Change

The state is not completely insensitive to the local mood or perspective. The criticism of the state policy in the ethnic area most often comes from local ethnic cadres. In other words, the local representative of the state is first to articulate the problems caused by the universal policy to the local communities. In the case of the aforementioned Chashan Yao, two officials belonging to this nationality expressed that what is important to them is not much about right or wrong, or if the view correctly represents all the Chashan Yao people. For them, it is more about the possibility of forming an ethnic perspective from the presumably distinctive Chashan identity. The Chashan identity thus proves to bear a discursive position to empower one to look at the state, instead of looking from it.

Self-empowerment is not necessarily self-conscious. Take the beginning of anise cultivation in Jinxiu, for example. This was a decision made against the state policy. Although not embedded in any ethnic consciousness, a local party secretary who insisted on developing anise was obviously acting out of the determination to change the life of his hometown, instead of any incentive provided by the state. The decision was made in 1972, but everybody did not thank him until a decade later.[13] For this reason, Jinxiu is now called "the Home of Anise" in the country, giving the local Yao a sense of pride. Although the local secretary's decision reflected some kind of individual agency for change, he was nonetheless an official representative of the state to execute the state policy. It was his position in the state that supported his decision, although not his risk-taking. Individual agency for change, leadership supported by the state, and the pride of the ethnic community together allude to the inability of the state to determine the results and the meaning of its development policy.

This is particularly true in the cultural arena. It is common among the villagers to see Yao schoolchildren perform cultural activities. The schedules of the performances are usually very timely. They are often done after state officials promulgate policies concerning the Three Represents or birth control. In the beginning, these cultural performances were instrumental in attracting villagers to policy promulgation. Theoretically, the cultural activities should be attached to policy promulgation, but in terms of motivation, the villagers are more interested in seeing their children perform. Thus, instead of the cultural activities being attached to the official policy, it is actually the other way around. The seemingly dominant state depends on the children to attract villagers' attention. Villagers only display their loyalty to the state by giving way to their children's performances, the ethnicity of which overshadows the concerns over unity.[14]

The state nevertheless intervenes directly in the reproduction of the Yao identity. This is clearly seen in the setting up of an ethnic school or ethnic classes in general school. Effectively promoting the traditional Yao medical culture, the state has recently recognized the medical practice of this nationality; thus, Yao doctors receive their licenses after passing the Yao medical examination. Furthermore, the Jinxiu County has a special budget to keep a Yao performing art team. When the county celebrated its fiftieth anniversary in 2002, the government allocated a special fund to build a presumably Yao-styled gate for the county office and a Yao-styled building in its hotel complex. Other buildings in the hotel facility are only named with meaningless numbers, but Building Number One has a proper name; it is called the "Nationality Building." The state's input in reproducing Yao ethnicity is essential to the state's claim to its universal position. The state must demonstrate its care for ethnic communities, and in return, ethnic communities must pay loyalty to the state.

The establishment of ethnic schools is the best policy to keep local communities' ethnic identities. Presumably, only the best get to study in ethnic schools, which are sponsored by the state. As students progress to higher education, they serve as models to their own groups. Breeding a multi-cultural atmosphere, the state then recruits these educated "elites" to work for the government. Some of them return home to become local officials or teachers. According to the principal of an ethnic school, returning home to teach is more common in their composition. Indeed, 70 percent of ethnic schoolteachers are Yao. This is a very high ratio as compared to other poor ethnic communities,[15] ensuring the reproduction of multiple identities embedded in the state's responsibility and Yao consciousness.

The county government is additionally involved in another culturally related work. The Bureau of Ethnic Affairs sponsors the editing of a book featuring the history of Jinxiu's Yao communities. The government has only a very limited budget, allocating not more than RMB50,000 for the editing work. However, the estimated expenditure is as high as RMB180,000.[16] Although the contents of the book, once printed, would be both too difficult to read for local residents and very conciliatory toward the state's universalist standpoint, it would still enhance Yao consciousness in the local community.

The Seemingly Weakened Yao Identity

The state-promoted discourse on development and the introduction of markets into the local communities affect the way the Yao people view themselves. Helping-the-Poor projects can make the people living in poverty feel that they are culturally inferior. As long as poverty is considered to bring a negative image, leaving the mountains, their homes, or the Yao communities seems to be a rational solution to escape inferiority. In this regard, the Yao people's sense of inferiority is not different from poor Han communities, except that the latter do not associate their ethnicity to inferiority. However, the desire to leave the mountains or their homes does not necessarily lead to a weakened ethnic identity in the long run. A case study of ethnic Dong immigrants in coastal cities suggests that these originally Hunanese mountain villagers pay more attention to ethnic festivals while working in Wenzhou, Zhejiang. Taking advantage of the Internet, ethnic college students are able to install Web sites that bear their ethnic consciousness. In the short run, though, those eager to meet the state-provided criterion of the modern citizen might want to escape their local, ethnic identity. Indeed, Yao college students who have already left Jinxiu rarely return.

Most Yao children are more or less exposed to national television programs. This is why they are able to understand Mandarin, even though they only speak the local Yao dialect at home. Young Yao people like those in other areas greatly enjoy pop songs and are even able to sing Taiwanese songs. In contrast, the Yao culture is not economically useful. In the past, young people volunteered to do a cultural performance. Today, however, most would expect some monetary return. Once relocated with their families outside the mountains, the young people quickly adapt to the popular culture. For instance, according to the Helping-the-Poor office, the six hundred villagers who were successfully relocated in 2002 now allegedly live well as immigrants.[17]

A schoolteacher takes a very negative attitude toward the Yao identities.[18] He said that all Yao communities have adopted the Han culture, so it no longer makes sense to claim the Yao identity. He also believes that the

Yao costume has begun to disappear. In the near future, no one would be able to make them any longer, he says. Currently, the Yao costume in each household was made by the mother in an earlier generation. According to his observation, no mother makes a Yao costume for her child today. Children have no Yao costumes for the spring festival unless their grandmothers are willing to make them. In some cases, however, children do not want to wear the costumes. The same teacher criticizes that the Yao festival has lost its ethnic characteristics. This is because there are too many Yao dialects, though no written language exists. For this reason, the tradition most likely might cease to continue without a written record to support it. Furthermore, in his neighborhood alone, there are parents who refuse to speak Yao to their children to make sure that the children speak fluent Mandarin.

Some schoolteachers have in their minds the mission to carry and promote the Yao tradition. In one conversation, they all agree that they need a basketball court urgently for the sake of physical education. Suddenly, one teacher recalls the idea of producing a set of Yao costumes for the children. This did not happen due to the lack of funding. Thus, when participating in competitions, Yao children would usually wear costumes their mothers prepared for them, which invariably comes in a variety of makes. Because of this, they often receive deductions as penalty for not having a complete uniform as a group.

According to a retired professor, a Jinxiu Yao's ethnic consciousness is much weaker than that of an American Yao.[19] The Yao immigrated to the United States about ninety years ago, with the fear of being "swallowed by the Americans." They thus struggled to keep the Yao language and customs alive, to the point of having Yao language classes for their children every week. Another retired Yao professor feels sad about receiving an American Yao to her town. She added that there will be no Chinese Yao in the future. The Yao nationality will exist only in the museum three hundred years from now, the professor says.

The former professor analyzes that the escape from Yao consciousness often results in self-pity. Yao people are afraid of being despised; this is why they want to hide their Yao identity. The same analysis may be gathered when interviewing officials of the Helping-the-Poor campaign. The Yao people refuse to leave the mountains, according to this logic, because they have no confidence in their ability to adapt to new environments. Moreover, a Yao priest believes this sense of inferiority has to do with the state's propaganda against superstition, as if all Yao customs are backward and feudal. Young people who were born after 1950 have had no chance at practicing Yao customs. Their negative attitude toward their parents' customs is the result of a political construction. The reason why Yao people, especially those cadres working for the state, try to get away from their Yao identities is to escape an inner sense of inferiority.[20]

The negative attitude toward one's own ethnic identities is not the same with weakened identities. If the identities were weakened, the need to hide would decrease. In any case, the loss of language, costume, and custom do not mean the end of the Yao identity. It can still be reproduced through some other mechanisms in the future.

Revived Yao Identities

Local Yao living customs are distinctive. Note the special diet of salted raw pork and baked capercaillie. Outsiders find difficulty adapting to these eating habits. However, catching capercaillies is also an environmental issue to the local people. Similarly, the technique of salting raw pork might seem easy, but for the Yao, it is a practice that needs to be respected. The survival of the local Yao identity depends on many of these local customs, which the state does not recognize. Also note that the nascent market for the Yao costume is way over the local capacity to supply. The aforementioned comment on mothers no longer making Yao costumes may also be correct when referring to handicraft. There is no guarantee that the development of tourism would not stimulate a different style of manufactured costume business.

The revival of religious activities is the most important sign of revived ethnic consciousness in Jinxiu. During the Cultural Revolution, ancestor worship continued in some villages. People did not practice it openly during the day, but still followed the procedure in a more simplified format during the evening. The two most important rituals are about one's funeral and manhood. The manhood ritual is for adolescents to caution them to abstain from their desire. Part of the ritual involves learning to read the Holy Bible. Rituals of this sort are conducted in Yao and are instrumental in the preservation of Yao consciousness. Ancestor worship associated with funerals should be more fundamental in this regard. Higher-level officials once commented that there are no religious activities going on in Jinxiu nowadays because only a few people still go to the temple. In actuality, it was precisely higher officials' religious engagement that bred the revival. Accordingly, the interviewed priest gives a completely different picture:

We believe that men have souls, so Yao people must have rituals of Dao. The priest performs for the living to watch. If the children of the dead do not invite the priest to comfort the soul of the dead, they feel uneasy inside. In 1958, this type of ritual was outlawed. In Jinxiu, people kept doing it during the evening despite the administrative order to ban it. Later, everything was confiscated. During the Cultural Revolution, all the Holy Bibles and the statues were confiscated. I returned from outside to find all these stuff still lying underneath some beds in the people's commune. I took them home to study. From 1985 onward, the ritual has returned. This proves that one extreme leads to another. The first one who openly and splendidly did it was the county official. Villagers saw him do it and they followed . . . 21

In the work of ethnic affairs, empathy is very important. When the policy and people's minds contradict, we are on the side of the idea as opposed to the material. We must acknowledge that there are superstitions in the Holy Bible to preserve materialism. However, we should also see that there are stories in the Bible that teach lessons similar to Confucianism and on how to be a benevolent person. The priest teaches the coming generations where they come from initially; they then view a big family picture and discuss the people in it. They also learn how their ancestors struggled to make their families grow.

In addition to religious rituals, the local scholars strive to prove that the Yao culture is not backward. One important cutting edge aspect that asserts the relatively advanced stage of Yao's history is the discovery of the institution of the village council and the village compact that the Ministry of Civil Affairs has promoted in the past decade, and that has had a long tradition in the Jinxiu communities. The Ministry of Civil Affairs claims that the institution of the village compact can be traced back to Wang Yangming, an official-scholar of the Ming Dynasty. The scholars in Jinxiu find that the institution of the stone compact was earlier than Wang Yangming. This initial conclusion was supported by the late Fei Xiaotong, the leading and the first scientific anthropologist of China. If Western scholars are at all interested in the institution of the village compact, Jinxiu should be the first to win recognition for being the most advanced.[22]

Indeed, it is most worthwhile to study the Yao culture in Jinxiu. Five different Yao divisions coexist in Jinxiu to give it the richest combination of the Yao culture. As scholars all over the world come to Jinxiu to study Yao, it is unlikely that the local community would continue to feel inferior. At the same time, the construction of Yao history is officially approved and is toward the demonstration of how Yao and the greater Chinese culture have mingled. The triad discourse of internationalization, acculturation to Han, and the rising Yao consciousness contradicts the stereotyped assumption that these three should be in conflict.

Not surprisingly, one's Yao identities cannot be easily forgotten. Those who shy away from the Yao identity become more conscious of it. The aforementioned school leader, for one, mentions repeatedly how Yao people would do things to discredit his earlier claim that one no longer presents one's Yao identities. For example, forgetting that girls have a more serious attendance problem, he insists that in Yao communities, the two genders are treated more equally than in Han communities. His evidence is that Yao men need to save more money than a typical Han before a girl would marry him. He also finds good sense in Yao mentality, for example, when an elder Yao would not allow all his children to leave home. It is Yao custom that at least a boy must stay to help prevent the old parent from being taken advantage of. Yet, this does not demonstrate how distinctive the Yao culture is. Rather, it is the claim that Yao culture is distinctive that matters to the revival of Yao consciousness. His claim that very few mothers still make costumes camouflages the fact that his mother still makes Yao costumes.

Conclusion

How and what ethnic people mean to the state and how the state means to ethnic people are two subjects worthy of research for both political scientists and anthropologists. In the case of Jinxiu, those officials who act in the name of the state, allocate resources, and formulate policies reduce ethnic communities to their performance on some universalist criteria. In their official capacity, they care most about how local cadres successfully develop the local economy and recruit the local children to attend school. History shows that some of these attitudes have transformed the local communities toward directions that were jettisoned later on. In particular, the Yao communities have been unable to present their suffering with the state in accordance with the universalist criteria. The state is becoming a hegemonic discursive system since it is ontologically prior to local ethnic communities.

On the other hand, Jinxiu communities show some agency for social change so that Yao officials do not become helplessly loyal to the state. Once in a while, they act outside of their official capacity. All kinds of seemingly trivial activities and ideas outside of the state reproduce the Yao identities and reframe the Yao's image. It is undeniable that a sense of inferiority motivates some Yao to shy away from home or their ethnic identities. At the same time, however, every occasion such as the promulgation of Three Represents, the once-gone religious ritual, the return of an American Yao, and the Helping-the-Poor project that distracts the state from cultural areas can be serviceable to the revival of Yao identities. Cadres that carry Yao identities will play an important role when they decide to take sides between the universalist state and the distinctive ethnic representation. They cannot act consistently as one or together all the time. Therefore, the state that they represent cannot monopolize the meaning of being Yao.

CHAPTER 12

Learning to Be Rational: Peasants' Responses to Marketization in Fenghuang

The Rational Peasant and the Moral Peasant

How rational peasants are, as opposed to their concern over justice and moral duty, is a long-standing issue of debate.[1] It is no surprise that the market reform in China since 1979 has incurred similar discussions on the rational peasant.[2] To what extent peasants are economically rational affects the judgment as to what motivates their seemingly social behavior. On one hand, there is the view that rational peasants continue to participate in the collective economic entity in order to avoid the risk of uncertainty generated by the arrival of the market economy.[3] From the rational peasant point of view, therefore, collectivism does not explain peasant behavior. It is an outcome rather than a cause that is to be explained by peasants' rational calculation. Collectivism is the condition of production to which peasants willingly subscribe to defend competition.

There is, however, the alternative view that collectivism means much more than a risk-sharing mechanism to peasants. Accordingly, social relationships mean different things to moral peasants. While the quest for profit that promotes participation in the market appears to be the goal, this should not overshadow the greater need for a social identity, which supports the sense of belonging as well as duty, or the greater anxiety toward the lack of just distribution. Although the profit incentive clearly exists, the profit is not the ultimate purpose. In brief, profit-driven behavior is a way of being social in the age of reform, so some sacrifice of personal or familial profit is always necessary to reconfirm one's identity in the collective life of the village.[4] Here, collectivism is a cause, not an outcome.

Each view portrays peasants in its specific ontology, with the first view treating peasants as self-centered, profit-maximizing beings and the second as other-oriented, morally dutiful social beings. This ontological difference pits the two views against each other. The first view draws on profit-driven behavior, which emerged after the market mechanism was introduced to the village. In addition to the rationalist interpretation of the productive relationship under the historical arrangement with landlords, this view explains the self-interested adjustment in peasant behavior during marketization. The second view depends on the stable social and reciprocal commitment more clearly before marketization than after, to show the subtle continuation of collective life. Could these two modes of ontology coexist? Or is it necessary that the economic, individualist ontology substitute the social, collective ontology in modern times?

This book presents a third view, exploring the symbiosis of the rational and the moral peasants. This means that peasants are able to shift from being rational individuals to being social beings, and vice versa, in responding to contexts. There is no need for them to choose between the two modes of existence most of the time, and when they do have to choose, there is no rule to constrain them from making a different choice of one over the other should the same situation take place again.

Since central authorities advocate market competition and profit-driven calculation, anyone who subscribes to collectivism must do so. To the extent that competing in the market is a response to the call of moral leaders in the center, to be rational in the market is at the same time to be social. Recall the example given in the introduction of this book, whereby restaurant owners refuse to charge villagers. This social behavior in the village is concomitant to the profit-driven behavior facing outside tourists. In other words, modern history does not have to be linear, but cyclical, so that marketization allows social needs other than driving for profit to intervene in reform from time to time at those points not to be anticipated in advance.

This chapter studies how the rational ontology, together with the moral ontology, makes village life sensible to peasants involved in marketization. The methodology of the book draws from cultural studies to the extent that the book places the origin of knowledge in peasants' practice as well as the interpretation of their positioning between the two modes of ontology, away from any external, analytical law of behavior.

Cultural studies provide a clue to the third approach that is in between the rational and the moral peasants. Scholars of cultural studies critically reflect upon the role of scholarship in the introduction of the market under their study. In the long run, the knowledge generated by scholars affects not only the choice of rationalist reference for self-judgment in the village but also the production of future scholarship. According to cultural studies, knowledge is not a medium between scholars and peasants under study. Academic knowledge hooks up the world of behavior to the identity of scholars in the name of scientific laws or principles through which peasants are able to achieve representations. Scholars teach the world about market rationality while at the same time studying the peasants who survive marketization, to the effect that their study is a self-study in a sense. Scholars and peasants thus become mutually constituted identities.

Accordingly, to judge peasants against the institutional reform that provides the profit-driven incentives mistakenly reproduces the image of the "naturalness" of such reform. Peasants have had no access to policy making that brings marketization. They therefore need quick and easy concepts to expedite and ease in the unavoidable adjustment that reform calls for. Scholarship incorporates peasant responses to marketization, which it shapes by spreading new concepts through policy documents or the mass media. Far from being natural, the new concepts demand drastic changes to the extent that they specifically ask the peasants to jettison certain ways of life, which are now called old customs.

Note that these old customs testify to a shared culture between reform scholars and peasants to make the call for changes meaningful to both. However, this shared culture likewise leaves room for peasants to give a different, moral reading to reform. Since such a reading does not comply with the identity of reform scholars, it escapes their attention.

Reform in the village is no longer faithfully celebrated, nor is it reconfirmed as promoted by scholars. How extensive peasants' rationale is under marketization is therefore not as relevant as how frequently it is applied. This is why this chapter would depend on peasants as sources of knowledge on reform, assuming that they, instead of pre-determined scientific laws of behavior, are the forces to choose between the two modes of ontology under the circumstances.

Logically inconsistent modes of ontology are layers added to peasants, making logical inconsistency irrelevant in their daily lives. To expand the category of peasants by including peddlers, cooperatives and agricultural companies, workers in the village, cadres, and dwellers in or even next to agricultural areas[5] greatly enriches the variety of possibilities concerning strategic decisions on one's choice of ontology in each different specific context. Villages and small cities surrounded by them share many social norms or mutual role expectations, obscuring the distinction between the peasants and those who are not and hence exposing the undecidable positioning of everyone between the two modes of ontology. In fact, at the center, the debate on anti-poverty policy sends the message of peasants and scholars' mutual constitution. How much commitment the Party should have toward the welfare of peasants as collective or individual peasants in extreme poverty is constantly a question that periodically interferes with the self-knowledge of the Party. Once marketization defines the Party, the strategic adaptation that shuns market competition might challenge the identity of the Party and those who study the peasants.

The thinking at the center used to be that the anti-poverty policy ought to enable peasants to profit from the market. In practice, anti-poverty has been more of a temporary relief from living conditions. Since the beginning of this century, the Party has been deciding that fighting poverty in the village must be the priority. The past emphasis on infrastructure proves insufficient in dealing with natural disasters or a backward culture in the village. The new leadership thus considers it critical that villagers develop a profiting capacity in the market. However, the villages usually lack such competitive consciousness. Helping-the-Poor teams sent to villages often complain that the stupidity of peasants impedes any effort at marketization.[6]

Some peasants are nonetheless successful in the market. They become the models of success. Many cadres and rich peasants feel that competitive consciousness is most important in their adaptation to competition. Their feeling implies that penetrating the market is a matter of learning a new game, not the emancipation of human nature from any institutional bondage. Rationality is an initially learned responsibility—it is not a given.

The following discussion relies on Helping-the-Poor team cadres and poor villagers in the ethnic Western Hunan County of Fenghuang to gather data and information regarding peasant rationality. The current chapter argues that there is no set law governing the choice between the rationalist ontology and the moralist ontology. The situation in which the specific peasants consider themselves involves allusions to the type of ontology on which they base their existence. Social relationships continue to constrain peasants' choice, while the newly imposed citizens' duty about reform complicates their interpretation of the situation. Peasants develop a range of responses to the expectations of marketization, suggesting that rational behavior can be learned. However, this learned behavior does not dictate how a particular peasant utilizes a specific situation to profit, nor predict how the same peasant might give up profit opportunities for the reproduction of other social relationships. In other words, entering the market is not any promise of linear staging.

Western Hunan is a nationally designated poor area. For the purpose of writing this book, visits to Western Hunan numbered more than eight times. This chapter draws particularly from the field research in Fenghuang, which is the capital county of Western Hunan Prefecture. Specifically, the trips to mountain villages included visits to Dawan Village of Guanzhuang Township and Kerong Village of Laer Mountain Township. The cadres interviewed came from the Office of United Front, the Office of Helping-the-Poor and Development, and Helping-the-Poor teams. They explained what they thought of profiting, from which this chapter infers why rationality is a learned culture and entering the market is a conscious choice, which is not to be narrated away from the concrete context of the choice.

The Helping-the-Poor Campaign in Fenghuang

The campaign against poverty began in Western Hunan in 1986. The campaign is in its third stage following the first two from 1986–1994 and 1994–2000. As of 2005, there remains a population of 750,000 in poverty. Of these, about 600,000 have an annual income below the poverty line of RMB880, and about 150,000 live in extreme poverty with an annual income of less than RMB625. About 85 percent of the villages have paved roads in the village area. All the neighborhoods that host a village council have electricity, and 95 percent of them have a minimal, though unsteady, supply of drinking water.

The Prefecture government guarantees a minimum of 0.4 acre of cultivable field free from the threat of flood or drought for each household. This is 0.1 acre short of the benchmark of 0.5 acre that the central government has set. The estimated annual income is intriguing in that it is potential income rather than real income. Since the peasants included in this study do not always sell their products, the income is the estimated revenue of crops if all are sold, including food stuff from the guarantee field, all the crops from other household land pieces, and the increase in livestock from the previous year.

Human judgment intervenes in the estimate of annual income everywhere in the process, making poverty hardly an objective condition. Crops such as older generations of corn that the state discourages are often not counted to make peasants appear poorer than they actually are. On the other hand, losses caused by price change or the low quality of electricity supply are beyond control, making peasants poorer than they appear.

Investments in infrastructure, such as roads, usually last only a short while as villagers are unable to maintain them. Most of these intra-village roads are short-lived because the collective fund of the village is rarely sufficient to sustain maintenance efforts. Marketization exacerbates the situation by dividing the previously public land, thus breaking productive teams into uncoordinated households. Consequently, the collective leadership and party organization collapse. Moreover, the historical practice of compulsory working days is no longer enforceable. As flood easily washes away the pavement, the lack of workers who are willing to remedy the situation in time renders the condition of the road even worse than trails.

The report of the local government to the superior on the campaign against poverty seldom mentions the failure with regard to infrastructure maintenance. The campaign does not begin from the poorest area anyway. Idiosyncratic factors influence where the campaign funds go—to those villages that are relatively geographically accessible, where there is the potential for profitable business, whose cadres actively strive for it or are socially well connected, and where the local authority can promise a supplementary investment.

In Western Hunan Prefecture, the Helping-the-Poor campaign includes four categories. In addition to infrastructure building, the other three are business development, occupational education, and export of labor. The purpose of business development is to establish a few major profitable products that can enhance market consciousness in the region. Over a decade of investment has witnessed success in marketing three major products— oranges, tobacco, and kiwi. The production of oranges in Western Hunan takes up to 10 percent of the total national production, occupying 13 percent of all the land for orange production in China. (Western Hunan is now called "the Hometown for Orange.")

Kiwi production is the result of research at the local ethnic Jishou University, and it is primarily processed into juice. Tobacco used to be the important source of tax revenues for the prefecture before the national campaign against smoking was introduced. Raising swine, oxen, and goats, the value of which reaches 13 percent of total agricultural products, and Chinese medicine have begun to replace tobacco as revenue makers.

The educational campaign is unique to the extent that it is not related to schooling in the pedagogical system. The major part of educational Helping-the-Poor project targets peasants, to bring them new technology or new crops. Each village now has two to three technicians. The same campaign also targets the school system by combining the more remote and smaller ones into larger compounds in order to cope with the drop of population due to birth control. The bolder part of this reshuffling is to transform all the classes above the third grade into boarding school. The most unique dimension of the educational Helping-the-Poor campaign, which began in 2003, aims at exporting labor.

In light of the large volume of workers from Western Hunan emigrating to coastal cities, the prefecture government launched a search for potential brokers who can provide a few months of training to middle-school graduates and place each of them into a job afterwards. Their educational level is so low, however, that to expect them to contribute to the family income is not realistic. In other words, this dimension of the Helping-the-Poor campaign does not aim to improve economic conditions. Rather, for these emigrants who are eighteen to thirty years old, the purpose is to reduce the demand for food at home. Over one thousand laborers were exported in the first year, and over six thousand in 2005.

The major research site for this chapter is Fenghuang County, under whose jurisdiction are thirty-one townships administrating 345 villages. The total agricultural population is 340,000, of which 69 percent are ethnic Miao. In 1986, Fenghuang was designated as a poor county at the provincial level. Since 2002, it has been in that state. There are 160 designated poor villages. Some 160,000 people are estimated to be living in extreme poverty.

The Office of Helping-the-Poor and Development opened in 1987 in order to enhance the Helping-the-Poor consciousness of the prefecture officials through on-the-job training, ad-hoc task forces, and short-term rustication. For the poor peasants, the Office provides technology training and introduces techniques in crop cultivation. The rationale of these training programs is to ameliorate the so-called culture of poverty of both officials and peasants.

Along the same line, the Office believes it is imperative to be strict on birth control in order to improve the quality of education in the future. In recent years, the Office has spent much effort on ecological education, hoping to transform all the low-producing fields into forests. The compensation that peasants receive for losing fields can become the initial investment in most profitable businesses.

The other functions of the Office include the typical construction of infrastructure, such as road paving, and electricity and water supply. In 2003, the prefecture celebrated its "grand" achievement of supplying electricity to all villages under its jurisdiction. (As of 2005, however, 240 villages have never had any access to roads.)

The Office also promotes economic crops such as orange and shaddock, developing over ten thousand acres for each type of crop. In addition, the Office identifies sale dealers and holds promotional fairs. Most importantly, the Office has intensified efforts to persuade peasants into cultivating the same crops that once faced the price drop crisis. To discourage poor peasants from abusing government investment, the Office now demands that the village provide at least 60 percent of the initial investment. On the other hand, with the mandate given by the superior government, the Office is responsible for making sure that funds allocated for helping the poor are not spent for other emergency uses.

Is Culture a Solution to Poverty?

The prefecture regards ethnic Miao culture as a point of fighting poverty. The construction of ethnic image depends greatly on the image of permissiveness. This means that culture and nature are not separable in Western Hunan. Though economically poor, Fenghuang is fortunately endowed with resources for ethnic tourism. Neighboring Zhangjiajie, an ethnic Tujia and Miao area, is a designated natural reserve. In the prefecture, there is the Xiaoxi natural reserve, another national reserve. Old town images of Wangcun Township regularly attract movie producers and photographers. Mengdong River drifting is among the designated sites of great interest to Olympic and aspiring athletes. However, the prefecture government considers its ethnic component as its most important attraction.

To cash in on ethnic tourism, the prefecture wants to minimize pollution as much as possible. Former Premier Zhu Rongji promised to restore Western Hunan forests to their once lush state. Again, this involves education initiatives. In contrast, Fenghuang County does not seem as interested in linking tourism to Helping-the-Poor, since major tourist sites in Fenghuang are far from the poor villages in remote mountains. The only benefit of tourism to poor villages in Fenghuang is improved sales of organic vegetables.

Specifically, Dawan Village of Guanzhuang Township has successfully been recovering from poverty. It is now well known for having established a cooperative of production and sale. When the Office of Helping-the-Poor and Development first brought the orange plan to the village and promised to invest, village cadres and party members had to take the lead as models for other generally conservative villagers. The county director moved to the village to persuade each village settlement to grow one common crop. The Office now offers four items for development—fruits, vegetables, pasturage, and Chinese medicine. Dawan decided to harness existing resources by cultivating orange trees. Once the average income rose above RMB850, Dawan began its experiment by organizing a cooperative that then independently chose its own crops.

In comparison, Laer Mountain Township did not have any economic projects, but since the last visit in 2001, it has successfully implemented an English training program which opens up new career possibilities for students. In Kerong village, the introduction of Golden Jade [jinyu] flower planting has begun to improve the residents' average income. However, most villagers remain economically unprepared to raise funds for the new crop project.

Prefecture officials are generally critical of the peasants' conservative mentality. In the past the local government, for political and bureaucratic reasons, indiscriminately mobilized the peasants into growing new crops only to end in failure. These past experiences hurt government credit. County officials similarly complain about the peasants' lack of cultural quality. Interestingly, they all hope that tourism, which brings in visitors from other parts of the country, will help in enhancing the culture of local peasant workers. Their effort to expand satellite television coverage is aimed at importing new cultural shows through channeled programs. Implicit in their remarks is that the culture they favor is primarily commercial or market oriented. This is how the short-term job training of junior high or occupational junior high graduates makes sense to them. The training should make them more competitive once they arrive in coastal cities. Nine companies have signed contracts with the prefecture government to recruit over fifty thousand laborers.

The government believes that the traditional thinking that only college education counts is not appropriate for local conditions. Parents do not invest in elementary education because they do not think their children can reach college level and, therefore, would rather stay in the mountains. Short-term job training for junior high graduates is now a short route to escape mountain life for the younger generations. Hopefully, parents will willingly begin to invest in education. Equally important is the hope of the government that these emigrant workers will eventually return home to bring new cultures to their respective hometowns.

"Cultural" renovation has been a continuing concern of local officials. The Associate Director of the Prefecture Office of United Front traces the line back to Deng Xiaoping's policy of openness to the outside world. He is confident that once students are out there, they will acquire new thinking, new concepts, and new ways of doing things and bring them home. Through this, the export of labor can ultimately be a way of enhancing culture at home.

A new project that recruits junior high graduates exclusively from the poorest villages began in 2005. The free training runs from three to six months. The fact is that all the success the prefecture has so far had in attracting outside investments has something to do with the feedback of those who have their hometowns in the prefecture. This is more a matter of hometown nostalgia than economic rationality. Similarly, despite the reality that most emigrant workers barely survive the labor market in coastal cities and do not send money back, early emigrants are always the brokers for latecomers in finding employment.

Social networking is a condition of export of labor without which latecomers might not even know there are such job opportunities. The national government decides that emigrant workers should be allowed to stay where they work if they choose. This has opened up a new channel of the Helping-the-Poor campaign. Simply moving to the cities and not returning when getting old is a way to relieve the burden of production at home.

The cultural dimension of labor export is different from that of tourism, with the former assuming local culture is too poor to support marketization, while the latter acknowledges that the local culture is attractive and economically exploitable. Through exchange, the ethnic culture that supports tourism is instrumental in introducing the new market culture brought to Fenghuang by tourists.

Since the function of ethnic culture is to attract a higher market culture and not to have merits of its own, local communities might gradually lose confidence in their own culture. One Miao lady, for example, who dresses in exotic Miao clothing and sells mineral water to tourists, ironically appeals not because of her ethnic attraction but because of her old age in exchange for sympathizers' attention. Nevertheless, ethnicity seems exploitable so that the three historical names that came from Fenghuang—Shen Congwen, the novelist; Xiong Xiling, the premier of Republican China; and Huang Yongyu, the artist—all have memorial homes. However, the tour guides know little about their respective careers and are more interested in selling souvenirs. The images of Miao women are on commercial display everywhere to be consumed freely in order to attract buyers of products carrying their images. Local culture is no more than an instrument to attract a "higher" market culture, while local officials understand that market culture involves the willingness to take some risk and to make money. Below the prefecture level, however, few Fenghuang officials speak on the overall orientation toward cultural renovation as their prefecture superiors do. They instead concentrate on cultural renovation at the village level.

After Fenghuang witnessed what the prefecture officials called the turnover of heaven and earth to become rich overnight, due to the influx of tourists, the neighboring township of Yongshun was reduced to the poorest region. Yongshun's strategy is to promote ecological Helping-the-Poor campaigns (see Chapters 3 and 6). It offers all sorts of policy incentives as well as disincentives to lure peasants into the project, for example, transforming the rice fields into woods or building a marsh gas tank from animal excrement so that the peasants no longer need to cut trees. At the same time, the Yongshun government closed down Yongshun Tobacco to control its pollution that is incompatible with ecological tourism.

The peasants appear backward because they resist marketization. However, many have responded actively, although not necessarily compliantly. In fact, neither rational ontology nor moral ontology denies peasants' agency for adaptation. Western Hunan officials have resorted to a great deal of face-to-face persuasion, policy incentives, and modeling by village cadres and administrative mobilization to increase the willingness of peasants to make investments in new crops. Peasant investors do not have enough savings. They rely on bank loans to take advantage of policy incentives. The risk thus incurred and which causes concern is not always market uncertainty. In fact, bad petty loans due to failure in the market are common in villages all over China. This is because the borrowers are often members of the village council; individual peasant households do not bear the risk directly. In Fenghuang, however, the Office of Helping-the-Poor and Development arranges for bank loans directly to benefit households. How has this arrangement affected the risk culture in the village?

In Kerong Village, there is a peasant who was granted a loan of RMB3,000 to clear the field where golden jades were cultivated. His family did not have enough rice fields, especially after newborns arrived. To participate in the golden jade project, in which seeds were supplied free, was his choice. What if his investment failed? His answer was simply that failure was the mother of success, so he would try again. He did not consider the risk of borrowing, which his neighbors refused to take. To improve his chances in the market, he did his homework. He went with the village director when the latter paid a learning visit to a neighboring community that was already cultivating golden jades. The interview took place in the second year of his investment. He hired a teacher from Fenghuang. It is not clear if the peasant interviewed was as much concerned with the risk in the market as with the unfamiliarity of the crop. Village cadres who invested first to assume political leadership also suggest that market risk is not the highest concern. However, if the investment failed either due to market uncertainty or lack of timely support from the government, even cadres would begin to resist further investment. Before failure, the peasants are not necessarily conservative.

Kerong is different from Dawan in the sense that Kerong's village director interpreted his own leadership differently. He had committed to a field of ten acres, ranking behind at least twenty other households. He invested much less than he had wanted because he was afraid that if he became rich too soon, his villagers would talk behind his back to make him lose legitimacy. He felt he should not be at the forefront. He reported that it was his villagers who pushed him to apply for the government project. A few households in his village nevertheless passed up the offer because, he explained, they did not have enough laborers at home. His explanation is problematic because one could always get a loan to hire laborers. The problem probably is that these households did not know how to manage the investment. In comparison, neighboring Dawan Village did not take advantage of the government offer in the beginning. In Dawan, the government persuaded the village director into investing in the new crop. His personal success later encouraged other villagers to follow suit.

While Dawan villagers responded to the government promotion much more slowly, some agency for change nonetheless picked up the momentum later. First of all, the retired village director is still active in bringing new technology. He emphasizes innovation and feels he is responsible for keeping his villagers updated. A breakthrough in organization took place in 2003 when a village cooperative's production and sale emerged. The new village director incidentally learned this type of organization when he negotiated for a bank loan in another village. He then did some research on cooperative management in magazines and newspapers. The village once tried to establish a company but failed due to lack of funding. This time, the cooperative had been a success. In 2004, the sale price of the same crop from Dawan fetched the highest prices in the country. The cooperative looks strong in the market, but it is based on the members' ability to fulfill their moral obligations.

The initial purpose of setting up the cooperative is not to negotiate a better price. It is primarily a production cooperative to organize individual peasant households into coming up with one standardized product to meet the demand of buyers. For individual procurers, joining the cooperative restrains their competitive relationship and alters their individualized productive habits. However, the establishment of the cooperative interestingly involved neither calculation by the individual villagers nor tedious negotiation. It was simply the decision making of the cadres to be followed by the trustful peasants. Accordingly, peasant cadres are rational, while peasant villagers are moral. Note that the cadres are rational in a peculiar way in the sense that their calculation attends to the village as a whole. Collectivism is hardly just an outcome in their way of being rational.

Profit consciousness is nonetheless clear on all the calligraphic works hanging in the cooperative office. Alongside profit consciousness is ancestor consciousness. The major one in the center reads: "Piling gold to exceed Dipper North, saving jade to cover Mountain South." Other examples include "Gold oven keeps fire for a thousand years, jade lamp brightens light for ten thousand ages"; "Newly lit incense thrives for a thousand years, long established heaven and earth prospers for ten thousand generations"; "Great happiness and fortune where there is no taboo in hundred matters in heaven, earth, yin, yang, year, month, day, and hours"; and "Heavenly respect and happiness for ancestors." Note that the expression of no taboo in several matters shows a strong attitude for reform, suggesting ancestors would not oppose the change, which will bring happiness back to ancestors. The change is obviously about the transformation of the rice fields into golden jade fields and is related to the productive function instead of the sale function.

The cooperative is at the same time a social organization that enforces disciplined cooperation among its members. The fifth item of the eighth clause stipulates that "members should not engage in activities that result in competition with the cooperative or that is detrimental to its interests." No member should supply to any other buyers or cooperatives. There is also a verbal consensus that if there should be anyone violating the rules, "other cooperative members could throw all his/her oranges into the rivers."

Similarly, the second item of the eighth clause requires the members to protect the interests and common assets of the cooperative. According to the ninth clause, when a peasant asks to withdraw, he or she is not entitled to his or her share in the cooperative or any part of the common asset of the cooperative. These rules imply that membership is an equally important value as compared to profit making. The cooperative and the members are not equal. Discipline is more important than the property rights of the members.

Although the cooperative is not a stringent requirement of the government, the Office of Helping-the-Poor and Development supports it. The peasants demonstrate that they are able to further protect collective interests by setting up the cooperative, which is not totally strange to them anyway since the cooperative used to be everywhere before reforms were instituted. The cooperative can coordinate enough producers to supply for difficult buyers who could order oranges in one size in a large amount.

The cooperative can also promote sales on the Internet to attract trade companies. The cooperative even provides after-sales service to deal with unsatisfied customers. Neighboring villages willingly join the cooperative, even though this means giving up the right to participate in cooperative decision-making.

Helping-the-Poor officials at the county level report an unexpected cultural development along with the rise of cooperative culture. For example, Dawan has established a music band. During the Dragon Boat Festival, for another example, a dragon boat team was organized through a fund raising effort, which collected RMB6,000. Dawan became the first team that did not represent a government branch but won the first prize.

Dawan also lends its expertise to help surrounding villages establish a ginger cooperative, a tree seed cooperative, and a kiwi cooperative. A total of 150 female peasants are also sent to neighboring provinces to teach productive technology, for an average income of RMB5,000.

Unlike other villages in Western Hunan where export of labor is an important source of income, Dawan villagers do not choose to work in coastal cities. One successful emigrant worker once offered an annual income of RMB50,000 to attract villagers to emigrate unsuccessfully.

Similarly in Laershan High School is the evolution of agency for change as a response to the external Helping-the-Poor project. Here is a unique project, sponsored by a foundation based in Taiwan, to support English education. In 2002, a seed fund of RMB25,000 from the foundation started the change. The school used a small portion of the fund to buy audio facilities and pedagogical tapes. Other parts of the fund have supported English teachers to take part in prefecture-level training or more advanced training programs in Shanghai. One of these teachers became the school principal in 2003. He designed a series of pedagogical reforms regarding English classes because English used to be the weakest pedagogical point in school. This changed dramatically in 2003.

First of all, there have been English-speaking and -listening contests, as well as conversation contests. Students have taken over a local channel to broadcast English programs. The principal feels that the teachers have shown a level of interest in their teaching that has never been seen before. Students have reported that improved English capacity helped their placement after graduation. All in all, three teachers each won an award from the provincial government for their research and writing on English teaching. Likewise, five students won an award in either a prefecture or county English competition. Most importantly, one student won a national award for English speaking and listening. Not only has Laer Mountain School never reached this level in its English teaching before, but no other subject has ever recorded such achievement. The school was ranked seventh in English teaching at the county level in 2004, up from its fifteenth place in 2002.

Apparently, historical or cultural contexts do not constrain the peasants from rationally calculating how to enhance their interests. However, this conclusion tells little about those villagers who do not respond to policy incentives provided by the government. Moreover, other villagers who have responded positively have done so in a variety of ways and at different timings. Dawan peasants who did not respond actively in the beginning, for example, were not sensitive toward the difference in price between orange and rice. In comparison with Dawan's development of a cooperative culture, individual villagers in Kerong differ from each other in their willingness to borrow a loan to begin the investment. In comparison, Helping-the-Poor cadres appear less active. For example, the cadres always complained about the lack of support from the superior government, meaning the money given was insufficient.

All of the interviewed government officials stress the achievement of specific villages or villagers while acknowledging that the overall situation remains serious. The basic-level cadres, however, criticize that the officials "tend to mistake policy goals for policy achievement." The diagnosis at the township level or below is invariably that the government should reallocate a bigger budget to the responsible villages, which are poorer than those who have received help. Likewise, for the Office of Helping-the-Poor and Development, the bottom line is that the superior government should give more, suggesting there is little to improve in terms of administration, or concrete strategy to cope with poverty.

It is the peasants in the field who are able to grasp policy incentives. A county official finds that the village leadership plays a critical role in determining the fate of the Helping-the-Poor campaign in each locality. A village director or a village party secretary must try to organize peasants to take advantage of policy incentives. In Kerong, the settlement is located in a compound; therefore, it is easier for a village director to persuade villagers into trying new crops.

In Dawan, whose villagers are spread widely, personal influence becomes critical. Lately, the rise of the cooperative suggests that some social connection is useful to marketization, though at the expense of individual rights in the market. Peasants always seriously consider their relationship with other villagers to the extent that the Kerong director decides to invest less than what is wished. Nevertheless, poor peasants can face the uncertainty brought about by marketization. They might respond more comfortably as members of a cooperative.

Conclusion

To understand marketization necessarily enlists perspectives that are already influential before they are introduced. Some peasants refuse to respond positively. This suggests that economic rationality is a learned component. At the same time, those who respond must be making a choice that is based upon a sensible pre-marketization culture, which could be reliant on government instruction, the unreserved trust in village leaders, the membership in collective cooperative, and so on.

These culturally based perspectives enable peasants to each face the introduction of marketization differently, and because of the undecidability among these perspectives as well as their interpretation, peasants are responsible for their choice of strategic adaptation.[7] Few of these perspectives come from marketization, although they affect the ways the peasants respond to it. The knowledge concerning either peasant rationality/morality or marketization is thus generated by the actual responses that the specific peasants make. There is no epistemic need to prioritize rationality vis-à-vis morality.

After rationality and morality, there is a third approach to peasant politics—learning rationality in the context of morality. Senior government officials who see peasants as culturally backward come from a mixed mentality of what rationality definitely is and how rational a peasant should definitely be. Peasants' ability, as a whole, to respond in many different ways to the government's call for reform and marketization reduces the government's view of rationality to at most a relative, not universal, position. In this relative position, superior government officials have already been active in that they pick up their own village of origin to take care of first, rely on top-down administration to promote marketization, compel village cadres to be the first to take the market risk as a model for other villagers, praise the highly disciplined cooperative (as opposed to competitive) arrangement, allow only positive views toward marketization, take advantage of hometown networking in exporting labors to coastal cities, and stress the critical role of village leadership in facilitating marketization. All these sporadic yet ubiquitous comments and analyses demonstrate how much government officials, village cadres, and poor peasants share a pre-market or market-unrelated culture.

Toward the end of the chapter, the readers' attention should also be drawn to those who pursue their personal interests, however defined. For example, the collectivist style of the cooperative organization achieves a much better negotiation position on pricing; some peasants want to move beyond the limitation of farmland to experiment with profitable crops without too much risk concerns; a good many of peasant women leave home to teach new crops in exchange for monetary reward; conservative peasants refuse to face the uncertainty of new crops; English teachers actively upgrade the level of their teaching; the retired director continues to look for innovation in productivity; and junior high school graduates eagerly explore job opportunities in faraway cities.

It is simply not sufficient to portray peasants as moral beings. The evidence presented here shows such a complexity and variety of peasant response that not even theory in its classic form can capture. To choose between the rational peasant and the moral peasant might tear apart the peasant. Morality in terms of reproducing just, social relationships is not to have a fixed form of expression, but a constantly revisable one through the introduction of market rationality in terms of risk calculation, willingness to compete, and an avenue with which to utilize profit incentive.

Conclusion

From Unity to Harmony
—Progress or Regress?

The focus of this book is that the Chinese State reaches out to ethnic communities through three different channels of autonomy, ethnicity, and poverty. However, each of these channels designates a submissive position to ethnic citizenship. The institution of autonomy is the most effective among the three in the field experiences in co-opting ethnic officials and cadres. This is because the autonomous status assigns an unmistaken identity to the local community, whose leaders the state recruit to serve government positions as the role model of their respective ethnic group. Moreover, policy privileges that aim at economic development and political recognition are contingent upon the autonomous status. Every few years on the anniversary of the granting of autonomous status by central authorities, each autonomous jurisdiction holds celebration. It is not exaggerating at all to say that in China, autonomy and unity are symbiotic concepts in the official discourses on ethnic minorities.

The campaign to alleviate poverty is the least successful in incorporating local communities into the state's political economic arena. As noted throughout this book, transforming local communities into ones that are prepared for market competition requires a lot of persuasion and learning, which always begins by condemning the cultural backwardness of indigenous societies. The difficulty that villagers encounter in learning to be modern often confirms their inferior self-images. As a result, the backward images—together with doubtful results—take away the subjectivities critical for any indigenous participant to think and act assertively in the politico-economic arena of the state. Accordingly, seemingly dependent and lethargic villagers reproduce the self-perception of being backward. At times, their frustration even infects the perspectives of those Helping-the-Poor teams that supposedly came to ameliorate local conditions. Politically, almost everybody involved in anti-poverty campaigns must satisfy their superior at home with images of success and yet these images are hollow since mountain villagers are simply not ready for market competition. The result might be a rising sense of alienation not only in the poor villages but also in the teams.

Fortunately, however, the phenomena previously mentioned are not social science laws. Backward self-images might become useful in breeding a sense of difference in local communities, such as in Xiaoxi, where an indigenous ecological view embedded in the nascent ancestor consciousness has emerged to fault the external helpers. Luocheng community is, for another example, able to find motivation under the autonomy system, and participates actively in the state-granted destiny of modernization and unity, even if many of the state's endeavors have not been effective. The devotion and the result, which do not match each other, show the power of identity that is not connected to the rational calculation of interests. In yet another example, some Western Hunan villages in poverty remain mum about their life as Helping-the-Poor teams come and go. The image of their culpable dependency might ironically exempt them from further intrusion. Nevertheless, growing out of poverty as the central authorities define it might continue to be simultaneously an attractive end as well as a source of frustration to the villagers. Lastly, the status of poverty has aroused Baise officials' ethnic consciousness that does not directly respond to the state's anti-poverty agenda.

The major point of the book is that amidst theoretical uncertainty on how the state has affected local communities, ethnic minorities can develop subjectivity. Through this, they can sincerely participate in the state's policy agenda, conveniently incorporate the state into the ethnic identity, give feedback to the state within the framework of official discourse, or hide behind the state to evade ethnic identification. Rather than finding a life outside the state, the ethnic communities can, in one way or another, position themselves inside the state.

Together, the three discursive schemata represent ethnic communities, with autonomy and ethnicity directly related, and poverty indirectly related to the construction of identity. At least in one area, all three discourses meet. This is about tourism. In only one of the research sites of this book—Yizhou's Shui communities—there is never a lack of discussion on tourism. Devising and selling exotic ethnicities under the guise of tourism seem to be the quickest way of beating poverty to arrive at the end of autonomy, which is integration into the mainstream Chinese nation, politically and economically. Ethnic culture, once reduced to the targets of tourism, is not ethnic anymore except in name, hence, compliance with the end of integration and unity. Paradoxically, the quest for pseudo-authenticity under tourism might lead to further alienation from the local conditions, since authenticity has to be defined and understood in terms of the distance from Han. In this regard, authenticity continues to be an act of performance to be consumed by outsiders as well as emigrants, who suffer nostalgia for some original objects. In return, consumers offer monetary reward to the show of authenticity.

Since Helping-the-Poor programs are ethnicity-blind, neither the unexpected rise of local consciousness nor the adaptation of street-level Helping-the-Poor teams to the self-consciousness of the local communities has ever represented a politically sensitive issue. Regarding the other two schemata—autonomy and ethnicity—ethnic communities practicing similar policy agendas do not share any similar results. The state simply cannot determine whether or not a specific community takes national unity as a strategic tool for social and economic development, or a serious mission that establishes its own identity. Even in the latter case, unity means something quite different from what the central government has in mind. Unity is accordingly an identity strategy that enables an ethnic community to construct almost anything by either eyeing an external target, or alienating an internal self with legitimacy. Unity is thus more than an unwelcome pressure to generate loyalty. It can be a mask that protects the local communities from over-interference by a statist, nationalist, or any fundamentalist agenda. It can also be a foundation for those lost in the quest of modernity to regain a sense of selfhood either because the state recognizes their differences, albeit nominally, or because they believe they are among the legitimate representatives of the Chinese nation.

From the minority point of view, therefore, their adaptation to top-down discourses and practices of identity involves little sense of resistance. Would this lack of resistance meet the value of harmony that the new leadership in Beijing has been promoting hard since 2005? As General Secretary/President Hu Jintao and Premier Wen Jiabao have reiterated, domestic harmony is predicated upon the balanced distribution of wealth and income. The economic growth of ethnic communities is necessarily a critical element in the building of a harmonious society. The two leaders stressed repeatedly that a harmonious society should be one of balance and affluence.

Evidence suggests that the misdistribution of income takes place within ethnic communities as well as between these and non-ethnic communities.

Township governments continue to extract resources from villages despite the waiving of all the levies by the central government. Township governments now collect fines to meet the target revenue imposed by county governments. The more effective but less available way of achieving affluence is to sell village land to the investing enterprises. The result is general poverty accompanied by sporadic cases of fast enrichment, hence the rising sense of relative deprivation within each ethnic community, and the false appearance of growth in the eyes of superior authorities. This topic is worth another book to discuss. However, to grow ethnic communities into affluent societies is not going to result in harmony. If this book is right in pointing out the irony that to be grown into affluence can be at times a process of alienation for ethnic groups, the implication that they are culturally backward inevitably triggers those strategies that can compensate for deprived self-respect. These strategies are by no means resistant in characteristics; they are usually not harmonious in essence, either.

In this book, there are numerous reports in which the situations are already incompatible with the notion of harmony—Jing people in Dongxing use the Chinese state to discriminate the culturally intimate Vietnamese; Xiaoxi tour guides' distinguishable ancestor consciousness thrives on the state's ecological discourse; Baise officials long for a higher social status for their group and claim dignity not bestowed by the central authorities; and, Buyi scholars' genealogical narratives pretend authenticity that cannot be easily harmonized. Even the loss of sensitivity toward one's ethnic identity in Yizhou's sporadic Shui community might challenge the pursuit of harmony, since balanced distribution requires Shui as a category of comparison to sustain. Hu and Wen's harmony imposes a mission on the ethnic communities, assuming they all want growth and will willingly perform unity in exchange for both political recognition and economic opportunities. If they do not know how to perform unity, there are always programs such as those in Guilin to perform unity on behalf of ethnic groups. There is no exit because the central authorities tell them that they are too backward to know their future. This could be true, though, if marketization is the only way to move forward.

The lack of resistance in word and deed camouflages the potential conflict within the mindset of each villager in the mountains. While entering unity through growth is only a theory at best, it nonetheless creates pressure for ethnic groups to take a stand on whether or not to transform present conditions. To some extent, their harmonious interactions with Helping-the-Poor campaigners destroy their internal harmony, which is now torn among modernity, ethnicity, poverty, unity, and autonomy. This book records only a very small portion of the stories of the villagers' adaptation. Nonetheless, one shared message is clear—they are making choices all the time despite the fact that these choices may not always be conscious. However, judgment must have been executed when they develop perspectives on the state and form identity strategies accordingly to understand why and how they belong to a certain ethnic group, both together and separately. The sheer existence of room for choices suggests the impossibility of achieving total unity. This is because different people make different choices. The appearance of harmony can still hold since they articulate whatever their choices are only within the discursive context of autonomy, ethnicity, and poverty.

In brief, the idea of harmony should not require minority groups to make changes. Rather, all should learn to adjust in order to remain respectful to one another. In reality, however, the pressure to change is much higher under the rules of harmony than under the discursive regime of unity. Achieving minimal unity is relatively easier because as long as there is no overt resistance, unity holds. Furthermore, resistance could be handled through coercive as well as material incentives. In comparison, harmony is more of a psychological state that demands cognitive adjustment in order to enable everyone to tune in to each other. Harmony thus implies equality of some sort so that tolerance of differences would appear legitimate and just. As a result, minority groups would have to remain different in one way and reach equality in another. From Hu and Wen's understanding, it is the minority groups' identities that should remain different, while it is their income that should become more equal. While growth might obscure ethnicity, autonomy would be helpful in the maintenance of at least nominal ethnicity. On the other hand, autonomy is also the channel of subsidy to guarantee minimal growth. This leads to the conclusion that autonomy is conducive to harmony.

Harmony is a mixed blessing. To perform harmony is to abide by the law of modernization. There is a good deal of self-criticism and transformation to be carried out. To the extent that harmony should not force a common agenda of transformation, the internal pressure to make choices would easily result in a variety of strategies. In combination, these strategies disclose that the position of making judgment continues to be in the hands of minority groups, although the execution of judgment is always partial in light of the state intervention in one way or another. Harmony could still be a progressive state if unity ceased to be the exclusive condition of making choices, allowing autonomy to gain substance.

Notes

Chapter 1

1. For example, Jock Collins, *Migrant Hands in a Distant Land* (Sydney: Pluto Press, 1991); W. Kymlicka, *Multicultural Citizenship* (Oxford: Oxford University Press, 1995); M. Zhou, "Segmented Assimilation," *International Migration Review* 31, no. 4 (1997): 975–1008; Stephen Castles and Alastair Davidson, *Citizenship and Migration* (London: Routledge, 2000); George Borjas, *Friends or Strangers* (New York: Basic Books, 1990).
2. The rule was that the authors should write on ethnic issues relating to their own countries. This left four overseas experts on Chinese ethnicity with no position to report their research. Instead, they served as chairs or discussants. Except for these four, Chinese scholars or officials did the rest of the chairing and discussing. Columbia University and the Science and Technology University of Hong co-sponsored the Workshop. Professors Morriss Rosabbi and Barry Sautman together provided the initial list of overseas participants. The second and the third conferences were held in Uppsala, Sweden in 2003 and 2004, respectively. No Chinese official was present at these subsequent meetings except a secretary.
3. Wen Jing, "The History and Experiences of China's Ethnic Regional Autonomy," in *Proceedings of International Workshop on Regional Autonomy of Ethnic Minorities*, ed. n.a., 3 (Beijing: Publisher, 2001).
4. Wen, 3.
5. Luoshang Zunzhu, "Road to Success of Common Development and Prosperity," in *Proceedings of International Workshop on Regional Autonomy of Ethnic Minorities*, ed. n.a., 154 (Beijing: Publisher, 2001).
6. Yang Lianfu, "Brief Notes on the Guarantee Effect of the Ethnic Regional Autonomy System on the Local Economic and Social Development," in *Proceedings of International Workshop on Regional Autonomy of Ethnic Minorities*, ed. n.a., 136 (Beijing: Publisher, 2001).
7. Wang Jianhua, "An Introduction on Autonomous Power and Democratic Power of Cadres of Ethnic Minorities," in *Proceedings of International Workshop*

on Regional Autonomy of Ethnic Minorities, ed. n.a., 129 (Beijing: Publisher, 2001).

8. Zhou Chuanbin, "The System of Regional Ethnic Autonomy and Social Harmony," in *Proceedings of International Workshop on Regional Autonomy of Ethnic Minorities*, ed. n.a., 51 (Beijing: Publisher, 2001).

9. Wu Shimin, "Functions of China's System of Regional Ethnic Autonomy," in *Proceedings of International Workshop on Regional Autonomy of Ethnic* Minorities, ed. n.a., 71.(Beijing: Publisher, 2001).

10. Wen Jing, 5.

11. Wen Jing, 5.

12. Zhou Chuanbin, 55.

13. Jin Binghao, "The Installation of Autonomous Regimes and the Execution of the Autonomous Power," *in Proceedings of International Workshop on Regional Autonomy of Ethnic Minorities*, ed. n.a., 35–36 (Beijing: Publisher, 2001).

14. Guo Hongsheng, "Ethnic Regional Autonomy and the Rights to Subsistence and the Rights to Development of China's Ethnic Minorities," in *Proceedings of International Workshop on Regional Autonomy of Ethnic Minorities*, ed. n.a., 41 (Beijing: Publisher, 2001).

15. Wu Shimin, 72.

16. Xie Re, "A Few Points about Doing Good Work on Regional Ethnic Autonomy in the New Era," in *Proceedings of International Workshop on Regional Autonomy of Ethnic Minorities*, ed. n.a., 81 (Beijing: Publisher, 2001).

17. Wu Guohua, "Making Full Use of Policy Advantages to Speed Up the Development of Ethnic Autonomous Regions," *in Proceedings of International Workshop on Regional Autonomy of Ethnic Minorities*, ed. n.a., 75 (Beijing: Publisher, 2001).

18. Zhang Beiping, "Regional Ethnic Autonomy and Poverty-alleviation Development," in *Proceedings of International Workshop on Regional Autonomy of Ethnic Minorities*, ed. n.a., 123 (Beijing: Publisher, 2001).

19. Bao Zhoding, "The Protection and Development of Ethnic Cultures by the Institution of Ethnic Autonomy," in *Proceedings of International Workshop on Regional Autonomy of Ethnic Minorities*, ed. n.a., 113 (Beijing: Publisher, 2001).

20. Chih-yu Shih, "The Problem of Sluggish Enrollment in Ethnic Schools," *Issues & Studies* 37, no. 2 (March/April 2000): 177–98; and "How Ethnic is Ethnic Education?" *Prospect Quarterly* 2, no. 3 (July 2001): 131–65.

21. Tie Muer, "The Reasons, Contents and Significant Meanings of the Revision of 'The Law on Regional Autonomy of the People's Republic of China,'" in *Proceedings of International Workshop on Regional Autonomy of Ethnic Minorities*, ed. n.a., 99 (Beijing: Publisher, 2001).

22. Wang Jianhua, 128.

23. Wang Xien, "Globalization and China's Regional Ethnic Autonomy," in *Proceedings of International Workshop on Regional Autonomy of Ethnic Minorities*, ed. n.a., 148 (Beijing: Publisher, 2001).

24. Ibid., 149.

25. Chen Jianyue, "Intergovernmental Financial Transfer Payment and the Practice of It in China's Regional Ethnic Autonomy," in *Proceedings of International Workshop on Regional Autonomy of Ethnic Minorities*, ed. n.a., 131 (Beijing: Publisher, 2001).
26. Ibid.

Chapter 2

1. For a pioneer discussion on this in the case of China, see Stevan Harrell, *Cultural Encounters on China's Ethnic Frontiers* (Seattle: Washington University Press, 1995); Mette Halskov Hansen, *Lessons in Being Chinese: Minority Education and Ethnic Identity in Southwest China* (Seattle: University of Washington Press, 1999).
2. For a similar concern, see Tim Oakes, *Tourism and Modernity in China* (New York: Routledge, 1998).
3. P. Steven Sangeren, "History and Rhetoric of Legitimacy," *Comparative Studies in Society and History* 30, no. 4 (1998): 674–97.
4. Norma Diamond, "The Miao and Poison," *Ethnology* 27, no. 1 (1988): 1–25.
5. For the use of alcohol in Chinese classic literature, see Chih-tsing Hsia, *The Classic Chinese Novel* (New York: Columbia University Press, 1968), 88–89
6. Esther Yao, "Is China the End of Hermeneutics? Or, Political and Cultural Usage of Non-Han Women in Mainland Chiense Films," *Discourse* 2, no. 2 (1989): 11–136.
7. For an argument on ethnicity as imagined genealogy instead of imagined common culture, see Chih yu Shih, "Voting for an Ancestor?" *Issues and Studies* 40, no. 3/4 (September/December 2004): 488–95.
8. For more discussions, see Wen-chi Kung, *Indigenous People and the Press* (Taipei: Hanlu, 2000).

Chapter 3

1. Hao Keming, "Preface," in *Face Poverty* ([*miandui pinqiong*]), ed. Zhang Li, 2. (Nanning: Guangxi Education Press, 1998).
2. *The Task Force on "Anti-Poverty" of the Institute of China's Reform and Development, The Governing Structures of Anti-Poverty in China* ([*zhonggua fan pinkun zhili jiegou*]) (Beijing: Chinese Economy Press, 1998), 3.
3. Quoted from the interview conducted in August 2003 of a Helping-the-Poor cadre in Yongshun County of Hunan Province.
4. The following analysis is from the interview with an official of the provincial government of Hunan, February 2003.

5. From the interview with a provincial official who once served on a Helping-the-Poor team in the Western Hunan Prefecture during his first year of assignment with the provincial government. The interview was conducted in February 2003.

6. Quoted from the interview of a Helping-the-Poor cadre sent by the provincial government to Western Hunan conducted in August 2003. The interviewee of this quote is not the same as previously mentioned.

7. *Wang Maolin, The Studies and Reflections on Hunan Economy—A Thesis on Mountain and Water Resources* ([*Hunan jingji yanjiu yu sikao—shan shui pian*]), (Changsha: Hunan Press, 1996): 304–5.

8. Quoted from the interview with a linguistic professor at Jishou University, conducted in January 2000.

Chapter 4

1. James Der Derian and Michael J. Shapiro (eds.), *International/Intertextual Relations: Postmodern Readings of World Politics* (Lexington, Mass.: Lexington Books, 1989); Michael J. Shapiro and Hayward R. Alker (eds.), *Challenging Boundaries: Global Flows, Territorial Identities* (Minneapolis: University of Minnesota Press, 1996); Cynthia Weber, *Simulating Sovereignty: Intervention, the State, and Symbolic Exchange* (New York: Cambridge University Press, 1995); Chih-yu Shih, *Navigating Sovereignty: World Politics Lost in China* (London: Palgrave, 2003); Yosef Lapid and Friedrich Kratochwil (eds.), *The Return of Culture and Identity in IR Theory* (Boulder: Lynne Rienner, 1997).

2. For more discussion on how the state discursively constructs ethnic citizenship, see Stevan Harrell (ed.), *Cultural Encounters on China's Ethnic Frontiers* (Seattle: University of Washington Press, 1995); Duara Prasenjit, *Rescuing History from the Nation: Questioning the Narratives of Modern China* (Chicago: Chicago University Press, 1995); Dru Gladney, *Muslim Chinese: Ethnic Nationalism in the People's Republic* (Cambridge: Council of East Asian Studies, 1991).

3. To disclose the arbitrary nature of the state in determining the identities of the border community and indirectly reinforce the image of an un-problematized state. For examples of this attempt at disclosing, see Colin Mackerras, *China's Minorities: Integration and Modernization in the Twentieth Century* (Hong Kong: Oxford University Press, 1994); Mette Halskov Hansen, *Lessons in Being Chinese—Minority Education and Ethnic Identity in Southwest China* (Seattle and London: University of Washington Press, 1999); Gerard A. Postiglione (ed.), *China's National Minority Education—Culture, Schooling, and Development* (New York and London: Falmer Press, 1999).

4. For research that sees from the eyes of those under study, see Louisa Schein, *Minority Rules: The Miao and the Feminine in China's Cultural Politics* (Durham: Duke University Press, 2000); Chih-yu Shih, *Negotiating Ethnicity in China: Citizenship as a Response to the State* (London: Routledge, 2002);

Uradyn E. Bulag, *Nationalism and Hybridity in Mongolia* (Oxford: Oxford University Press, 1998).

5. For more discussion, see Thomas M. Wilson and Hastings Donnan (eds.), *Border Identities: Nation and State at International Frontiers* (New York: Cambridge University Press, 1998); Christian P. Scherrer, *Ethnicity, Nationalism, and Violence: Conflict Management, Human Rights, and Multilateral Regimes* (Burlington, VT: Ashgate, 2003); Andreas Wimmer, *Nationalist Exclusion and Ethnic Conflict: Shadows of Modernity* (New York: Cambridge University Press, 2002).

6. For illustration, see the discussion by Mathias Albert, David Jacobson, and Yosef Lapid (eds.), *Identities, Borders, Orders: Rethinking International Relations Theory* (University of Minnesota Press, 2001); Benedict Anderson, *Imagined Communities: Reflections on the Origin and Spread of Nationalism* (New York: Verso, 1991).

7. The Yanbian Korean Autonomous Prefecture has stipulated in Clause 20 of its education law that Korean schools should teach using the official Korean language; occupational schools, technical schools, and middle-specialized schools can use Mandarin in addition to the official Korean language.

8. This should be an internal report. The preliminary result was revealed by an attendant of the review committee.

9. Zhang Zhaohe (Cheung Siu-woo), "Local Development, National Consciousness and Folk Religion: A Case Study of a Vietnamese Community in Guangxi," *Journal of History and Anthropology* 2, no.1 (April 2004): 122.

10. Zhang Zhaohe believes that the historically intense relationship poses a challenge to the official construction of Jing ethnicity. His historiography is based upon Yan Xuejun, "An Investigation of the Conditions of Vietnamese in Fangcheng," in *Editorial Board of Guangxi Zhuang Autonomous District, An Investigation of the History and the Society of the Guangxi Jing People* (Nanning: Guangxi Ethnic Press, 1987 [1953]).

11. From Zhang Zhaohe's field interview report quoted in "Local Development, National Consciousness and Folk Religion: A Case Study of a Vietnamese Community in Guangxi," 105–10.

12. From Zhang Zhaohe's field interview report, 106.

Chapter 5

1. Some argue that this is because the Chinese culture is all-embracing; see Zhou Xing, *New Theses on Ethnology* [*minzuxue xin lun*] (Xian: Shanxi People's Press, 1992), 28. Others argue that this is because the Chinese culture is close to the outside world; see Zhu Riyao, Cao Deben, and Sun Xiaochun, *The Contemporary View of China's Political Cultural Tradition* [*zhongguo chuantong zhengzhi wenhua de xiandai sikao*] (Changchun: Jilin University Press, 1990), 29.

2. In fact, in the Western literature, a nation is likewise a modern invention; see Liah Greenfeld, *Nationalism: Five Roads to Modernity* (Cambridge: Harvard University Press, 1992), Introduction.

3. Chen Daluo, *Historical Review of Chinese Nation Building* [*zhonghua minzu ronghe licheng kaoshu*] (Taipei: Editorial Committee of Chinese Series, National Institute for Compilation and Translation, 1979).

4. Fei Xiaotong described the Chinese nation as "multiplicity into unity" [*duoyuan yiti*], which witnesses the process of mix as Fei says, "you come then I go; I come then you go; I have you in me and you have me in you." See Fei Xiaotong, "The Structure of Multiplicity into Unity of the Chinese Nation" ["*zhonghua minzu de duoyuan yiti geju*"], *Beijing Daxue Xuebao* 4 (1989): 1, 11.

5. Fei actually had a theory of anomaly, which was rarely attended. He specifically argued that there were two forces in the process of national building—centripetal and centrifugal. Fei believed that this was why a nation could rise or fall and form or split. He encouraged newcomers to study this subject. See Fei Xiaotong, "A Brief Review and Recollection of My Ethnological Studies" ["*jian shu wode minzu yanjiu jingli he sikao*"], *Beijing Daxue Xuebao* 2 (1997), 1–4.

6. "The Huishui Society of Buyi Studies," in *Huishui Buyi Nationality* (Guiyang: Guizhou People's Press, 2001), 24.

7. *Huishui Buyi Nationality*, 91–97.

8. *Huishui Buyi Nationality*, 17.

9. Benedict Anderson, *Imagined Communities: Reflections on the Origin and Spread of Nationalism* (London: Verso, 1991).

10. One of the most famous late Qing/Republican writers Ling Qichao was among those who praised the converging power of the Chinese culture. Liang saw the Chinese culture as the single most important force in forming the Chinese nation. His remark of this sort is widely taught in class by the Chinese professors on nationality.

11. For more discussion, see Chen Yongling, "Exploring a Few Questions about the Research on Han Ethnology" ["*tansuo hanzu minzuxue de yanjiu de ji ge wenti*"], in Yuan Shaofen and Xu Jieshun (eds.), *Han Studies* [*hanminzu yanjiu*] 1 (Nanning: Guangxi People's Press, 1989).

12. Lucian Pye, "China: Erratic State, Frustrated Society," *Foreign Affairs* 69, no. 4 (1990): 56–74.

13. Wu Yiping, *A Brief Review of the Relationship between the Great Chinese Nation and Its Culture* [*da zhonghua minzu yu qi wenhua zhi guanxi shu lyue*], (Tainan, Taiwan: Wendao, 1970), 94–95.

14. This is exactly opposite to the popular theme of the end of history. Once they reach great harmony, men no longer live just for the interests of their own or their inner circle.

15. Mellissa Brown, *Is Taiwan Chinese?: The Impact of Culture, Power, and Migration on Changing Identities* (Berkeley: University of California Press, 2004).

16. For how the Manchurian court struggled to demonstrate to the Han subjects its assimilation into the Confucian culture, see Jonathan Spence, *Treason by the Book* (New York: Penguin, 2002).

17. Yu Yingshi, "The Concept of Nation-state and National Consciousness" ["*guo jia guannian yu minzu yish*"]), in *Cultural Reviews and Feelings toward China* [*wenhua pinglun yu zhongguo qinghuai*], ed. Yu Yingshi, (Taipei: Yunchen, 1988), 19.

18. See the discussion in Ross Terrill, *The New Chinese Empire: And What It Means for the United States* (New York: Basic Books, 2003); Lucian Pye, The Spirit of Chinese Politics (Cambridge: MIT Press, 1968).

19. As mentioned in Chapter 4, a Yao teacher told his guest that nobody in his community is still self-identified as Yao; a Tujia school principal told me nobody in his community wanted to still speak Tujia. Both claim that this is because of cultural assimilation. Others comment that they either suffer from inferiority complex or simply try to avoid discrimination.

20. Liu Xiaomeng, "The Formation of the Chinese Nation in Modern History" ["*zhonghua minzu zai jindai lishi zhong de xingcheng*"], *The Formation and the Growth of the Bonding Power of the Chinese Nation* [*zhonghua minzu ningju lixingchen yu fazhan*], ed. Ma Rong and Zhou Xing, (Beijing: Beijing University Press, 1999), 116–19.

21. Concerning the complicated relationship between Westernization and nationalism, see Liu Dengge and Zhou Yunfang, *The Western Knowledge Coming Eastward and the Eastern Knowledge Going Westward* [*Xi xue dong jian yu dong xue xi jian*] (Beijing: Chinese Social Science Press, 2000), 97–125.

22. The famous mortuary drama of Yellow River condemns the Chinese culture and calls for an "ocean-oriented" or "blue" renovation. The text was later published and reprinted again and again by a Taiwanese press. See Su Xiaokang and Wang Ruxiang, *Death Song of the River* [*he shang*] (Taipei: Fenyun Shidai, 1988).

23. The major task is to refute the theory that the Chinese originally come from Egypt, India or Babylonia. See Wang Ling, Wei Kaizhao and Wang Caimei, *Yellow River, Yellow Soil and the Children of Emperors Yan and Huang* [*huang he, huang tudi, yan huang zisun*](Beijing: China Bookstore, 1991), 3–12.

24. Gao Bingzhong, "The Diverse Characteristics of the Chinese Culture and the Sharing of Culture among Nationalities" ["*zhongguo wenhua de duoyang xing yu zu ji wenhua gongxiang*"] in *The Formation and the Growth of the Bonding Power of the Chinese Nation*, ed. Ma Rong and Zhou Xing 246–53 (Beijing: Beijing University Press, 1999).

25. Genealogy is the indicator of diasporic community. Children of early immigrants remain diasporas because of genealogy. The genealogy argument is the basis for discussion of model minority or model immigrant. See the discussion of Ruth in Old Testimony in Bonnie Honig, "Ruth, the Model émigré: Mourning and the Symbolic Politics of Immigration," in *Moral Spaces:*

Rethinking Ethics and World Politics, ed. D. Campbell and M. J. Shapiro, (Minneapolis: University of Minnesota Press, 1999),184–210.

26. He used the term "serious" to describe the loss of authenticity of the Buyi culture.

27. Quoted from the interview with a scholar from the Guizhou Social Science Academy, who escorted me to Huishui in April 2003.

28. For more discussion, see Suo Xiaoxia, *Amorphous Links: Succession and Modernization of Ethnic Minorities' Culture in Guizhou* [*wuxing de lianjie: guizhou shaoshu minzu wenhua de chuancheng yu xiandaihua*] (Guiyang: Guizhou Nationality Press, 2000), 187–200.

29. The same decoration can be seen in Uygurs, Tujia, Miao, and Qiang villages.

30. This is also true elsewhere. See my discussion *in Negotiating Ethnicity in China: Citizenship as a Response to the State* (London: Routledge, 2002).

31. Huishui Buyi Nationality, 331.

Chapter 6

1. See for example,–*The Issue Research Team on Helping the Poor at the Academy of Chinese (Hainan) Reform and Development, The Governance Structure of Helping the Poor in China*–([*zhongguo fan pinkun zhili jiegou*]) (Beijing: Chinese Economic Press, 1998); Zhang Li (ed.),–*Facing Poverty: The Background of Educational Development in China's Poor Areas* ([*miandui pinkun: zhongguo–pinkun diqu jiaoyu fazhan de Beijing*]) (Nanning: Guanxi Education Press, 1998); The Chinese Communist Supervisor Office of Western Hunan Prefecture and The Office of Advancing Helping-the-Poor at the Most Difficult Stage of Western Hunan Prefecture (eds.),–*The Great Melody of Advancing at the Most Difficult Stage* ([*gong jian zhuang ge*]) (1996).

2. Wang Lichuan, "The Standing Committee of Political Bureau on How to Benefit the Disadvantaged People" ([*zhengzhi ju chang hui taolun zhogu ruoshi zuqun*]), United Daily (2002.12.13): 13.

3. The following summaries are drawn from the report to the National People's Congress prepared by Township Diector Ru Chengui. He also uses this report as a public relations script for any visitors to the township. (mimeo).

4. Interview with the Director of the Bureau of Finance of Yongshun County (2003.9.2).

5. Interview with the Associate County Director of Yongshun County (2003.9.2).

6. Interview with the B & B owner (2003.8.29).

7. Interview with a B & B owner (2003.8.30).

8. Interview with villagers (2003.8.31).

9. For a similar conclusion from a different story, see Tang, Ching-Ping and Shui-Yan Tang, "Negotiated Autonomy: Transforming Self-governing Institutions for Local Common-Pool Resources in Two Tribal Villages in Taiwan," *Human Ecology* 29, 1 (2001): 49–65.

Chapter 7

1. See Wu Shimin, ed., *Zhongguo minzu zhengce gailan* [*On Chinese Nationality Policy*], 21–25 (Beijing: Renmin chubanshe, 1995).
2. See Au Junde, *Zhonghua renmin gongheguo minzu quyu zizhifa shiyi* ([*A Review of vague points of the Law of Ethnic Regional Autonomy of the PRC*]) (Beijing: Minzu chubanshe, 2001), 9–10.
3. Zhou Yong, "Probing into the Road of Combining China's 'Regional Autonomy' and 'Ethnic Autonomy,'" in *Wu*, op. cit. 114–18.
4. Zhou Yong, "Exploring the way of Combining of Chinese "Regional Autnomy" and "National Autonomy," in *Proceedings of International Workshop on Regional Autonomy of Ethnic Minorities*, ed. n.a., 3 (Beijing: Publisher, 2001), 114–18.
5. I chose Longsheng because it is the last county that still carries the word "multiple" (ge) in its name, making it an extreme example of the politics of representation in autonomous regions.
6. According to the information I gathered during previous research trips to other parts of the country, this ratio is consistently inflated.
7. Chih-yu Shih, *Negotiating Ethnicity in China: Citizenship as a Response to the State* (London: Routledge, 2002), chapters 6 and 13.
8. See Shih, *Negotiating Ethnicity in China*, chapter 12.
9. Edward W. Said, *Orientalism* (New York: Random House, 1979).
10. The local teacher salary ranges from roughly five hundred yuan per month to less than one thousand yuan.
11. Zheng Yuntao and Shi Donglong, "Chengxian qihou, jiwang kailai —relie qingzhu Longsheng gezu zizhi xian chengli wushi zhounian" ([Taking from the predecessors, opening up for the latecomers, following the past, creating the future—warmly celebrating the fiftieth anniversary of the establishment of the Longsheng Multi-ethnic Autonomous County]), *Minzu zhi sheng* (*Voices of Nationalities*), 2001, no. 5: 3–5.

Chapter 8

1. Edward Said, *Cultural Imperialism* (New York: Vintage Books, 1991), 311–12.
2. In opposition to multi-culturalism, Homi Bhabha attributes the inexpressible postcolonial position to one of in betweenness; see his "The World and the Home," *Social Text* 31–32 (1993): 141–53.
3. Edward Said, *Orientalism* (New York: Vintage Books, 1979).
4. Albert J. Paolini, *Navigating Modernity: Postcolonialism, Identity, and International Relations* (Boulder: Lynne Rienner, 1999).
5. For example, see Rey Chow, *Alternative Perspectives on Hong Kong Culture* [*xie zai jia guo zhi wai*] (Hong Kong: Oxford University Press, 1995); Louisa Schein, *Minority Rules: The Miao and the Feminine in China's Cultural Politics* (Durham: Duke University Press, 2000); Fred Y. L. Chiu, "Politics and the

Body Social in Colonial Hong Kong," in *Formations of Colonial Modernity in East Asia*, ed. T. Barlow, (Durham: Duke University Press, 1997).

6. For criticism of this sort, see Dirlik Arif, "The Postcolonial Aura: Third World Criticism in the Age of Global Capitalism," in *Dangerous Liaisons: Gender, Nation and Postcolonial Perspectives*, ed. A. McClintock, A. Mufti, and E. Shohat, 501–28 (Minneapolis: University of Minnesota Press, 1997); Andrew Linklater (ed.), *International Relations: Critical Concepts in Political Science* (Boulder: Routledge, 2000).

7. For more of these research sites, see my *Negotiating Ethnicity in China: Citizenship as a Response to the State* (London: Routledge, 2002).

8. Quoted from the interview with an official in March 2002.

9. An interview reported in my "A Research Note on the Evening Spent in the ethnic Qiang village of Erchahe: The Micro View of the Boundary of the Chinese State" [*erchahe qiang zhai dasu zhaji: zhongguo guojia jiexian de weiguan kao cha*], *Chinese Affairs Quarterly* [*zhongguo shiwu jikan*] 1 (2000), 90.

Chapter 9

1. Chih-yu Shih, "The Society That Does Not Speak: Approaching Poverty in Western Hunan," presented at the Conference on Reforms and Institutional change in China, The Protestant Academy of Loccum, Loccum, Germany, 25–27 February 2005.

2. Interview with an official sent to the Office of Helping-the-Poor of Tianyang County.

3. Interview with the Director of Bureau of Tourism of Tianyang County.

4. The same bias appears in many other poor villages the author visited in the past.

5. Interview with the officials of the Office of United Front.

6. Interview with the county official in Tianyang.

7. For more discussion on cadres between the state and the society, see Vivien Shue, *The Reach of the State* (Stanford: Stanford University Press, 1988).

8. Interview with Mr. NH.

9. Interview with Mr. TH.

10. The author had encounters with a multi-ethnic community such as Longsheng Autonomous County, an ethnic Yao community such as Jinxiu Autonomous County, a diasporic ethnic Shui village around Yizhou city, and a newly installed ethnic Mulao community such as Luocheng Autonomous County. All these communities are multi-cultural to the extent that both Han and Zhuang are always among their major identities.

11. Interview with Associate County Director of Tianyang.

12. Interview with Director of the Bureau of Tourism.

13. There is a park built specifically for memorializing the uprising.

14. Interview with Associate County Director of Tianyang.

15. Interview with the head of the Office of United Front of Baise City.

Chapter 10

1. For the original version of the "rational new institutional" approach, see Ronald Coase, "The Nature of the Firm," *Economica* 16 (1937): 386–405; Ronald Coase, *The Firm, the Market and the Law* (Chicago: Chicago University Press, 1988).

2. For the advocacy of the "historical new institutional" approach, which stresses the institutional path, see Douglas North, "Government and the Cost of Exchange in History," *Journal of Economic History* 44 (1984): 225–64; Douglas North, *Structure and Change in Economic History* (New York: Norton, 1981).

3. For intellectual intervention in China's institutional reform, see Steven Cheung, "Will China Go Capitalist?" *Hobart Paper 94, The Institute of Economic Affairs* (Norfolk: Thetford Press, 1982).

4. For intellectual intervention from the historical institutional perspective, see Yushan Wu, *Comparative Economic Transformation: Mainland China, Hungary, the Soviet Union and Taiwan* (Stanford: Stanford University Press, 1994).

5. The recognition of those purposes outside of the mainstream discourse on institutional reform constitutes a philosophical proposition that attends to the factor of undecidability of human decision. For more discussion, see Michael J. Shapiro, "The Ethics of Encounter," in *Moral Spaces*, ed. D. Campbell and M. J. Shapiro (Minneapolis: University of Minnesota Press, 1999), 57–91.

6. Unless otherwise noted, all the interpretations of field experiences in the following discussion are drawn from Chih-yu Shih, *Negotiating Ethnicity in China: Citizenship as a Response to the State* (London: Routledge, 2002).

7. For more discussion on diasporic Shui community in Yizhou, Guangxi, see my "Lost Agency for Change: The Diasporic Identity in Yizhou's Shui community," *Social Identities* Vol. 11, no. 4 (2005): 381–93.

8. This is ironic in light of the publication of books on Mulao ethnicity one after another; see, for example, Luo Shiqing (ed.), *Guizhou Mulao Nationality* ([*Guizhou Mulao zu*]) (Guiyang: Bureau of Legal and Political Affairs of Commission of Civil Affairs, Guizhou, 1997); Chen Zhengjun, *The History and Culture of Guizhou Mulao Nationality* [*Guizhou Mulao zu lishi wenhua*] (Guiyang: Guizhou Nationaliaty Press, 2003).

9. Wu Baohua and Hu Xiqiong (eds.), *The History and the Culture of Mu Lao Nationality* ([*Mulao zu de lishi yu wenhua*]) (n.p.: Guangxi Nationality Press, 1993), 2.

10. Quoted from the interview with an official of ethnic affairs at Luocheng County conducted in March 2002.

Chapter 11

1. For criticism of political science research in this regard, see David Campbell, *National Deconstruction: Violence, Identity and Justice in Bosnia* (Minneapolis: University of Minnesota Press, 1998); Yosef Lapid and Fridrich Kratochwill (eds.), *The Return of Culture and Identity in IR Theory* (Boulder: Lynne Rienner, 1996); Yosef Lapid, "Theorizing the 'national' in International Relations Theory," in *International Organizations*, (New York: HaperCollins, 1996), 20–31.

2. Unless otherwise noted, the reports on other ethnic communities throughout the chapter are drawn from my *Negotiating Ethnicity in China: Citizenship as a Response to the State* (London: Routledge, 2002). Also see "The Problem of Sluggish Enrollment in Ethnic Schools: The Case of One Dong Village in Shaoyang, Hunan," *Issues & Studies* 37, no. 2 (March/April 2001), 177–98; "How Ethnic Is Ethnic Education: The Issue of School Enrollment in Meigu's Yi Community," *Prospect Quarterly* 2, no. 3 (July 2001), 131–65; "Assimilation through Ethnicity: Chinese Ethnic Language Policy in Yunnan and Shenyang," *International Journal on Minority and Group Rights* 7, no. 3 (2000), 189–206.

3. Interview with an official of Ethnic Affairs of Guilin City to whose jurisdiction Jinxiu belongs.

4. Interview with an official of the Bureau of Enterprise of Jinxiu County.

5. Ralph Litzinger, *Other Chinas: The Yao and the Politics of Belonging* (Durham: Duke University Press, 2000).

6. The analysis was made by an official of Ethnic Affairs of Jinxiu County.

7. Interview with a county official of Jinxiu County.

8. Interview with a self-identified Chashan Yao official in Jinxiu.

9. Pan Nianying, *Hand Notes on Helping the Poor* [*fu pin shou ji*] (Shanghai: Shanghai literature and Art Press, 1997).

10. This is not done in any official document since the Chinese state literature is always careful to be even-handed. Besides, a low culture level often means less education or slower economic development. That said, officials at the county level or higher as well as Helping-the-Poor teams take the word literally to mean inferiority.

11. Interview with the Associate Director of Ethnic Affairs of Jinxiu County.

12. Interview with a Helping-the-Poor cadre.

13. Interview at a local township office.

14. Incidentally, a Taiwan Affairs, official at the Chinese Academy of Social Science (CASS), who is an old friend, formally criticized a draft version of this chapter to be delivered at a CASS, conference for ridiculing Jiang Zemin's Three Represents Theory into something parallel to children's play. He remains a friend afterwards, though.

15. Interview with a Township official responsible for education.

16. Said by the Associate Director of Ethnic Affairs of Jinxiu.

17. From a group interview in a village.

18. Interview with a local schoolteacher who accompanied the researcher to a number of village schools.

19. Both he and his wife are students of the Founding Father of Chinese anthropology, Fei Xiaotong.

20. Interview with a priest at his home.

21. Quoted from the interview with the priest on the second floor of his house where he kept all the necessities for the performance of a ritual. The interview was conducted in March 2002.

22. Interview with the professors at their house. The wife made the remark. She recalled that Fei Xiaotong had agreed with her thesis. She raised her arms and clapped after finishing her remarks to the visitor.

Chapter 12

1. James C. Scott, *The Moral Economy of the Peasant: Subsistence and Rebellion in Southeast Asia* (New Haven: Yale University Press, 1976).

2. For more discussion, see Daniel Little, *Understanding Peasant China: Case Studies in the Philosophy of Social Science* (New Haven: Yale University Press, 1989).

3. For more discussion, see Jean Oi, "Rational Choice and Attainment of Wealth and Power in the Countryside," in *China's Quiet Revolution: New Interactions between State and Society*, ed. D. Goodman and B. Hooper, 64–79 (New York: St. Martin, 1994); Victor Nee, "A Theory of Market Transition: From Redistribution to Markets in State Socialism," *American Sociological Review* 54, no. 5 (1989): 663–81.

4. See Tang Chou, "Back from the Brink of Revolutionary-'Feudal' Totalitarianism," in *State and Society in Contemporary China*, ed. D. Mozingo and V. Nee, (Ithaca: Cornell University Press, 1983), 53–88. Also, Fong Hsiaw-chian's "Exchange Structure and Property-Rights Patterns in Sunan and Wenzhou," *Mainland China Studies* 45, no. 4 (2002, 7–8):1–13; Chih-yu Shih, "New-institutionalism in China Studies: Reflection on Literature with a Special Attention to the English Work by Chinese Writers," *The Journal of Post-communist and Transition Studies* 15, no. 2 (June 1999), 126–45.

5. The definition of peasant involves serious political and policy repercussions in China. The peasant [*nongmin*], the village [*nongcun*], and agriculture [*nongye*] are three closely related concepts in the Chinese context of "*nong.*" The "peasant problem" is about poverty; the "village problem" is about development, and the "agricultural problem" is about budget and revenue.

6. The Issue Research Team on Helping the Poor at the Academy of Chinese (Hainan) Reform and Development, *The Governance Structure of Helping the Poor in China* [*zhongguo fan pinkun zhili jiegou*] (Beijing: Chinese Economic Press, 1998), 3; Hao Keming, "Preface," in *Facing Poverty: The Background of Educational Development in China's Poor Areas* [*miandui pinkun: zhongguo*

pinkun diqu jiaoyu fazhan de Beijing] (Nanning: Guanxi Education Press, 1998), 2; Peng Boming, *Thought and Analysis on Economics of the Mountain Areas* [*shan qu jingji si bian*] (Beijing: The Weather Press, 1997), 92.

7. This undecidability is not unlike the argument about the agency of the weak to make use of the situation or the ideology imposed upon them for their own needs, which shift across situations. See more discussion in James C. Scott, *Weapons of the Weak: Everyday Forms of Peasant Resistance* (New Haven, Yale University Press, 1985).

References

Albert, Mathias, David Jacobsen, and Yosef Lapid, eds. 2001. *Identities, borders, orders: Rethinking international relations theory.* Minneapolis: Univ. of Minnesota Press.

Anderson, Benedict. 1991. *Imagined communities: Reflections on the origin and spread of nationalism.* London: Verso.

Au Junde. 2001. *Zhonghua renmin gongheguo minzu quyu zizhifa shiyi [A review of vaguepoints of the law of ethnic regional autonomy of the PRC].* Beijing: Minzu chubanshe.

Bao, Zhoding. 2001. "The protection and development of ethnic cultures by the institution of ethnic autonomy." Paper presented at the Proceedings of International Workshop on Regional Autonomy of Ethnic Minorities, Beijing, June 22–25.

Bhabha, Homi. 1993. "The world and the home," *Social Text* 31–32:141–53.

Borjas, Goerge. 1990. *Friends or strangers.* New York: Basic Books.

Broderstad, Else Grete, and Nils Oskal. 2001. "Human rights as providing limitations and necessary conditions for ethnic regional autonomy." Paper presented at the Proceedings of International Workshop on Regional Autonomy of Ethnic Minorities, Beijing, June 22–25.

Brown, Mellisa. 2004. *Is Taiwan Chinese? The impact of culture, power, and migration on changing identities.* Berkeley: Univ. of California Press.

Bulag, Uradyn E. 1998. *Nationalism and Hybridity in Mongolia.* Oxford: Oxford Univ. Press.

Campbell, David. 1998. *National deconstruction: Violence, identity and justice in Bosnia.* Minneapolis: Univ. of Minnesota Press.

Castles, Stephen, and Davidson, Alastair. 2000. *Citizenship and migration.* London: Routledge.

Chen, Daluo. 1979. *Historical review of Chinese nation building ([zhonghua minzu ronghe licheng kaoshu]).* Taipei: Editorial Committee of Chinese Series, National Institute for Compilation and Translation.

Chen, Jianyue. 2001. "Intergovernmental financial transfer payment and the practice of it in China's regional ethnic autonomy." Paper presented at the Proceedings of International Workshop on Regional Autonomy of Ethnic Minorities, Beijing June 22–25.

Chen, Yongling. 1989. "Exploring a few questions about the research on Han ethnology" ([*tansuo hanzu minzuxue de yanjiu de ji ge wenti*]). In *Han Studies* ([*hanminzu yanjiu*]) 1, Eds. Yuan Shaofen and Xu Jieshun. Nanning: Guangxi People's Press.

Chen, Zhengjun. 2003. *The History and culture of Guizhou Mulao nationality* ([*Guizhou Mulao zu lishi wenhua*]). Guiyang: Guizhou Nationaliaty Press.

Cheung, Siu-woo. 2004. "Local development, national consciousness and folk religion: A case study of a Vietnamese community in Guangxi." *Journal of History and Anthropology* 2, 1:89–132.

Chiu, Fred Y. L. 1997. "Politics and the body social in colonial Hong Kong." In *Formations of Colonial Modernity in East Asia*, Ed. T. Barlow. Durham: Duke Univ. Press.

Chow, Rey. 1995. *Alternative perspectives on Hong Kong culture* (xie zai jia guo zhi wai). Hong Kong: Oxford Univ. Press.

Coase, Ronald. 1937. "The Nautre of the firm," *Economica* 16:386–405.

———. 1988. *The Firm, the market and the law*. Chicago: Chicago Univ. Press.

Cogo, Margherita. 2001. "Peaceful co-existence and co-operation of different groups." Paper presented at the Proceedings of International Workshop on Regional Autonomy of Ethnic Minorities, Beijing, June 22–25.

Collins, Jock. 1991. *Migrant hands in a distant land*. Sydney: Pluto Press.

Danspeckgruber Wolfgang. 2005. "The model of *self-governance* and regional integration as an instrument to enhance peace, stability, and prosperity." In *Autonomy, self-governance and conflict resolution: Innovative approaches to institutional design in divided societies*. London: Routledge.

Derian, James Der, and Michael J. Shapiro, eds. 1989. *International/intertextual relations: Postmodern readings of world politics*. Lexington, MA: Lexington Books.

Diamond, Norma. 1988. "The Miao and poison." *Ethnology* 27, 1:1–25.

Dirlik, Arif. 1997. "The postcolonial aura: Third world criticism in the age of global capitalism." In *Dangerous liaisons: Gender, nation and postcolonial perspectives*. Minneapolis: Univ. of Minnesota Press, 501–28.

Elisabeth Nauclér. 2001. "Presentation of the åland autonomy." Paper presented at the Proceedings of International Workshop on Regional Autonomy of Ethnic Minorities, June 22–25, Beijing.

Fei Xiaotong. 1989. "The structure of multiplicity into unity of the Chinese nation" ([*zhonghua minzu de duoyuan yiti geju*]). *Beijing Daxue Xuebao* 4:1–11.

———. 1997. "A brief review and recollection of my ethnological studies" ([*jian shu wode minzu yanjiu jingli he sikao*]). *Beijing Daxue Xuebao* 2.

Fong Hsiaw-chian. 2002. "Exchange structure and property-rights patterns in Sunan and Wenzhou." *Mainland China Studies* 45, 4:1–13.

Gao Bingzhong. 1999. "The diverse characteristics of the Chinese culture and the sharing of culture among nationalities" ([*zhongguo wenhua de duoyang xing yu zu ji wenhua gongxiang*]). In *The formation and the growth of the bonding power of the Chinese nation*. Beijing: Beijing Univ. Press.

Gladney, Dru. 1991. *Muslim Chinese: Ethnic nationalism in the people's republic*. Cambridge: Council of East Asian Studies.

Greenfeld, Liah. 1992. *Nationalism: Five roads to modernity*. Cambridge: Harvard Univ. Press.

Guo Hongsheng. 2001. "Ethnic regional autonomy and the rights to subsistence and the rights to development of China's ethnic minorities." Paper presented at the Proceedings of International Workshop on Regional Autonomy of Ethnic Minorities, June 22–25, Beijing.

Hansen, Mette Halskov. 1999. *Lessons in being Chinese—Minority education and ethnic identity in southwest China*. Seattle: Univ. of Washington Press.

Hans-Joachim Heintze. 2001. "Autonomy in international law." Paper presented at the Proceedings of International Workshop on Regional Autonomy of Ethnic Minorities, June 22–25, Beijing.

Hao Keming. 1998. "Preface." In *facing poverty: The background of educational development in China's poor areas* ([*miandui pinkun: zhongguo pinkun diqu jiaoyu fazhan de Beijing*]), Ed. Zhang Li. Nanning: Guanxi Education Press.

Harrell, Stevan, ed. 1995. *Cultural encounters on China's ethnic frontiers*. Seattle: Univ. of Washington Press.

Honig, Bonnie. 1999. "Ruth, the model émigré: Mourning and the symbolic politics of immigration." In *Moral spaces: Rethinking ethics and world politics*. Minneapolis: Univ. of Minnesota Press, 184–210.

Hsia, Chih-tsing. 1968. *The classic Chinese novel*. New York: Columbia Univ. Press.

Issue Research Team on Helping the Poor at the Academy of Chinese (Hainan) Reform and Development. 1998. *The governance structure of helping the poor in China* ([*zhongguo fan pinkun zhili jiegou*]). Beijing: Chinese Economic Press.

Jin Binghao. 2001. "The installation of autonomous regimes and the execution of the autonomous power." Paper presented at the Proceedings of International Workshop on Regional Autonomy of Ethnic Minorities, June 22–25, Beijing.

Kefale, Asnake. 2001. "The federal option and ethnic autonomy in Ethiopia since 1991." Paper presented at the Proceedings of International Workshop on Regional Autonomy of Ethnic Minorities, June 22–25, Beijing.

Kristen Trolle. 2001. "Greenland home rule: Experiences from the implementation of autonomy for the population of Greenland within the Danish realm." Paper presented at the Proceedings of International Workshop on Regional Autonomy of Ethnic Minorities, June 22–25, Beijing.

Kung, Wen-chi. 2000. *Indigenous people and the press*. Taipei: Hanlu.

Kymlicka, W. 1995. *Multicultural citizenship*. Oxford: Oxford Univ. Press.

Lapid, Yosef, and Kratochwill, Fridrich, eds. 1996. *The return of culture and identity in IR theory*. Boulder: Lynne Rienner.

———. 1996. "Theorizing the 'national' in international relations theory." In *International organizations*. New York: HarperCollins.

Li, Zhang, ed. 1998. *Facing poverty: The background of educational development in China's poor areas* ([*miandui pinkun: zhongguo pinkun diqu jiaoyu fazhan de Beijing*]). Nanning: Guanxi Education Press.

Linklater, Andrew, ed. 2000. *International relations: Critical concepts in political science*. Boulder: Routledge.

Little, Daniel. 1989. *Understanding peasant China: Case studies in the philosophy of social science*. New Haven: Yale Univ. Press.

Liu Dengge and Zhou Yunfang. 2000. *The Western knowledge coming eastward and the eastern knowledge going westward* (Xi xue dong jian yu dong xue xi jian). Beijing: Chinese Social Science Press.

Liu Xiaomeng. 1999. "The formation of the Chinese nation in modern history" ([*zhonghua minzu zai jindai lishi zhong de xingcheng*]). In *The formation and the growth of the bonding power of the Chinese nation* ([*zhonghua minzu ningju lixingchen yu fazhan*]). Beijing: Beijing Univ. Press.

Luo Shiqing, ed. 1997. *Guizhou Mulao nationality* ([*Guizhou Mulao zu*]). Guiyang: Bureau of Legal and Political Affairs of Commission of Civil Affairs, Guizhou.

Luoshang Zunzhu. 2001. "Road to success of common development and prosperity." Paper presented at the Proceedings of International Workshop on Regional Autonomy of Ethnic Minorities, June 22–25, Beijing.

Lyu Yi. 2004. "Do not cut the foot to fit the shoes when facing history." *Lianhe Zaobao* July 5. http://www.zaobao.com

Mackerras, Colin. 1994. *China's minorities: Integration and modernization in the twentieth century*. Hong Kong: Oxford Univ. Press.

Manion, Melanie. 2004. *Corruption by design: Building clean government in mainland China and Hong Kong*. Cambridge: Harvard Univ. Press.

Naughton, Barry, and John McMillan. 1992. "How to reform a planned economy: Lessons from China." *Oxford Review of Economic Policy*, 8, 1 (Spring).

Nee, Victor. 1989. "A theory of market transition: From redistribution to markets in state socialism." *American Sociological Review* 54, 5:663–81.

North, Dougglas. 1981. *Structure and change in economic history*. New York: Norton.

———. 1984. "Government and the Cost of Exchange in History." *Journal of Economic History* 44: 225–64.

Oakes, Tim. 1998. *Tourism and modernity in China*. New York: Routledge.

Oi, Jean. 1994. "Rational choice and attainment of wealth and power in the countryside." In *China's quiet revolution: New interactions between state and society*. New York: St. Martin.

Osaghae, Eghosa E. 2003. "The sate and ethnic autonomy in Nigeria." *Regional and Federal Studies*, 13, 2:84–105.

Pan Nianying. 1997. *Hand notes on helping the poor (fu pin shou ji)*. Shanghai: Shanghai Literature and Art Press.

Paolini, Albert J. 1999. *Navigating modernity: Postcolonialism, identity, and international relations*. Boulder: Lynne Rienner.

Peng Boming. 1997. *Thought and analysis on economics of the mountain areas* (shan qu jingji si bian). Beijing: The Weather Press.

Postiglione, Gerard A., ed. 1999. *China's national minority education—Culture, schooling, and development*. New York: Falmer Press.

Prasenjit, Duara. 1995. *Rescuing history from the nation: Questioning the narratives of modern China*. Chicago: Chicago Univ. Press.

Pye, Lucian. 1968. *The spirit of Chinese politics*. Cambridge: MIT Press.

———. 1990. "China: Erratic state, frustrated society." *Foreign Affairs* 69, 4:56–74.

Ramzy, Austin. 2004. "Rewriting history: China and the Koreas feud over the ancient kingdom of Koguryo." *Time Asia*. August 16.

Said, Edward. 1979. *Orientalism*. New York: Vintage Books.

———. 1991. *Cultural imperialism*. New York: Vintage Books.

Sangeren, P. Steven. 1998. "History and rhetoric of legitimacy." *Comparative Studies in Society and History* 30, 4:674–97.

Schein, Louisa. 2000. *Minority rules: The Miao and the feminine in China's cultural politics*. Durham: Duke Univ. Press.

Scherrer, Christian P. 2003. *Ethnicity, nationalism, and violence: Conflict management, human rights, and multilateral regimes*. Burlington, VT :Ashgate.

Scott, James C. 1976. *The moral economy of the peasant: Subsistence and rebellion in southeast Asia*. New Haven: Yale Univ. Press.

———. 1985. *Weapons of the weak: Everyday forms of peasant resistance*. New Haven: Yale Univ. Press.

Shapiro, Michael J. 1999. "The ethics of encounter." In *Moral Spaces*. Minneapolis: Univ. of Minnesota Press.

Shapiro, Michael J., and Alker, Hayward R., eds. 1996. *Challenging boundaries: Global flows, territorial identities*. Minneapolis: Univ. of Minnesota Press.

Shih, Chih-yu. 2000. "A few nights with the Qiang peasants in erchane village—A research note on the micro-limit of the Chinese state" ([*erchahe qiang zhai dasu zhaji: zhongguo guojia jiexian de weiguan kao cha*]). *Chinese Affairs Quarterly* (zhongguo shiwu jikan) 1:79–91.

———. 2000. "Assimilation through ethnicity: Chinese ethnic language policy in Yunnan and Shenyang." *International Journal on Minority and Group Rights* 7, 3:189–206.

———. 2001. "How ethnic is ethnic education: The issue of school enrollment in Meigu's Yi community." *Prospect Quarterly* 2, 3:131–65.

———. 2001. "The problem of sluggish enrollment in ethnic schools: The case of one dong village in Shaoyang, human." *Issues & Studies* 37, 2:177–98.

———. 2002. *Negotiating ethnicity in China: Citizenship as a response to the state*. London: Routledge.

———. 2003. *Navigating sovereignty: World politics lost in China*. London: Palgrave.

———. 2004. "Voting for an ancestor?" *Issues and Studies* 40, 3/4:488–95.

Shue, Vivien. 1988. *The reach of the state*. Stanford: Stanford Univ. Press.

Spence, Jonathan. 2002. *Treason by the book*. New York: Penguin.

Steven Cheung, 1982. "Will China go capitalist?" *Hobart Paper* 94, The Institute of Economic Affairs (Norfolk: Thetford Press).

Su Xiaokang, and Wang Ruxiang. 1988. *Death song of the river* ([*he shang*]). Taipei: Fenyun Shidai.

Suo Xiaoxia. 2000. *Amorphous links: Succession and modernization of ethnic minorities' culture in Guizhou* ([*wuxing de lianjie: guizhou shaoshu minzu wenhua de chuancheng yu xiandaihua*]). Guiyang: Guizhou Nationality Press.

Tang Chou. 1983. "Back from the brink of revolutionary—'Feudal' totalitarianism." In *State and Society in Contemporary China*. Ithaca: Cornell Univ. Press.

Tang, Ching-Ping, and Tang, Shui-Yan. 2001. "Negotiated autonomy: Transforming self-governing institutions for local common-pool resources in two tribal villages in Taiwan." *Human Ecology* 29, 1:49–65.

Terrill, Ross. 2003. *The new Chinese empire: And what it means for the United States*. New York: Basic Books.

The Chinese Communist Supervisor Office of Western Hunan Prefecture and The Office of Advancing Helping-the-Poor at the Most Difficult Stage of Western Hunan Prefecture, eds. 1996. *The great melody of advancing at the most difficult stage* ([*gong jian zhuang ge*]). N.p.: n.p.

The Huishui Society of Buyi Studies. 2001. *Huishui Buyi nationality*. Guiyang: Guizhou People's Press.

Tie Muer. 2001. "The reasons, contents and significant meanings of the revision of 'the law on regional autonomy of the People's Republic of China.'" Paper presented at the Proceedings of International Workshop on Regional Autonomy of Ethnic Minorities, June 22–25, Beijing.

Wang Jianhua. 2001. "An introduction on autonomous power and democratic power of Cadres of ethnic minorities." Paper presented at the Proceedings of International Workshop on Regional Autonomy of Ethnic Minorities, June 22–25, Beijing.

Wang Lichuan. 2002. "The standing committee of political bureau on how to benefit the disadvantaged people" ([*zhengzhi ju chang hui taolun zhogu ruoshi zuqun*]). *United Daily* December, 13.

Wang Ling, Wei Kaizhao, and Wang Caimei. 1991. *Yellow river, yellow soil and the children of emperors Yan and Huang* ([*huang he, huang tudi, yan huang zisun*]). Beijing: China Bookstore.

Wang Xien. 2001. "Globalization and China's regional ethnic autonomy." Paper presented at the Proceedings of International Workshop on Regional Autonomy of Ethnic Minorities, June 22–25, Beijing.

Weber, Cynthia. 1995. *Simulating sovereignty: Intervention, the state, and symbolic exchange*. New York: Cambridge Univ. Press.

Wen Jing. 2001. "The history and experiences of China's ethnic regional autonomy." Paper presented at the Proceedings of International Workshop on Regional Autonomy of Ethnic Minorities, June 22–25, Beijing.

Wilson, Thomas M., and Donnan, Hastings, eds. 1998. *Border identities: Nation and state at international frontiers.* New York: Cambridge Univ. Press.

Wimmer, Andreas. 2002. *Nationalist exclusion and ethnic conflict: Shadows of modernity.* New York: Cambridge Univ. Press.

Wolff, Stefan. 2002. "Autonomy in ethnically plural societies." Paper presented at the Association for the study of Nationalities, Annual World Convention, New York.

Wu Guohua. 2001. "Making full use of policy advantages to fasten the development of ethnic autonomous regions." Paper presented at the Proceedings of International Workshop on Regional Autonomy of Ethnic Minorities, June 22–25, Beijing.

Wu Shimin, ed. 1995. *Zhongguo minzu zhengce gailan* ([On Chinese nationality policy]). Beijing: Renmin chubanshe.

Wu Shimin. 2001. "Functions of China's system of regional ethnic autonomy." Paper presented at the Proceedings of International Workshop on Regional Autonomy of Ethnic Minorities, June 22–25, Beijing.

Wu Yiping. 1970. *A brief review of the relationship between the great Chinese nation and its culture* ([da zhonghua minzu yu qi wenhua zhi guanxi shu lyue]). Tainan, Taiwan: Wendao.

Wu, Yushan. 1994. *Comparative economic transformation: Mainland China, Hungary, the Soviet Union and Taiwan.* Stanford: Stanford Univ. Press.

Xie Re. 2001. "A few points about doing good work on regional ethnic autonomy in the new era." Paper presented at the Proceedings of International Workshop on Regional Autonomy of Ethnic Minorities, June 22–25, Beijing.

Yan Xuejun. 1987 [1953]. "An investigation of the conditions of Vietnamese in Fangcheng." In *An investigation of the history and the society of the Guangxi Jing People.* Nanning: Guangxi Ethnic Press.

Yang Lianfu. 2001. "Brief notes on the guarantee effect of the ethnic regional autonomy system on the local economic and social development." Paper presented at the Proceedings of International Workshop on Regional Autonomy of Ethnic Minorities, June 22–25, Beijing.

Yao, Esther. 1989. "Is China the end of hermeneutics? Or, political and cultural usage of non-Han women in mainland Chinese films." *Discourse* 2, 2:11–136.

Yu Yingshi. 1988. "The concept of nation-state and national consciousness" ([guo jia guannian yu minzu yishi]). In *Cultural reviews and feelings toward China* ([wenhua pinglun yu zhongguo qinghuai]). Taipei: Yunchen.

Zhang Beiping. 2001. "Regional ethnic autonomy and poverty-alleviation development." Paper presented at the Proceedings of International Workshop on Regional Autonomy of Ethnic Minorities, June 22–25, Beijing.

Zheng Yuntao, and Shi Donglong. 2001. "Chengxian qihou, jiwang kailai—relie qingzhu Longsheng gezu zizhi xian chengli wushi zhounian" ([Taking from the predecessors, opening up for the latecomers, following the past, creating the future—warmly celebrating the fiftieth anniversary of the establishment of the Longsheng Multi-ethnic Autonomous County]). *Minzu zhi sheng* (Voices of Nationalities), 5:3–5.

Zhou Chuanbin. 2001. "The system of regional ethnic autonomy and social harmony." Paper presented at the Proceedings of International Workshop on Regional Autonomy of Ethnic Minorities, June 22–25, Beijing.

Zhou Xing. 1992. *New theses on ethnology* ([*minzuxue xin lun*]). Xian: Shanxi People's Press.

Zhou Yong, "Probing into the road of combining regional autonomy with ethnic autonomy," Paper presented at the Proceedings of International Workshop on Regional Autonomy of Ethnic Minorities, June 22–25, Beijing.

Zhou, M. 1997. "Segmented assimilation." *International Migration Review* 31,4:975–1008.

Zhu Riyao. 1990. *Cao Deben and Sun Xiaochun, The contemporary view of China's political cultural tradition* ([*zhongguo chuantong zhengzhi wenhua de xiandai sikao*]). Changchun: Jilin Univ. Press.

Index